# PRAISE FOR
## A+ Marketing: Proven Tactics for Success

*For many years, Andrea Eliscu has been a trusted advisor [as well as] our eyes and ears in the community ... Her book will educate the reader ... We are thrilled to share Andrea's strategies and vision for our practice [in this book] in the hope that it will stimulate others to do the same.*

**Robert S. Gold, M.D.**
Physician Partner
Eye Physicians of Central Florida
Orlando, Florida

*Compared to other marketing books I've reviewed, this book is, by far, the most comprehensive guide to marketing physician practices. It will ... help any medical practice—solo or group. This resource gives physicians the knowledge and tools to develop their own step-by-step marketing programs. A must read for all physicians.*

**Tina M. Hogeman, CPA, MS, MT**
Health Care Consultant
Denver, Colorado

*Excellent resource for any medical practice professional. The specific role of marketing in the strategic planning process is often overlooked and this book not only emphasizes this point but gives direction on how to move forward.*

**Jeff Brockette**
Chief Administrative Officer
Texas Retina Associates
(15 FTE physicians)
Dallas, Texas

*In practice management, we continually seek to expand our knowledge through conferences, books and networking, hoping to get that one key tidbit of information that will make a difference in our practice. I found that Ms. Eliscu's book provided not one, but many of these key tidbits of valuable information that I can implement in the management of our practice.*

**Brenda K. Merchberger**
Chief Administrative Officer
Osler Medical
Melbourne, Florida

*I thoroughly enjoyed reading Andrea's book. As an administrator of a practice, I loved that she was able to get down to the basics of marketing. Her ideas are simple and easy to implement and very compelling. The book really dealt with understanding patient satisfaction and how to increase overall patient approval. Andrea put meeting patient's needs as a top priority in her book. Her thoughts and ideas are forward thinking and will help us better market for future success of the practice. I would recommend the book as a must read!*

**Charla Ferchow, COE**
Administrator
Eye Physicians of Central Florida
Orlando, Florida

... It has become more expensive to practice, harder to get paid and more competitive. Marketing and taking steps to retain patients have become absolute necessities. A+ Marketing: Proven Tactics for Success *is a must read for physicians and their office managers. "The Four A's"—Access, Availability, Accountability and Accommodation should be the basis for any successful medical practice or clinic.*

A+ Marketing: Proven Tactics for Success *should be considered an invaluable book that covers all the key elements from building a good practice identity, addressing patient needs and good customer service, increasing referrals, advertising, internet and much more. Ms. Eliscu has outlined the systems and techniques that have worked so well ... I highly recommend this book for all those who want to reposition themselves to meet the needs of practicing medicine in the 21st Century.*

**Donald Rauhofer**
Publisher
M.D. News
Florida

# A+ Marketing
## Proven Tactics for Success

ANDREA T. ELISCU, BS, RN

Medical Group Management Association© (MGMA©) publications are intended to provide current and accurate information and are designed to assist readers in becoming more familiar with the subject matter covered. Such publications are distributed with the understanding that MGMA does not render any legal, accounting, or other professional advice that may be construed as specifically applicable to an individual situation. No representations or warranties are made concerning the application of legal or other principles discussed by the authors to any specific factual situation, nor is any prediction made concerning how any particular judge, government official, or other person will interpret or apply such principles. Specific factual situations should be discussed with professional advisors.

**Production Credits**
Publisher: Marilee E. Aust
Project Editor: Anne Serrano, MA
SME: David Highbee Smith, MBA
Composition: Virginia Howe, McIntire Publishing Services
Copy Editor: Jenifer Walker, Cartref Communications
Proofreader: Mary Kay Kozyra, Valley Editorial Services
Indexer: Carolyn G. Weaver, Weaver Indexing Services
Cover Design: Ian Serff, Serff Creative Group, Inc.

**Library of Congress Cataloging-in-Publication Data**

Eliscu, Andrea T.
 A+ marketing : proven tactics for success / Andrea T. Eliscu.
   p. ; cm.
 Includes bibliographical references and index.
 Summary: "This easy, practical, how-to guide helps the practice administrator or physician manager understand the importance of marketing, build the right foundation for needed projects, and prepare the tools required to implement them. The author describes how to achieve these goals using the Four As--Access, Availability, Accountability, and Accommodation"--Provided by publisher.
 ISBN 978-1-56829-291-5
 1. Medical care--United States--Marketing. 2. Medicine--Practice--United States--Management. 3. Patient satisfaction--United States. I. Medical Group Management Association. II. Title. III. Title: A plus marketing.
 [DNLM: 1. Marketing of Health Services--methods--United States. 2. Practice Management, Medical--United States. 3. Public Relations--United States. W /4 AA1 E43a 2008]
 RA410.56.E36 2008
 362.1068'8--dc22
                2007049857
Item #6709
ISBN: 978-1-56829-291-5

Copyright © 2008 Medical Group Management Association


All rights reserved. No part of this publication may be reproduced, stored in a retrieval system, or transmitted, in any form or by any means, electronic, mechanical, photocopying, recording, or otherwise, without the prior written permission of the copyright owner.


Printed in the United States of America
10 9 8 7 6 5 4 3 2 1

# Acknowledgments

I feel truly blessed. It's not often that one has the opportunity to tell his or her "story" to friends and colleagues and those eager to begin a journey of health care marketing. I've had that experience three times now, and I recognize it's because I have a wonderful team to encourage me and lend their support and expertise to accomplish it.

I thank each and every one of you with special thanks to: Richard J. Walsh, Frans Wester, Lori Johnson, John Bruns, Michael Lowe, Kristin Weissman, Bob Kodzis, Tom Calato, Annetta Wilson, Richard Sandlin, Mary K. Scott, Debbie Muse, and Robert Lussendum.

This book would not be useful as a teaching tool without the wonderful clients who graciously allowed me to share examples of their leadership. I offer a very special thanks to them for allowing me to share their marketing stories with you. They are Jay Pearce; Jeff Brockette; Bobby Gold, MD; David Auerbach, DO; Louis Blumenfeld, MD; Victor Thomas, MD; Larry Lewis, OD; Charles Garnette, MD; Nicholas Abrudescu, MD; and Nancy Brown, MD.

Finally, I'd like to say a special thanks to my late husband, Edward H. Eliscu, MD, who shared his vision, support, and understanding of the health care community and its changing ways, even as he traveled on his own journey.

Additionally, I want to thank the visionary and supportive team at MGMA. They were champions in encouraging me to update *Ready-Set-Market!* Special thanks go to Marilee Aust, MGMA's publisher, who gave me the opportunity to write another book about marketing for MGMA's audience; and to Marilee's team of consummate editorial and production professionals including Anne Serrano, information products manager; and Jennifer Dysert and Julie Sommer, marketing managers.

# Contents

Acknowledgments .......................................... iii
Introduction ............................................. ix

**Chapter 1 ■ The Power of the Basics—A Few Important Points** ...... 1
    Building Your Practice Identity .............................. 2
        *Exhibit 1.1 Sample Service Statement*
    50 Basic Marketing Tips for Health Care Providers ........... 3
        *Exhibit 1.2 Strategic Action Plan*
        *Exhibit 1.3 Strategic Plan: Objectives, Strategies, and Participants/Notes*

**Chapter 2 ■ Gaining a Fresh Understanding of Your Patients** ........ 23
    Building Better Customer Service ........................... 23
    Patient Satisfaction ....................................... 25
    Meeting Patient Needs ..................................... 26
        *Exhibit 2.1 Patient Satisfaction Survey*

**Chapter 3 ■ Providing POW! Customer Service** ..................... 35
    John Bruns: Customer Satisfaction ......................... 38
        *Exhibit 3.1 The SPC Model*
    Summary ................................................ 42

**Chapter 4 ■ Diagnosing Your Practice—A Simple Guide to Effective Practice Assessment** .......................... 45
    Assessing Your Practice .................................... 47
        *Exhibit 4.1 Practice Assessment Guidelines*
    Your Audit List ........................................... 51
    Assessing Your Practice Identity ............................ 51
        *Exhibit 4.2 Sample Practice Assessment*
        *Exhibit 4.3 How to Differentiate Your Practice*

Assessing Your Logo.......................................... 55
    *Exhibit 4.4 Sample Group Practice Logos*
Assessing Your Staff.......................................... 56

**Chapter 5 ■ Developing Bulletproof Referral Relationships**.......... 61
Bob Kodzis: The Power of Great Relationships ............... 61
Navigating the Wide Spectrum of Relationships............. 65
    *Exhibit 5.1   The Relationship Continuum*
Fostering Postive Referral Relationhips....................... 70
    *Exhibit 5.2   Referral Enhancement Behaviors for Physicians*
    *Exhibit 5.3   Case Example: Referral Enhancement Program*
    *Exhibit 5.4   A Typical Letter to Referring Physicians About a New Associate Joining the Practice*
    *Exhibit 5.5   A Referral Physician Newsletter Introducing a New Associate*
    *Exhibit 5.6   The Same Referral Physician Newsletter Introducing Another Associate Customized for Another Community*
    *Exhibit 5.7   An Announcement Card for a New Associate*
    *Exhibit 5.8   Ad to Introduce a New Associate*
    *Exhibit 5.9   A Clinical Trial Newsletter*
    *Exhibit 5.10 Referral Pad and Thanksgiving Card Showing Communication with Referring Physicians*

**Chapter 6 ■ Putting Our Heads Together—A Guide to Practice Retreats** ......................................... 85
To Retreat or Not to Retreat? ................................ 85
    *Exhibit 6.1 Strategic Planning Facilitation and Consultation Proposal*
    *Exhibit 6.2 Staff Retreat and Brainstorming Session*
    *Exhibit 6.3 Staff Retreat Survey*
    *Exhibit 6.4 Staff Retreat Summary Report*
    *Exhibit 6.5 Staff Follow-up Retreat*

**Chapter 7 ■ Telling Your Story—Practical Approaches to Managing Your Media Message** ......................... 115
Annetta Wilson: Media Messages ........................... 116

Real-Life Case................................................. 120
    *Exhibit 7.1 News Release*
    *Exhibit 7.2 Article from* Orlando Sentinel, *October 2006*
Making Television Work for Your Practice...................... 127
Tom Calato: Television—Using the Medium Well ............ 128
Summary...................................................... 142
    *Exhibit 7.3 Sample Ads*
    *Exhibit 7.4 Sample Talking Points*

**Chapter 8 ■ Reaching Out—A Guide to Community Relations**....... 149
    Kristin Weissman: Crafting the Message .................... 150
    Case Studies................................................. 153
        *Exhibit 8.1  Marketing and Public Relations Plan (24 Months)*
        *Exhibit 8.2  Action Plan*
        *Exhibit 8.3  New Logo and Letterhead/Their Corporate Identity*
        *Exhibit 8.4  Patient Letter*
        *Exhibit 8.5  Additional Opportunities*
        *Exhibit 8.6  Thank-You for Nurses*
        *Exhibit 8.7  Steps for the Office Manager to Implement Nurse "Thank-You" Plan*
        *Exhibit 8.8  Talking Points on Why to Advertise*
        *Exhibit 8.9  Sample Ads*
        *Exhibit 8.10 Patient Survey*

**Chapter 9 ■ Expecting the Unexpected—A Guide to Meeting Specific Challenges** ....................................... 187
    Challenge #1: Using the Internet to Market Your Practice .... 187
        *Exhibit 9.1 A Typical Contract to Enhance an Existing Website*
    Kristin Weissman: The Internet is Here to Stay .............. 192
    Challenge #2: Opening a New Office......................... 195
        *Exhibit 9.2 New Office Briefing*
        *Exhibit 9.3 Action Plan for Office Opening*
        *Exhibit 9.4 Ad to Introduce the New Office in Community Newspaper*
        *Exhibit 9.5 Direct Mail Postcard*
        *Exhibit 9.6 Ad Integrating Community Service to Neighborhood Church*
        *Exhibit 9.7 "Our Newest Office" Poster*

**Chapter 10** ■ **Maximizing Your Practice's Profit Potential—
A Guide to Retail Medicine** .............................. 205

Richard Sandlin: Real-World Advice for Physicians Seeking to
Establish and Market Their Retail Medicine Ventures ...... 208
Legal Aspects of Retail Medicine........................... 214
Michael R. Lowe: Health Law .............................. 214
Summary................................................... 228

Exhibit 10.1   *Marketing Plan*
Exhibit 10.2   *Newly Created Logo*
Exhibit 10.3   *Map*
Exhibit 10.4   *Ad in High School Booklet*
Exhibit 10.5   *Press Release*
Exhibit 10.6   *Letter Sent to Coaches and Trainees on Letterhead*
Exhibit 10.7   *Flyer Used as Community Handouts*
Exhibit 10.8   *Ad Placed in Middle School Planner*
Exhibit 10.9   *Managed Care "Blast Fax"*
Exhibit 10.10  *Ad on Website*

**Chapter 11** ■ **Final Words of Advice** .................................... 245

**About the Author** ......................................... 247

**Index** .................................................... 249

# Introduction

When I sat down to write this book, I couldn't help but reflect on my 25 years of advising physicians about how to market their practices. And it immediately occurred to me that the old saying, "The more things change, the more they stay the same," is absolutely true when it comes to medical marketing.

Of course, the health care field itself has changed dramatically since the 1980s. As a leader in health care management, you know more than most about the difficult struggles that practices face today. These include several noted in my book, *Ready-Set-Market!*[1] as well as others:

- Health care has become more bureaucratic
- Consumers play a greater, more assertive role in decision-making
- Third-party payers continue to increase their demands on hospitals and physicians
- Government regulations continue to increase and intrude in group practice operations at an escalated rate
- Medicare and Medicaid continue to lower reimbursements
- The cost of pharmaceuticals continues to increase
- Medical excellence and patient service continue to be a focal point of competition
- Technology has made enormous inroads into patient care and expectations
- Insurance company profits have increased relative to physician payments
- General and baby boomer populations have grown
- Medical malpractice issues complicate care
- Physician recruitment is difficult in certain states
- There is employer backlash over benefits

Regardless of these factors, physicians continue to practice medicine and plan to control their own destinies. In fact, it's because of all these factors that medical marketing has taken on an even more important role than most of us could have imagined.

The idea of medical marketing was an almost novel concept 25 years ago. Most physician practices at the time were very reluctant to take such a drastic step. But when we managed to convince a brave physician or practice manager to make the revolutionary decision to market the group, we recommended three important steps. First, the group had to practice quality medicine. Second, it had to develop brand-name identity. Third, it had to focus on patient/customer service.

In my two previous books published by Medical Group Management Association (MGMA), *Position for Success: Strategic Marketing for Group Practices* and *Ready-Set-Market!*, I covered these fundamentals—along with the rationale for marketing, how to "think" marketing and how to achieve specific marketing goals. I also presented several case studies to illustrate the basics.

Although many things have changed along the way, these three vital components of medical marketing have not. Certainly things are different now, but the essential elements of successful medical marketing remain virtually the same. Only the specific strategies that are used to achieve your goals may have changed.

What physicians once resisted—marketing and communicating to meet the needs of their patients/customers—is now an important part of everyday business. Instead of a bold move on the part of a medical practice, today it's virtually a necessity to establish and maintain a successful practice.

That said, there's one important thing that has changed tremendously over the past few years. As I emphasized in *Ready-Set-Market!*, medical marketing has become more and more about the third element—patient/customer service. Today it's increasingly about serving patients and it's more patient-directed as opposed to physician-directed, as it was in the past.

Although the first two elements are still important, I'll go so far as to maintain that medical marketing today is all about customer service.

This is largely a direct result of our changing American culture and demographics. Over the past 25 years, patients have changed. They're younger, better educated, better informed, and more inclined to take control of their own health care. A high percentage of them research physicians and health conditions before choosing a provider. And with the advent of the Internet, it's easier than ever!

In their book, *YOU The Smart Patient,* Michael F. Roizen, M.D., and Mehmet C. Oz, M.D.,[2] write about the "Marcus Welby era ... when physicians were seen as supreme authorities." Those days are over, they admit, and I've also found that to be true.

Although some of the older generation still may see physicians as all knowing and therefore are willing to tolerate a non–service-oriented practice, our booming younger population comes with an entirely different mentality. Their attitude is more likely to be, "Give it to me now and give it to me quickly," as well as "I expect the same kind of service you expect because I'm just as important as you."

Furthermore, patients come to practices armed with mounds of information they've gathered from the Internet (some accurate, some not), and they demand answers and service like never before.

Roizen and Mehmet say this phenomenon made them realize that "Marcus Welby had officially retired to his cabin in the woods, not to be seen again. This was the new world order in medicine—one in which empowered patients called the shots and regularly questioned us."[3]

Of course, books such as Roizen's and Mehmet's and others, along with medical television shows and other sources, also have contributed to the proliferation of so-called Smart Patients. And although some practices may find this troubling, they should realize that these well-educated patients are more likely to be compliant, which can only contribute to better outcomes. In our daily rush, we sometimes may forget this.

But let's face it, that's what we're all working toward, isn't it? Patients engaged in their health care issues who proactively work with their doctors to resolve those issues.

My goal in this book is to help make practical marketing more accessible for you as physician marketer or practice administrator and/or your internal marketing staff. The ideas I present are things that you and the practice can implement on your own with minimal assistance.

Even more focused, the topics covered in this book are the usual and customary marketing tactics that happen on a day-to-day basis across the United States. They're marketing opportunities that you'll easily be able to find and they're totally focused on meeting the needs of and serving your target audience, whether it's patients, referring physicians, internal staff, or others.

As I said, everything has changed but, in essence, it's still the same. We've gone through diagnoses-related groups, business health care coalitions, managed care plans, independent practice association networks, mergers and acquisitions, consolidation of medical group practices, the breakup of those same consolidations, the use of electronic medical records, handheld personal digital assistants (PDAs), and an increasing baby boomer population.

What used to be viewed as huge, aggressive hurdles to marketing are now seen as basic fundamentals. Such items as these are now considered the norm: creating a logo, creating a mission statement, creating a vision statement and defining core values of the practice, developing a marketing plan or plan of action, designing and implementing strategies and tactics, and assigning someone to follow through on these projects.

Although there are other important elements that I believe should be part of a good marketing program—research, marketing retreats, and a comprehensive marketing plan—I understand that these often do not happen in today's practical world.

Instead, I see practices simply decide they want to accomplish certain specific marketing projects. Then they focus on defining those projects and coming up with a plan of action to make them happen. The plan of action may include one project or enough projects that it takes two years to complete.

I don't see this project-only orientation as a major stumbling block to the overall goal of marketing. I believe it's a simple evolutionary step that makes sense in today's practical reality.

As I emphasized in *Ready-Set-Market!*, customer service is one of the most important elements—if not the most important element—in medical marketing today. It's all about understanding what your customer wants and providing it at a reasonable price—or at a price your customer feels is reasonable—and at the level of service that satisfies your customer.

That's the very simple key to successful health care marketing. And the cornerstone to achieving that goal today is what I call **The Four A's— Access, Availability, Accountability,** and **Accommodation.** Many traditional marketing books and educational classes teach the Four P's of marketing: product, price, place, and promotion. **The Four A's** are today's new customer service issues. They include everything that makes marketing a practice successful and, obviously, they're interrelated. There are times when **Access** and **Availability** seem to be the same, and there are times when **Accommodation** is really about **Availability** and **Access.**

After you understand this concept, your approach to marketing and the implementation of projects will be less stressful and less expensive. And your marketing also will be much more successful.

In today's business environment—and make no mistake about it, medicine today is a business—all the marketing in the world won't make you succeed if you fail to remember your customers are your number one priority. Quite simply, if you don't keep them happy, they'll find someone who will.

It's easier than ever today when health care is being delivered at locations by publicly traded companies sitting right inside your community. Families can now receive health care at Super Wal-Mart, Walgreen's, CVS Pharmacy, Target, and—in some communities—even in grocery stores. And they're sometimes willing to accept what we might consider a lower (or at least, different) quality of care in exchange for simply having **Access, Availability, Accommodation,** and someone who will accept **Accountability.**

My goal for this book is simple. I want to provide an easy, practical, "how-to" guide that will help you—the practice administrator or physician manager—understand the importance of marketing, help you build the right foundation for the projects you want to accomplish, and help you prepare the tools that you need to implement them. I believe that's what it takes to find success, both for you and for your patients/customers.

And please note that although I've used the words "customers" and "patients" almost interchangeably, you should realize that you have any number of other customers besides patients, such as referrers, internal staff, vendors, and others.

I've included many examples of action plans and other materials from different types of specialty group practices. I've also tried to illustrate how you can put these strategies to work and how they might look in your practice. You also may note that I've said similar things in different ways in different chapters. This is primarily for emphasis but also to illustrate multiple points where certain goals, objectives, or strategies may apply. In addition, I've called on respected colleagues in several areas—customer service, community relations, television, strategic planning, retail medicine, and the Internet—to offer marketing secrets from their diverse perspectives.

I hope you find my book a friendly marketing tool, and I hope you find my recommendations easy to implement in your practice.

So let's get started. The first step is to decide what you want to achieve, and I strongly encourage you to initiate that process today. After you know your goals, you can take charge of your dream, investigate how to achieve it, and finally, achieve everything you can, based on your available budget.

Good luck!

## REFERENCES

1. Eliscu, Andrea T., *Ready-Set-Market!* Medical Group Management Association, Englewood, Colo: 1999. p. vii–ix.
2. Roizen, Michael F., and Mehmet C. Oz, *YOU The Smart Patient.* Free Press, A Division of Simon & Shuster, Inc., New York: 2006. p. 3.
3. Roizen, Michael F., and Mehmet C. Oz, *YOU The Smart Patient.* Free Press, A Division of Simon & Shuster, Inc., New York: 2006. p. 6.

CHAPTER 1

# The Power of the Basics— A Few Important Points

Far from being a novel concept, medical marketing today is a subject discussed in scores of books, including the two I've written previously for MGMA. If you're looking for basic information, I refer you to an excellent chapter in MGMA's *Medical Practice Management Body of Knowledge Review: Planning and Marketing, Volume 7.*[1]

Rather than reiterate the fundamentals, I'd like to reinforce several important elements that you must understand and utilize if your marketing program is to succeed. Primarily, I want to help you understand that marketing means meeting the needs of your customers, and I want to empower you to take charge in your practice.

My aim for this book is to present the kind of information that both will help you develop the specific goals you want to achieve and develop a plan of action toward achieving these goals. When you review your plan 12 months from now, I want you to see that you've made positive progress in achieving your goals. Toward that aim, I'll also present practical marketing opportunities that you can easily implement within your practice.

As you proceed, please keep in mind what I call the new cornerstones of physician practice marketing: **The Four A's—Access, Availability, Accountability,** and **Accommodation.**

As you plan your strategies and tactics, ask these questions each step of the way: "As our practice initiates this marketing plan of action, how many of these four cornerstones have we addressed? Will this marketing project allow **Access** for our customers? Will we be **Available** to our patients? Will our staff, both professional and clerical, be

**Accountable**? And can we **Accommodate** our customers?" Traditionally two of the methods used to measure a service organization's success were timeliness and accuracy. Now with **The Four A's** we have great opportunities for additional measurements to consider in meeting the needs of our clients.

Remember, it does no good to spend creative energy and financial resources without first being in touch with your target markets and their needs. Without that information you will never achieve the outcome you desire.

## BUILDING YOUR PRACTICE IDENTITY

Although I won't be discussing the basics, there is one of the very specific, fundamental goals of marketing that I do want to talk about. The subject is the necessity to build brand-name identity, which I believe is a vital element of customer service.

You must establish and build your brand name, which is another term for your practice identity, within your community (or multiple communities if you have multiple community offices). And I strongly encourage you to use the term *community offices* rather than *satellite offices*. The latter term connotes something less in quality or status than the primary office. It's just as easy to speak of your community offices, based on their locations.

Building brand-name identity, or managing your brand, is a promise to deliver a health care experience for your patients that is specific and unique to your practice. You're essentially making a promise no one else can make. It's the essence of how your practice delivers health care and service. And it requires that you recognize what patients want, both in the functional delivery of care and their emotional relationships with your practice. This is what is known as a gap analysis in finding what you can do and what you can't do in comparison to your competitors. What you do the same as your competitors is just as important as what you do better and what you don't do.

To build brand-name identity, you first must determine who you are and how you want to be perceived by your customers. Whether your customers are patients, referring physicians, employers, managed care companies, or internal staff—or as is usually the case, a combination of these and perhaps others. Whatever the case, you must know what you stand

> **EXHIBIT 1.1 ■ Sample Service Statement**
>
> Our group will do everything possible to help provide our patients with superior services, innovative thinking, and efficient operations. We know that our success and our survival depend on how well we consistently serve our customers whenever they are involved with our practice. We understand that each employee's job has an impact on the timeliness, quality, empathy, and service that we offer. We will respect and have concern for our patients' needs. We understand that one negative patient encounter is one error too many. We will strive to do our job right the first time and to continually seek performance improvement.
>
> A.T. Eliscu, Ready-Set-Market! Medical Group Management Association, Englewood, CO: 1999. p. 23. Reprinted with permission from the Medical Group Management Association, 104 Inverness Terrace East, Englewood, Colorado 80112. 877.ASK.MGMA. www.mgma.com Copyright 1999.

for, as well as your practice focus and your service commitment. And of course, you must communicate it to your customers. See Exhibit 1.1 for a Sample Service Statement.

If you don't define yourself, other practices within your specialty will do it for you. And that is *not* something you want to happen.

I also believe that marketing planning retreats are very valuable. However, only about one of eight groups I work with actually conduct them. (I'll discuss this in-depth in Chapter 6.)

Just remember, if you want to move forward before (or without) a marketing retreat, I suggest you determine three or four goals and projects you need or want to accomplish within a year and concentrate all your efforts on them. This helps enhance your brand-name identity in the marketplace while allowing you to control your level of service to the patients and others using your practice.

## 50 BASIC MARKETING TIPS FOR HEALTH CARE PROVIDERS

Here are a few very simple tips that will be useful in your practice—and help alleviate your concerns about marketing. You may find some or all appropriate for your practice. As you study these tips, think how they encompass **The Four A's.** You'll realize that these elements must play an integral role of any plan that meets the needs of both your practice and your target groups.

## Market Research

1. Start by finding out who your target audiences are, what they want, and how they perceive your practice. Gather information from your local Chamber of Commerce, Census Bureau, hospital, the Economic Development Commission in your area, or local university or college, and other sources. Medicare and Medicaid also might be good sources.
2. Know your competition, how they are expanding, who they are hiring—and what they're doing.
3. Survey your patients to determine what they think about your practice.

## Strategic Planning

4. If you don't know where you're going, you won't know how to get there. Begin with a well-thought-out strategic marketing plan that's designed to create awareness, project a positive image, and increase usage of your services.
5. Build in a system of tracking to measure your progress against your plan. Make sure you understand the reasons for any deviation.
6. When your budget is limited, determine the most important marketing project and implement it with appropriate resources. As your practice grows, map out when you can begin the next project; keep moving your marketing projects forward so that at the end of a year, you can review how far you've come and what should be repeated or deleted from your plan.

## In-Office Marketing

7. Make your reception area a pleasant, informative place for your patients. Remove the frosted glass left over from the 1980s.
8. Be sure your staff greets each patient by name within 20 seconds of his or her arrival—and with a smile.
9. In addition to the usual and current magazines, stock some on health care topics and areas that may be of interest to your patients, such as golf, tennis, travel, fishing, cycling, and autos.
10. Place a toy box full of child-safe toys in your reception area. Be sure to include children's books on your shelves. Give children a small puzzle or coloring book imprinted with your practice name to take with them.

11. Keep patients informed on the status of their appointment if you know they're going to be delayed. Learn to sincerely apologize and problem-solve with your patients if your office is running behind schedule. Offer patients a chance to reschedule in a timely manner. Remember **The Four A's—Access, Availability, Accountability,** and **Accommodation.**

## *Patient Communication*

12. Create a Website that represents your practice in a patient-useful manner. Update it frequently, especially when you open a new office, add physicians or physician extenders, or when you add or change office hours. Create links to interesting and informative health care articles or specific procedures or treatments related to your practice. Think of your Website as a marketing tool with a variety of capacities that can tie you to patients and that can include: personal health record applications, scheduling appointments, MapQuest® directions, policies, video files, and an interactive 24-hour service that provides sources of information to all Website readers.
13. Prepare and distribute a patient handbook to introduce your practice, explain your office policies, and list special services and procedures.
14. Periodically publish a patient newsletter to provide information about your practice, staff, and patients. Include many photos, case studies, and health care news your patients can use. Remember, consistency is more important than frequency—so start with a quarterly or biannual issue. Post this newsletter on your Website.
15. Develop a professional-looking, consistent stationery package that includes logo, letterhead, envelope, business cards, appointment cards, note card and envelopes, mailing labels, prescription pad, and referral pads and folders, if appropriate for patient handouts.
16. Regularly review all materials (such as Yellow Pages®, patient education sheets, Website addresses, and community ads) to assure accuracy and consistency.
17. Have your receptionist give every new patient a copy of your handbook and other policies and procedures when handing out your medical information form. If your patients register

online, offer them the brochure as a part of your new patient welcome package.

18. Have personalized business cards printed for all your staff. Encourage them to use them with patients and everyone else they come in contact with.
19. Listen to what your patients ask you. Establish eye contact with them and use their names to show your concern for them.
20. Send a follow-up note to new patients, thanking them for choosing you and welcoming them to your practice. Reiterate the importance of follow-up appointments (if appropriate) and regular check-ups.

## *Customer Service*

21. Remember that it costs 10 times as much to acquire a new patient than it does to keep an existing one.
22. Be concerned that 91 percent of unhappy patients will never visit again, but that they will make their dissatisfaction known to at least nine other people. That means if you turn off 1 patient, you discourage 10!
23. Call patients the day after they've had surgery or an office procedure to see how they're doing. You'll be surprised at the positive effect this has on patients.
24. Survey a sample of your patients each year to learn more about their needs, wants, and expectations regarding your services.
25. Periodically send a brief postage-paid evaluation card or survey to each patient after his or her visit. Use responses to praise outstanding employees and correct any negative responses.
26. Make it convenient for patients to see you. Evaluate whether you should set practice hours for select evenings, one lunch period per month, and one or two Saturdays per month to accommodate people who can't get to your office during weekdays.
27. Personally give all patients your business card. Thank them for choosing you for their care.
28. Have your staff acknowledge all callers and wait for a response before putting patients on hold.
29. Ask patients if they understand their diagnosis and instructions. Listen to what they tell you.

## Referral Physicians

30. Make referrers feel as if they're part of the team—report to them promptly and send their patients back to them.
31. Send a thorough response—a detailed, diagnostic report—for every referral. Include an executive summary at the beginning of the report.
32. Be available to referring doctors. Set aside a specific time to return calls.
33. Schedule referred patients as quickly as possible. Set aside a block of time each day for this purpose—and let referrers know about it.
34. Hold an annual educational seminar about your specialty. Arrange for continuing medical education credits.
35. Make sure regular referrers know that they are important to you. Stay in touch and thank them regularly with a note or small gift or invite them to a special event.
36. Thank the staff of referrers by doing something special for one office each month. Send an appropriate gift to the office or have your staff take their staff to lunch.

## Internal Relations

37. Review all staff policies and procedures regularly.
38. "Recharge batteries" with staff retreats.
39. Make sure you or your office manager belong to a national professional organization and encourage him or her to keep up to date and attend their meetings.
40. Reward long-time employees with incentives (such as a lapel pin or a restaurant gift certificate).
41. Hire the right staff. Research and use some of the assessment tools available to help you hire the correct person for specific job responsibilities.
42. Have written job descriptions, hold meaningful staff meetings, and create an employee handbook.
43. Teach your staff to answer the phone cheerfully and professionally. Write a script that everyone can follow easily.
44. Make sure your staff returns patient phone calls promptly and cheerfully. Don't ever make a patient feel like a nuisance.

45. Empower your staff to make decisions. (Be sure to set up the necessary systems.)

## *Community Relations*

46. Build time into your schedule to integrate you and your practice into the community.
47. Sponsor a community league or team.
48. Contact your local, state, and national politicians and ask them to keep you up to date on any legislation that might affect your practice. Communicate with them about issues that affect health care delivery.
49. Check with industries near your office. Volunteer to contribute health care articles for their monthly newsletters.
50. Make friends with the media.

See Exhibits 1.2 and 1.3 for a sample plan that was used in a highly competitive community for a very successful group practice that wanted to stay that way.

## EXHIBIT 1.2 ■ Strategic Action Plan

**EYE PHYSICIANS OF CENTRAL FLORIDA STRATEGIC PLAN OF ACTION FOR PUBLIC RELATIONS AND MARKETING**

*Current Position*

Eye Physicians of Central Florida is an established ophthalmology practice with two offices in a medium-sized metro area. The practice has three board-certified ophthalmologists and two optometrists in addition to appropriate, trained support staff.

Eye Physicians of Central Florida is a full-service eye practice, handling general ophthalmology and optical care such as glasses and contacts, but the ophthalmologists are also specialists in the areas of pediatrics, neuro-ophthalmology, oculoplastics, and adult eye muscle disorders.

Patients come to Eye Physicians of Central Florida seeking ongoing, routine eye care, but many more are referred by other physicians who seek temporary specialty expertise for their patients.

Eye Physicians of Central Florida is studying the possibility of opening another office in a southwest suburb in the near future.

*Strengths*

- Eye Physicians of Central Florida can handle all routine and many specialty eye care procedures.
- They participate in most major insurance plans.
- They accept new patients and can arrange an appointment within hours or one–two days for new as well as established patients.
- The practice has already begun the process of updating its logo, practice name, and correspondence collaterals.
- Eye Physicians of Central Florida is doing preliminary research on how its performance is perceived by referring physicians.

*Weaknesses/Challenges*

- The practice has no established practice brand.
- The practice is generally not known outside the circle of existing clients (physicians and patients).

*(continued)*

## EXHIBIT 1.2 ■ **Strategic Action Plan** *(Continued)*

- There are two messages to either market separately or merge: full-service eye care and eye specialist center.
- Eye Physicians of Central Florida does not have the collaterals and tools to market itself effectively to its physicians and patients.
- Eye Physicians of Central Florida has done no research to determine its strengths, weaknesses, and value to its patients so it can focus its efforts.
- Both offices are located to the north of the city, leaving many residents too far from an office to make Eye Physicians of Central Florida a convenient option.
- The practice is ready to expand, adding another ophthalmologist and another office, yet marketing and public relations operations, including customer service protocols, are incomplete within the existing framework.

*Unknowns*
- Do doctors in the pool of potential referrers know Eye Physicians of Central Florida? What would it take to get non-referring doctors to sample Eye Physicians of Central Florida?
- What is the patient experience like at Eye Physicians of Central Florida? How can it be improved?
- What is the Eye Physicians of Central Florida budget to establish its goals?

*Competition*
(Information provided from Eye Physicians of Central Florida physician survey results)
- Two other pediatric ophthalmologists
- One other neuro-ophthalmologist

*Current Marketing, PR Programs, and Techniques*
(Information provided from Eye Physicians of Central Florida physician survey results)
- Personal networking
- Print advertising
- Participate in health fairs
- Conduct vision screening
- Visiting/communications with referring doctors
- Speaking in the community
- Brochure about our practice
- Sent out a Botox mailer to patients (failure)
- Donate Botox to charity and school fundraisers

*Current Goals*
- Update the brand identity of Eye Physicians of Central Florida.
- Increase physician referrals in our major areas of specialization.

*Potential Future Goals*
- Increase referrals in less prominent areas of specialization.
- Increase general optometric and optician practice volume.
- Increase patient self-referrals.

*Target Audience*
- Existing and potential referring physicians: pediatricians, neurologists, internists, family practitioners, and endocrinologists
- Existing patients

*Objectives*
- Create the *brand* of Eye Physicians of Central Florida: identify the niche, the strengths, and the advantages of this practice over others for patients and for referring physicians.
- Evaluate and strengthen practice procedures as they relate to marketing and public relations.
- Internal relations, including procedures to build and maintain referral relationships (also noted below)
- Patient service and education protocols (separate from medical practice protocols), including but not limited to patient education collaterals
- Reception comfort, appearance, pediatric orientation, and utilization as it relates to marketing
- Other related areas so that the operation of the practice supports the mission and reinforces the brand
- Communicate the brand to the audiences—physicians and patients—initially and on an ongoing basis.
- Communicate the revised brand to established and potential referring physicians.
- Create ongoing protocols for securing and cementing referral relationships.
- Communicate the brand to patients in-house.

*(continued)*

### EXHIBIT 1.2 ■ Strategic Action Plan *(Continued)*

- Use the introduction of the new physician to reinforce the brand.
- Use the opening of the new community office to reinforce the brand.
- Use selected media when appropriate to communicate the brand.

*Effects on Strategic Plan*

- Evaluate all stock letters sent to referring doctors to be sure each adequately thanks the doctor for the referral. Create a list of different "thank you concluding sentences" to be rotated by the staff for fresh, personal-feeling correspondence.
- Encourage Eye Physicians of Central Florida physicians to include a personal note (i.e., person-to-person specific comment) on each correspondence to a referring physician.
- Implement other personal contacts for physician communication, such as a birthday commemoration (a card, a plant, a donation to an appropriate charity, etc.). These can be done by staff, but the Eye Physicians of Central Florida doctors must know about them in case it comes up in conversation.
- Rethink the newsletter and postcard, perhaps using an abbreviated format.
- Create a schedule of workshops—to be held at large referrers' offices whenever possible.
- Create a record-keeping system to be sure all professional correspondence pertaining to referral patients is handled promptly, professionally, thoroughly. It is very important to the referring doctors.
- Create a database of potential referring physicians and lapsing referring physicians and initiate personal contact to remind them of Eye Physicians of Central Florida's doctors, skills, and commitment to delivering prompt, professional care to their patients.
- Follow up with personal thanks when new or lapsed physicians do refer.
- Create a convenience packet to be distributed by the referring physician to increase the possibility that patients with a choice will select Eye Physicians of Central Florida. Include a patient handbook with map, information about various eye disorders if possible, appointment card, and "welcome letter."

**CONVERSATIONS WITH REFERRING PHYSICIANS**

*Summary*

Physicians who responded:

Kramer Smith, DO (family practice)

Jon Olson, MD (pediatrics)
Caroline Butler, MD (pediatrics)

- All respondents refer to Dr. T, one uses Dr. R, and one used Dr. C when he was in a previous practice, plans to refer to him now at Eye Physicians of Central Florida.
- All cited the fact that Eye Physicians of Central Florida physicians see their patients promptly as a primary reason for continuing referrals. Professionalism, good work, prompt communication are other reasons. One doctor said Dr. R has a good personality. They trust them professionally: two of them see Dr. T for their own eye care.
- Note: One doctor said that on a recent occasion, a patient who was supposed to see one of the doctors saw an optometrist instead. He plans to discuss this with Dr. T.
- Feedback from their patients is always favorable. Specifically, the doctors and their staff are friendly.
- Eye Physicians of Central Florida—specifically Dr. T—shows his appreciation to referral doctors by thanking them when he sees them in person. One referrer said, "No other thanks are necessary." One said that the letter that follows the consultation is an appropriate form of thank you.
- Doctors sometimes refer to other eye specialists...for emergencies and because of insurance or geography reasons. One doctor generally gives his patients several names and allows the patient to select, so Eye Physicians of Central Florida may not get the referral in those cases.
- None of the referrers felt they needed additional information on the range of services offered by Eye Physicians of Central Florida. They know when to refer. (Listing this material in physician and patient handbooks would be for the benefit of new potential referrers and all new patients.)
- All three doctors said they get more mail than they care to read and were negative on a physician newsletter or case study, although each of those ideas received a lukewarm, "Yes, I'd read it." One said both ideas are "A waste of time."
- All three were enthusiastic about the idea of occasional seminars. One doctor specified that they should be held onsite in the referring doctors' offices. One doctor said they would be especially helpful if they fell under CME guidelines, as all need that.

*Used with permission of Eye Physicians of Central Florida.*

EXHIBIT 1.3 ■ **Strategic Plan: Objectives, Strategies, and Participants/Notes**

| Objective | Strategy | Participants/Notes |
|---|---|---|
| (1) Create the *brand* of group | (1a) Re-examine and solidify the focus of the practice, by writing/revising current *mission* and *vision* statements. Also put to paper and pen a *two-year vision*. Full participant buy-in is essential. | Can be done with MMI facilitation or by EG. Note general ophthalmic, optician, and specific specialties. |
| | (1b) Conduct a referring physician phone survey to determine from their perspective what are the strengths and challenges of the existing practice.<br>Share results with staff; use to edit these brand materials and for more effective on-going referral physician communications. | Responsibility of marketing consultant or internal marketing staff person.<br><br>Two hours to contact 4–6 doctors, add results to this plan. |
| | (1c) Create updated logo, tagline, and all related correspondence collaterals that are consistent with the brand of the practice. | |
| | (1d) As above, creat a template to be used for future production of patient education and other materials; stationery for personal correspondence from physicians to referrers, convenient referral pads (including map to offices), and add Website to all materials. | |
| | (1e) Create a 1–2 sentence summary of the practice to be used on media releases and from which brand-accurate and consistent phrases can be drawn for other materials. | Consultant or practice can write. |

| Objective | Strategy | Participants/Notes |
|---|---|---|
| | **(1f)** Create a 1–2 sentence *referral philosophy statement*. Content: while EG does routine eye care, it respects the physician-patient relationship of its referral patients and their primary eye doctors and regards its role as complementary and supportive. This statement needs to be carefully crafted with the endorsement of all at EG, to be used on all appropriate referral communications. | Consultant or practice can write, either based on EG input or by creating several options. |
| **(2)** Evaluate and strengthen internal relations | **(2a)** Perform a strategic analysis of current protocols to find areas that need to be strengthened to facilitate excellent patient care and to accommodate growth, consistent with mission and vision. | Refer to consultant. |
| | **(2b)** Create a survey to determine strengths and challenges of the existing practice from patient perspective. Give or mail to patients after treatment, include return envelope. EG staff member coordinates results, share results and suggestions at staff meetings. | Create patient questionnaire.<br><br>Layout by artist, TBD.<br>Print or copy onto letterhead. |
| | **(2c)** Implement those improvements that reinforce the mission and vision and facilitate excellent patient care and effective referral relationships. | |

*(continued)*

EXHIBIT 1.3 ■ **Strategic Plan: Objectives, Strategies, and Participants/Notes** *(Continued)*

| Objective | Strategy | Participants/Notes |
|---|---|---|
| | **(2d)** Survey existing and lapsed referring physicians to determine how EG is and is not meeting the needs of referring doctors. | Calls made by consultant. |
| **(3)** Communicate the brand to the audiences—physicians and patients—initially and on an ongoing basis. | | |
| Audience: Patients | **(3a)** Create patient handbook, including information about the practice, what to expect at a visit, contact procedures, payment policy, physician photos and bios, and other relevant data. | Staff provides photos, bios/CVs, office procedures, etc. Write and expect to revise two times. Artist: include maps. Printer: TBD |
| | **(3b)** Create fact sheets or brochures on the EG areas of specialty, including the most common eye conditions within each. Display in reception area. | Consultant to write: 1–2 hours each dependent on how much original research. If there are fact sheets, print them onto templates. |
| Audience: Physicians | **(3c)** Create a referring physician handbook, highlighting the areas of specialty at EG, the quality of care, mission, physician CVs, and other factors. Include referral philosophy as noted above. | Design so one panel has contact info to be revised as new office opens, one panel includes physicians to be revised as MDs, staff grows. |

| Objective | Strategy | Participants/Notes |
|---|---|---|
| Communicate the revised brand to established and potential referring physicians. | **(3d)** Prepare mailing to current referring physicians introducing new physician, spotlighting new focus of practice, inviting inquiries, encouraging referrals. Include cover letter, new physician CV, referral physician handbook, referral pads, Website, **and/or** | 1. Write letter<br>2. Determine target market<br>3. Coordinate and collate<br>4. Mail |
| | **(3e)** Above: to current referring practices, include a thank-you gift, for example, carrot cake muffins. Include clever note. Hand deliver if possible. (Muffins are more fun than carrots.) | 1. Write letter<br>2. Coordinating, collating<br>3. Delivery |
| | **(3f)** Above: to targeted (high-volume) practices that don't refer, hand deliver packet, with different cover letter, with carrot cake muffins. Include clever note. | 1. Write letter<br>2. Coordinating, collating<br>3. Delivery |
| | **(3g)** Above: to remaining potential referring physicians, packet with above cover, without muffins. | 1. Write letter (use above letter)<br>2. Coordinating, collating<br>3. Mailing |
| | **(3h)** In initial mailing to referring physicians—or in follow-up in conjunction with new MD or new office—include small stacks of specialty fact sheets/brochures (listed above) to distribute to patients they will refer. | |

*(continued)*

**EXHIBIT 1.3** ■ **Strategic Plan: Objectives, Strategies, and Participants/Notes** *(Continued)*

| Objective | Strategy | Participants/Notes |
|---|---|---|
| Use selected media | **(3i)** Create media release on new doctor. Include press pack on practice (fact sheet, patient handbook). | 1. Create<br>2. Collate<br>3. Disseminate |
| | **(3j)** Create ad for placement in select print media on new doctor, spotlighting practice brand, tagline. | 1. Write, design<br>2. Place |
| Physicians | **(3k)** Arrange personal visits to select large practices to introduce doctor, reinforce brand. | EG |
| | **(3l)** When new doctor gets new referral to EG, he or she should hand write a personal thank you. | EG |
| Use selected media | **(3m)** Look for news/feature angle on specialty areas to pitch to appropriate media. | |
| | **(3n)** Write inspirational or other story on specialty case for placement in niche print media (such as family publications). | Consultant or practice will write: client to supply information and support materials! |
| Use the addition of the new physician to reinforce the brand | **(3o)** Create an announcement card with the doctor's photo, key CV points, and contact information; send to all potential referring physicians in target area. | Artist<br>Printer<br>Mail house<br>Postage |
| | **(3p)** Create a media release with information about the physician, the practice. Release in small publications with appropriate readership. | Write and distribute |

| Objective | Strategy | Participants/Notes |
|---|---|---|
| | Consider effects of EMR solution to share more information with physicians including PHR (personal health record) solution. | |
| | **(3q)** Schedule introductory meetings, bringing the new physician to select large referring practices for a face-to-face invitation to refer. | In house/staff |
| **(4)** Use the opening of the new office to reinforce the brand Physicians | **(4a)** Create list of potential referring physicians in new area; highlight those of highest priority. | In house/staff |
| | **(4b)** Prepare packet for high-potential referring physicians in the new area, introducing the practice, inviting inquiries, encouraging referrals. Include cover letter, referral physician handbook, referral pads, and Rolodex card. Include info sheets on eye specialties, with offer to supply more for each office. Hand deliver with carrot muffins. | 1. Prepare<br>2. Collate<br>3. Deliver |
| | **(4c)** Prepare mailing for remaining potential referring physicians in new area, introducing practice, inviting inquiries, encouraging referrals. Include cover letter, referral physician handbook, referral pads, and Rolodex card. Include info sheets on eye specialties with offer to supply more for each office. | 1. Prepare<br>2. Print, collate<br>3. Mail |

*(continued)*

## EXHIBIT 1.3 ■ Strategic Plan: Objectives, Strategies, and Participants/Notes *(Continued)*

| Objective | Strategy | Participants/Notes |
|---|---|---|
| Patients | **(4d)** Prepare a mailing to existing and previous patients in the new area, telling of your new, closer location, listing services, with motivator for friend-friend referrals. | 1. Write (1 hour)<br>2. Produce on oversize postcard or on letterhead with business card |
| Use selected media<br>New office<br>New doctor | **(4e)** Prepare and disseminate media release to outlets in new area<br>■ Include fact sheet on practice.<br>■ Include practice handbook.<br>■ Include cover letter offering EG services as expert on pediatric and neuro eye care. | Media release:<br>Fact sheet:<br>Cover letter: |
|  | **(4f)** Prepare and run print ads in selected media in new area. | Artist<br>Ad cost |
| **(5)** Media—ongoing | **(5a)** Train staff and physicians to watch for interesting cases, medical advances in EG specialties that could become potential news or feature stories. MMI prepare pitch to appropriate reporters. | Consultant |
| **(6)** Create on-going protocols for securing and cementing referral relationships. | **(6a)** Organize continuing medical education seminars for referring physicians, either in the offices of large practices or in a convenient mutual location. | EG to organize as is appropriate |
|  | **(6b)** Create quarterly newsletter, brief and succinct, with updates on key issues and progress in specialty ophthalmology, send to current and potential referring physicians. | Referring physicians report that they already receive too much mail, so this must be useful and concise. |

| Objective | Strategy | Participants/Notes |
|---|---|---|
| | **(6c)** Create a periodic case study postcard to spotlight one of the following: new procedures in EG repertoire, partnership w/local MD that resulted in superior patient care, new study results or participation, etc. Include EG contact info. | Create template to be followed in subsequent editions so doctors can skim the familiar format. Include valuable info such as upcoming conferences, etc. as well as new procedures and services at EG. Newsletter depends on how much material. Case study dependent on how much info provided by client |
| | **(6d)** Consider combining newsletter and case study: one 8.5 × 11 page, folded, with case study always in prominent location. | Need to discuss. See report from referral survey of 3 physicians. |
| Physicians | **(6e)** Follow up on "x" number of referral doctors' offices each month to be sure EG is meeting their needs and exceeding their standards. Track in-house. | In-house |
| Physicians, patients | **(6f)** Physicians write personal thank you notes for physician and patient referrals. | In-house |

*Abbreviations*

| | | | | |
|---|---|---|---|---|
| CV: | Curriculum Vitae | | MMI: | Medical Marketing Inc. |
| EG: | Eye Group | | TBD: | to be determined |
| EMR: | Electronic Medical Record | | | |

*Used with permission of Eye Physicians of Central Florida.*

## REFERENCES

1. Oetjen, Reid M. and Dawn M. Oetjen, *Medical Practice Management Body of Knowledge Review: Planning and Marketing, Volume 7.* Medical Group Management Association, Englewood, Colo. 2006, p. 17–22.

CHAPTER 2

# Gaining a Fresh Understanding of Your Patients

Naturally, patients are your practice's most important customers. They're the reason you and your group's physicians go to work, continue to update your education, plan for the future, spend your creative and financial resources to upgrade your facilities, and stay compliant with the law.

Patients also are one of the primary reasons you must market your services. **The Four A's—Access, Availability, Accountability,** and **Accommodation**—are all about how empowered patients have become.

As I said in my second book, *Ready-Set-Market!*,[1] when you think about marketing, you should first concentrate on meeting the needs of your patients or customers. Obviously, their needs can vary from the very complex to the very simple. And although some may require a sophisticated response, most can be met easily—and inexpensively.

## BUILDING BETTER CUSTOMER SERVICE

From a functional perspective, patients primarily want to find out if they're ill and, if so, how your practice physicians or extenders will create a plan to make them better.

From an emotional perspective, patients want to be able to have **Access** to an appointment *when it's important to them*. They also want both phone and face-to-face exchanges to be unhurried and compassionate, and they want to feel engaged and personally recognized during the time they're connected with your practice.

Here are a few basic strategies that can help you foster better customer/patient service in your practice.

1. Make customer service a priority, but first make sure that everyone you employ knows what service means and how it should be carried out within your practice.

2. No matter how briefly your staff interacts with patients or other customers, train them to use the patient's or customer's name. Your goal is to make everyone feel his or her needs are important to your practice.

3. Give customers extra value. Find ways to recognize long-time patients and referrers for their loyalty to your practice. This can be as simple as a personal handwritten note from the physician.

4. No matter what the size of your group, information systems and documentation are critical. By keeping records of patients and referring physicians, you can identify trends that foretell customers' changing needs. And don't just read reports—take action from the information you extract from them. Assign someone to review trend reports and recommend actions for the group.

5. Use technology wisely. It's as important as intellectual capital in today's complex world.

6. Pay attention to all components of your practice, not just the external side the patients see. Your infrastructure, processes, systems, and people support the culture of your organization.

7. Don't compromise on quality in products, services, or people—especially people. As in any other industry, creating a valued service experience in health care is an exercise in thoughtful details. These experiences support your group's brand name identity and service excellence, which is critical to your success.

8. Find out what your customers experience at your practice. Hire a mystery shopper to become your patient, have that person evaluate interactions and experiences, and then have him or her report back to your group. Also offer all your patients a chance to tell you how they believe you're meeting their needs by implementing a patient survey to provide patient feedback.

9. Track and identify the department that reports the most patient complaints each month. Use the staffing in that area of your practice to help come up with solutions.

municate problems and patient concerns, don't criticize. You want them to reveal any mistakes they've made rather than hide them for fear of disciplinary action.

11. Every chance you get, demonstrate your commitment to customer service, thoroughly and intently, to your staff, your patients, and others with whom you do business. Seek anecdotes, stories, and ideas from your staff, patients, vendors, and competitors that will allow you to enhance your service.

12. Casually experience your competitors. Find out what they offer that could attract patients, managed care, or employers to do business with them rather than with your practice.

13. Consider having alert patients willing to see a doctor soon in the event that there is a no-show. Some computer systems allow for this.

## PATIENT SATISFACTION

Patients and employees who are purchasing managed care benefits or are selecting health plans want to find providers with whom they're familiar. And they want their fears and concerns addressed. They've heard or read that health care reform will give them less choice, so they're concerned that gatekeepers will reduce health care resources to save money or to line their own pockets.

In addition to familiarity and assurance, patients also look for trust and name recognition (brand-name identity). They want to believe that they're with quality doctors who will provide **The Four A's—Access, Availability, Accountability, and Accommodation.** Patients want to believe that their doctors will choose to reduce overhead to become "lean and mean" through business operations, rather than by withholding clinical resources.

As I said earlier, some things have changed in the past decade. On the other hand, many items have not changed. The following list of today's patient preferences reflects the results of numerous focus groups and interviews. Although it's by no means all-inclusive, this list will give you a good idea of what most patients want. (Note that many of the items are related to what is of value to the patient who uses the services and the expertise provided by medical practices.)

- Patients want to be able to reach you when they need you.
- Patients want the phone answered by a friendly voice that understands the nature and urgency of their problems.
- Patients want to know how long it will take for someone to return a phone call.
- Patients want to have the ability to e-mail questions and get responses, rather than wait for phone calls to be returned at the end of the day.
- Patients want to feel valued by all staff, no matter how brief a visit. They do not want to feel like a commodity that simply passes through a doorway with an overhead sign that says "Doctor's Office."
- Patients do not want to believe that every interaction they have with your practice is about money—a deductible, a cost of service, a prepayment before a procedure. If your practice makes a call to welcome a new patient to the practice, that is a "value added" service instead of calls about how a procedure will be financed.
- Patients also want other information, such as:
  - Do you accept their insurance?
  - What will happen to them during their visit?
  - When will they have results of diagnostic tests? If you don't reach them immediately, and their test results are problematic, they want to be assured you'll continue to attempt to reach them until you've made a connection.
  - Does your office accept patient e-mail to their doctors or to extenders?
  - Does your practice have a Website?

## MEETING PATIENT NEEDS

Satisfying these preferences is simple, really. Most are just common-sense measures that can be implemented easily by almost any practice in the United States, no matter how large or how small. They're the minimum you can do to meet the needs of those with whom you do business. Think of this as a review chart—an exercise checklist to be included in your practice assessment.

- Be sure your reception area is a pleasant, tidy area for patients. Provide patients with a phone to make local calls.

- If you know your practice always runs late and patients back up, provide coffee or fruit juice for patients and visitors in your reception area.
- Update magazines in your reception area so they are no more than 90 days old. Remove old issues and donate them to school libraries. Purchase a subscription to the daily paper and have it available for patients to read.
- Create a display in the reception area that highlights your physicians with photos and specialty descriptions. Patients enjoy knowing what their physician looks like before their first meeting.
- Develop a one-page fact sheet that describes your physician providers, your subspecialties, and the services available within your group.
- Have one-page articles available to provide health education. This may include seasonal information and facts about procedures or screenings available within your practice.
- Place long-lasting fresh flowers in your reception area at the beginning of each week. At the end of the week, invite patients to take flowers as they leave the practice.
- Have a suggestion box in your reception area with three-by-five cards on which patients can jot down ideas and comments to improve your practice's patient service. Also provide an area on your Website for patients to contact your practice.
- At least once a month, sit in your reception area. Use this time to read the magazines available for patients, look at the décor, and notice what it's like to be a patient in your practice. Change those things that don't make you feel good.
- Invest in some coloring books, paper dolls, and other child-safe toys to keep children and parents happy while they're waiting to be seen.
- Make it your goal to have no patient wait longer than 15 minutes during an appointment. Encourage patients to notify your staff if the wait is longer.

## One Example

How do you know how your patients perceive you? Ask them. See Exhibit 2.1 for how Texas Retina Associates surveys its patients.

**EXHIBIT 2.1** ■ **Patient Satisfaction Survey**

# PATIENT SATISFACTION SURVEY

***To Our Valued Patient:*** Your opinion counts so we invite your comments. At Texas Retina Associates, our goal is to provide you with the highest quality eye care and patient safety. To help us serve you better, please take a few minutes today and complete our patient satisfaction questionnaire. Your responses are completely confidential and anonymous. Your input about our service to you, allows us to utilize your opinions to make positive changes in our practice. We thank you in advance for completing our survey.

| | | |
|---|---|---:|
| My appointment is with | Dr._____ | 1 |
| My appointment is at the | _____office (location) | 2 |
| The amount of time the doctor spent with me was adequate for my needs. | ☐ Yes<br>☐ No | 3 |
| The physician treated me with dignity, respect and patience. | ☐ Yes<br>☐ No | 4 |
| Why do you have an appointment with Texas Retina Associates? | ☐ New Patient ☐ Referred by another physician<br>☐ Follow up visit as ☐ Other_____<br>  an established patient *(Please specify)* | 5 |
| Who referred you to us? | ☐ Primary Care Physician ☐ Friend<br>☐ Ophthalmologist ☐ Relative<br>☐ Optometrist ☐ Other? Who | 6 |
| How many days did you wait to get today's appointment? | _ _ _ days *(write in number)* | 7 |

### ARRIVAL AND CHECK IN

| | | |
|---|---|---:|
| Did you wait past the time of your scheduled appointment? If so how long? | _ _ _ minutes *(write in number)* | 8 |
| Were our financial policies clearly explained to you? How could this experience be improved? | ☐ Yes<br>☐ No | 9 |
| Were you asked for your current insurance information? | ☐ Yes<br>☐ No | 10 |

# Patient Satisfaction Survey

Please rate the following aspects of your visit by circling the appropriate number after each statement below, according to this scale:

| Strongly Agree | Agree | No Opinion | Disagree | Strongly Disagree |
|---|---|---|---|---|
| ① | ② | ③ | ④ | ⑤ |

## Arrival and Check In

| Statement | Strongly Agree | Agree | No Opinion | Disagree | Strongly Disagree | # |
|---|---|---|---|---|---|---|
| The person who set up my appointment was helpful, patient and courteous. | ① | ② | ③ | ④ | ⑤ | 11 |
| The office location was convenient. | ① | ② | ③ | ④ | ⑤ | 12 |
| Parking was convenient. | ① | ② | ③ | ④ | ⑤ | 13 |
| Our receptionist was helpful, patient and courteous. | ① | ② | ③ | ④ | ⑤ | 14 |
| The length of time I waited in the reception area was reasonable. | ① | ② | ③ | ④ | ⑤ | 15 |

| My appointment was: | on time | 15 minutes late | 30 minutes late | 16 |
|---|---|---|---|---|

## Office Visits

| Statement | Strongly Agree | Agree | No Opinion | Disagree | Strongly Disagree | # |
|---|---|---|---|---|---|---|
| The medical assistant who prepared me for my exam was friendly, patient and courteous. | ① | ② | ③ | ④ | ⑤ | 17 |
| The physician gave me time to ask questions. | ① | ② | ③ | ④ | ⑤ | 18 |
| The instructions I received about follow up care were clear and easy to understand. | ① | ② | ③ | ④ | ⑤ | 19 |
| I was provided with written instructions for my follow up care. | ① | ② | ③ | ④ | ⑤ | 20 |
| The follow up instructions I received were easy for me to understand. | ① | ② | ③ | ④ | ⑤ | 21 |

*(continued)*

**EXHIBIT 2.1 ■ Patient Satisfaction Survey** *(Continued)*

# PATIENT SATISFACTION SURVEY

## OFFICE VISITS

| Question | Rating | # |
|---|---|---|
| The medical assistants showed concern for me as a patient. | ① ❷ ③ ❹ ⑤ | 22 |
| The reception area was clean and pleasant. | ① ❷ ③ ❹ ⑤ | 23 |
| The treatment room was clean and pleasant. | ① ❷ ③ ❹ ⑤ | 24 |
| The restrooms were clean and had necessary supplies. | ① ❷ ③ ❹ ⑤ | 25 |

## LAB / PROCEDURES

| Question | Rating | # |
|---|---|---|
| The lab/photography staff who helped with my care was friendly, patient and courteous. | ① ❷ ③ ❹ ⑤ | 26 |
| The lab staff explained what was going to happen during my procedure. | ① ❷ ③ ❹ ⑤ | 27 |
| The lab staff answered my questions until I was clear about my procedure. | ① ❷ ③ ❹ ⑤ | 28 |

## CHECK OUT AND DEPARTURE

| Question | Response | # |
|---|---|---|
| Was our staff available and helpful to answer your questions about our billing procedures? | ☐ Yes  ☐ No | |
| The manner in which financial arrangements were made was professional. | ① ❷ ③ ❹ ⑤ | 29 |
| I would recommend Texas Retina Associates to my friends without hesitation. | ① ❷ ③ ❹ ⑤ | 30 |
| My visit would have been improved if | _____ | 31 |

# Patient Satisfaction Survey

Do you have any suggestions as to how we might improve our services to you?

_____ 32
_____
_____

Please make any additional comments you would like us to know.

_____ 33
_____
_____

**Dallas — Main**
7150 Greenville Avenue, Suite 400
Dallas, Texas 75231
**214.692.6941 • 800.695.6941**
214.739.5797 fax

**Dallas — Baylor**
3600 Gaston Avenue, Suite 1055
Dallas, Texas 75246
**214.821.4540 • 214.821.9073 fax**

**Arlington**
1001 N. Waldrop Drive, Suite 512
Arlington, Texas 76012
**817.261.9625 • 817.261.9586 fax**

**Plano**
1780 Coit Road, Suite 215
Plano, Texas 75075
**800.695.6941**

**Lubbock**
3802 22nd Street, Suite B
Lubbock, Texas 79410
**806.792.0066 • 806.792.2446 fax**

**Corsicana**
301 Hospital Drive
Corsicana, Texas 75110
**903.872.4611 • 903.872.4573 fax**

**OPTIONAL**
If you would like someone from our practice to contact you about this survey or for other information, please print the following:

name _____

address _____

phone number _____

email address _____

**Sherman**
2627 Masters Drive
Sherman, Texas 75090
**903.893.8443 • 903.893.6468 fax**

**Denton**
2210 San Jacinto Blvd., Suite 1
Denton, Texas 76205
**800.695.6941 • 940.383.2608 fax**

Would you like to receive updates and information regarding Texas Retina via email?    ☐ Yes    ☐ No

**Wichita Falls**
5800 Kell Blvd. Suite 100
Wichita Falls, Texas 76310
**940.691.3232 • 800.695.6941**
940.691.5535 fax

**Paris**
575 DeShong, Suite B
Paris, Texas 75462
**903.739.8321 • 903.783.1546 fax**

Thank you for participating in our survey

_Used with permission of Texas Retina Associates._

## Other Ways to Meet Patient Needs

Quite often, patients are the driving force behind the evolution of health care. One example of this is retail medicine, which I'll discuss in greater detail in Chapter 10.

This phenomenon has led to the opening of primary health care centers in grocery stores and drugstores. And it happened because patients could not get **Access** to their regular physicians in a time they felt was reasonable. An opportunity was created to meet patient needs, and it's really become quite sophisticated. As with some of the other opportunities that have evolved to compete with group practices, this has come about because of **The Four A's.** It's a result of patients wanting **Access, Availability, Accountability,** and **Accommodation.**

This particular retail medicine concept was originally created in 2000 because a parent named Rick Krieger took his sick son to an urgent care center and had to wait 2 hours to get a test for strep throat. Mr. Krieger decided there had to be a quicker and more convenient way to get care.

A year later, he and his new partners—one of which was a physician—founded QuickMedx, the retail health care clinics that became Minute Clinic. Their first health care centers opened in Minneapolis in Cubb food stores. They focused on seven common acute medical conditions that patients often suffer from—including strep throat, mono, bladder infections, ear infections, sinus infections, pregnancy testing, and the flu. Now, Minute Clinic has added health care centers in several Target stores and CVS Pharmacies.[2]

The situation is really very simple. Your patients want to get in to see you on what they consider to be a reasonable time schedule. If they, their child, or their spouse is ill, they want to be seen by a physician or a health care extender who can prescribe medication or treat their problem.

What you must realize is that patients are no longer necessarily loyal to their personal physician practices. If you don't meet their needs—if they can't be seen when they want to be seen—they'll look for a way to be accommodated. And unlike a decade ago, it's often right at their fingertips.

In many communities, they can go to their grocery store, their pharmacy, or a Target or Wal-Mart store, for example, and be seen quickly. Some places, they're given a beeper so they can go and shop while they wait to be called to the health care provider. They have absolutely no wait, *no wasted time*. And you know as well as I do that's an important consideration to today's busy, overscheduled moms and dads.

Then they can move directly from the caregiver to the pharmacy to get a prescription filled and pick up Gatorade, throat lozenges, or whatever else they need to make their life a little more comfortable. They can pay with their credit card or with cash and hope their insurance company will cover it, and then go home to wait until they feel better.

In these retail health care facilities, we frequently find happy, pleasant workers. It doesn't seem to be a state of frenzy and rushing. Patients are addressed by name and for that short period, they feel that they're really being listened to and accommodated.

The policy and advocacy section of the American Academy of Family Physicians even sets forth an entire set of attributes that they believe is important in retail health care centers. They developed these attributes as a guideline for family practice physicians who may be working directly with or overseeing them.

That certainly gives a level of respect to the fact that these clinics are meeting the needs of people in our community. And it seems they're here to stay. As you face this and other competition to traditional group practice care, you must be sensitive to the things that are of value to your patients. And you would be wise to plan your marketing activities accordingly.

## REFERENCES

1. Eliscu, Andrea T., *Ready-Set-Market!* Medical Group Management Association, Englewood, Colo. 1999; p. 18–19.
2. www.minuteclinic.com

CHAPTER 3

# Providing POW! Customer Service

One of the most important tenets of marketing maintains that you must know your customers. As discussed, health care marketing "customers" primarily translate to patients, but they also include your referrers and others, including your staff. And after you know them well, you must try your best to meet their wants and needs, even as your practice evolves. Toward this goal, many practices create mission statements and vision statements; some even define their core values.

No matter what the process, successful practices find a way to address customer service issues because they realize that's the cornerstone of their success. Although some of these issues may not sound important, they are vital to your patients. Some of these issues include the following:

- How long it takes to get an appointment
- How long callers spend on hold
- How long it takes to see a physician or extender beyond the time of an appointment
- How quickly phone calls are returned
- If physicians call back a family caregiver in a timely way
- Whether parking is readily available
- Whether signage is friendly and easy to read
- Whether staff exhibits a patient-friendly attitude

Even when you try hard to meet customers' needs, sometimes it can seem like an impossible task. How can your practice focus on serving patients when your physicians are focused on practicing medicine? After all, they still have to concentrate on making the right diagnostic and treatment decisions, keep up with changing regulations, and understand and manage overhead costs. All this while they watch their incomes being compromised and creative competitors carve away at what once was a stable patient base.

That said, I'm sure you realize that marketing and communications are fundamental factors in the business of medicine. And customer/patient service is *the single most important element* of any marketing program.

How do others do it? Here's an example from the restaurant industry that's known for its excellent customer service: Red Lobster, which is owned by Darden Restaurants, the leader in the casual dining market. I believe their methods are easily extrapolated to health care.

Red Lobster was founded in 1968 and has grown to more than 600 restaurants. Obviously, consumers' tastes have changed over the past 40 years; to succeed, Red Lobster has had to change with them. As an example, consumers are much more health-conscious today. So Red Lobster altered its menus to offer seafood and other entrees prepared in a variety of ways, such as grilled and steamed, to meet these newly defined customer preferences.

If Red Lobster had not asked questions and stayed alert to customers' needs and desires, the popular restaurant may not have recognized the growth opportunities at its door. In the highly competitive food service field, it may have failed to even survive.[1]

What can you learn from this example that will help you improve your practice? First and foremost, understand that providing service and managing your brand in the face of cultural, behavioral, and economic shifts is an ongoing, evolutionary process. Then, continually plan for changes that translate into service and accommodation for your customers/patients, just as Red Lobster does for its dining guests.

Let's look at another example, this one from the hospitality industry. Hyatt Hotels understands what its customers want and knows how important it is to provide those services throughout its many locations. Hyatt is **Accessible, Available,** and **Accommodating.** And every employee throughout the chain wears a name badge that tells where they "used" to live. This assures that the employee can be identified for **Accountability** and also provides an opportunity for discussion if clients are so minded.

In addition, Hyatt offers services it knows its customers appreciate, such as AAA discounts, senior rates, a Hyatt.com rate, spa services, golf, family discounts, Hyatt-at-Home (the ability to buy Hyatt home products), Gold Passport bonuses for frequent users, and Web check-in. There's something for everyone, because Hyatt understands its customers' desires. Consequently, customers feel well served.

If these two industries realize how important it is to serve their customers, perhaps we in health care can learn a lesson or two from them. In *Ready-Set-Market!*, John Bruns, then general manager of The Ritz-Carlton, Cleveland, discussed how that hotel chain became an icon for service in the hotel industry. It was under his leadership, in fact, that the Ritz-Carlton, Cleveland, won the coveted Baldridge Award, the hospitality industry's highest honor for quality and service.

In Chapter 1 of *Ready-Set-Market!*,[2] John discussed how he found employees with the core values to meet the Ritz-Carlton's mission statement. He also disclosed how he motivated new hires and young staff people to do their best jobs.

John, who also served as vice president of development for Renaissance Hotels International and as general manager of the Stouffer Renaissance Chicago hotel, shared his prospective from the hotel industry viewpoint. His other experience includes general manager of the Stouffer Nashville hotel and management positions with Westin Hotels and Resorts in San Francisco, Seattle, Detroit, Cincinnati, and Chicago.

If you haven't read his contribution in *Ready-Set-Market!*, I encourage you to. I believe you'll see a connection between his perspective and your role as leader of your health care organization or group practice.

In 2000, John was lured away from Ritz-Carlton by Las Vegas–based Harrah's Entertainment. Building on the strong cultural foundation of the Ritz-Carlton Hotel Company and with 10 years of innovative process work opening two hotels as its general manager, John applied his Baldridge training to a gaming company committed to leveraging service as a competitive advantage.

When John joined the company, Harrah's owned and operated 28 casinos in 12 states across the United States. Headed by Chairman, Chief Executive Officer, and President Phil Satre and Chief Operating Officer Gary Loveman, Harrah's was a solid pure-play gaming company whose business model was based on the Service Profit Chain. Loveman, previously an associate professor in the Service Management Group at Harvard University, was eager to demonstrate the linkage between service, customer loyalty, and profits.

John's operational experience made him the perfect choice to fulfill Loveman's passion for great service. And now, eight years later with service clearly a cornerstone of Harrah's core capabilities, he offers his overview of how customer satisfaction at Harrah's has improved for 24 consecutive quarters. In late 2007, John was been promoted yet again and now is headquartered in London, England, to handle Harrah's international gaming facilities.

## JOHN BRUNS: CUSTOMER SATISFACTION

### Background

Harrah's measures customer satisfaction assurance (CSA) rigorously, sending out more than 2 million surveys per year with a response rate of more than 20 percent. Each survey measures the two critical attributes to a gamer: friendly/helpful behavior of the employee and wait time (WT), how long the customer waits to be served.

Each casino property generally measures 10 operating departments (such as cashiers, beverage, slots, total rewards, buffet). During a typical year, Harrah's collects more than 8 million datapoints in CSA. The CSA survey rating scale is just like school:

- A = Excellent
- B = Good
- C = Satisfactory
- D = Poor
- F = Failure

Harrah's only counts top box A scores, because B scores, or merely good service, is not a strong enough score to bring the customer back or create loyalty in a customer. In 2000, Harrah's percentage of top box A scores on a company-wide basis was 38 percent, meaning 62 percent of all customers rated service as a non-A. Non-A customers, by definition, were not loyal to Harrah's and were at risk to competitive attack, usually manifested as direct mail offers and promotions designed to take customers and market share from Harrah's.

## EXHIBIT 3.1 ■ The SPC Model

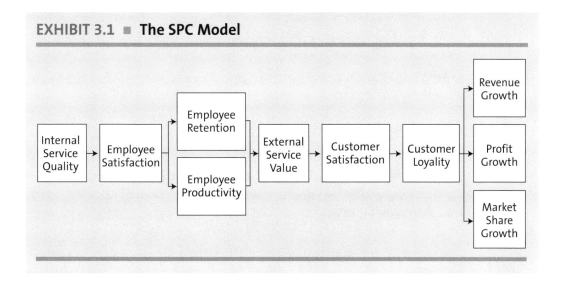

## *Service Profit Chain Business Model*

Since Loveman's arrival at Harrah's in 1998, casino operators had struggled to improve service. While Loveman was preaching the service profit chain (SPC) model, operators were failing to get traction and improve service. From 1998 to 2000, scores were flat at 36 to 38 percent "A's." (See Exhibit 3.1.)

Clearly, the service profit chain needed new strategies and tactics to engage employees and deliver an improved customer experience.

Feeling slightly overwhelmed, I had the daunting task to improve service through 45,000 employees to more than 5 million frequent players carrying the Total Rewards Loyalty Card.

To overcome the fear, I did two important things. First, I started reading books related to service. I started with classics such as *Moments of Truth* by Carlzon; *The Service Profit Chain* by Heskett, Sasser, and Schlesinger; *The Loyalty Effect* by Reichheld and Teal; *The Customer Delight Principle* by Keiningham and Vavra; and *Managing the Customer Experience* by Wheeler and Smith, among others.[3-7]

Second, I hit the road. Traveling more than 150,000 miles domestically, he visited all the casinos to listen to *his* customers—the casino operators.

For 5 months, I discussed strategy, tactics, standards, measurements, accountabilities, consequences, data integrity, and reporting with general managers and casino executive teams. As I moved from property to property—from team to team, collaborating with all levels of property management—a strategy emerged. Named Strategy for Success, this unifying vision was destined to bring the SPC to life and to guide management and employee behaviors for years to come.

### CSA Strategy for Success

1. Service culture: philosophies, beliefs, and values that guide behavior
2. Service process: dynamic delivery systems to match capacity demand

### Leveraging the Strategy for Success and SPC

Internal Service Quality has six components:

1. Selection and development
2. Information and communication
3. Recognition and reward
4. Job design
5. Workplace design
6. Tools and systems to serve the customer

### Service Culture

The friendly/helpful behavior of all employees is brought to life at Harrah's through the employees' experiences, beginning at selection and development. Harrah's knows that friendly/helpful behavior is the most important aspect of customer service. Accordingly, the company instituted "panel auditions" in which applicants answer questions and play games in front of senior management as part of the interview process. Thus applicants must demonstrate a friendly/helpful attitude to proceed to the next step.

The development of the employee-friendly/helpful behavior is continued in orientation, department skill training, and daily preshift department meetings called buzz sessions. Benchmarked from the Ritz-Carlton Line-Ups, Harrah's buzz sessions are designed to provide information, communication, and recognition for the employees on a daily basis.

Harrah's understands that employees come to work with problems, and the buzz sessions are designed to transition the employee from home to work. Typical problems that employees come to work with include the following.

1. Child care (sick child at home)
2. Health care (employee, child, aging relative)
3. Transportation (car breaks down, bus/train late)
4. Financial (living hand-to-mouth)

Harrah's buzz sessions are designed to transition the employee—put him or her in a state of readiness to serve the customer and get "every brain in the game." Buzz sessions have five building steps:

1. Listen—to employee's suggestions—and act!
2. Communicate—what's important today on the floor
3. Reinforce—upbeat/positive attitude and behaviors valuable to customer
4. Recognize—service stars and read customer testimonials
5. Have fun—energize the team

So, with one operationally effective tactic—buzz—Harrah's is able to execute a strategy designed to build employee satisfaction and engagement by reinforcing selection, development, information, communication, and recognition in one daily activity.

## *Service Process*

Job design, workplace design, and tools to serve the customer are typically related to service process, meaning repeatable steps of a service delivery system. Harrah's recognized early on that for the employee to deliver a Moment of Truth that exceeded customer's expectations, the customer had to be in a state of readiness to *receive* a great Moment of Truth.

This notion of customer readiness is centered on the understanding that *if* the customer waits too long to be served, *then* the employee will not be able to overcome customer anger with an upbeat/positive attitude. WT, therefore, was studied in the context of three types.

1. Transaction time
2. Time in line or time to be acknowledged
3. Number of people in line

Based on Disney's knowledge, described in *The Service Profit Chain*, Harrah's believed that transaction time is the least important time to a customer because "it takes as long as it takes" to complete a personalized transaction. Although time in line is difficult to measure on an ongoing basis, acknowledgment time is important in departments such as slots and beverage where the customer is waiting to be served. Number of people in line, the number ahead of you versus the number of agents available to serve, also directly impacts the customer's perception of WT.

Harrah's realized that it needed to set WT service standards to protect the customers from unreasonable waits and thus corresponding anger. Analysis of WT data by department led Harrah's to a concept called Cliff of Dissatisfaction. Simply said, there comes a time when the customer has waited so long (unreasonable WT) that he or she will never give you an "A" (excellent) score on WT.

Subsequently, WT Cliffs of Dissatisfaction were discovered in each operating department in terms of maximum wait time. Importantly, the Cliffs were turned into service standards, clearly communicating *the time to beat* to protect the "A."

## *Conclusion*

Harrah's entertainment analysis of empirical customer survey data led it to develop service standards, strategies, and tactics to improve the customer experience. Selecting and developing employees with friendly/helpful behavior and then holding management accountable for designing delivery systems that protect the WT "A" proved to be a combination that customers valued.

Overall customer satisfaction "A" scores moved from 38 percent to 54 percent over the past 6 years. That translates into 25 consecutive quarters of year-over-year improvement. And it means that John gets to keep his job!

## SUMMARY

So what can you learn from these models that will help you improve your practice? Look closely and you'll see how the major points of each can positively impact your relationships with patients, referring physicians, and other customers.

Simply stay alert to your customers' needs and desires as Red Lobster did; understand the importance of **The Four A's: Access, Availability, Accountability,** and **Accommodation** as Hyatt did; recruit, motivate, and retain good employees as the Ritz-Carlton did; and finally, develop service standards, strategies, and tactics to improve your customers' experiences as Harrah's did.

If you provide services and manage your brand as well as these companies do, you'll have no trouble maintaining your current patient base and growing your practice if you desire.

## REFERENCES

1. Darden Restaurants 2005 Annual Report. Darden Restaurants, Orlando, Fla. 2005.
2. Eliscu, Andrea T., *Ready-Set-Market!* Medical Group Management Association, Englewood, Colo. 1999.
3. Carlzon, Jan, *Moments of Truth.* Ballinger Publishing Company, Cambridge, Mass., 1987.
4. Haskett, James L., Earl W. Sasser, and Leonard A Schlesinger, *The Service Profit Chain.* The Free Press, New York, 1997.
5. Reichheld, Frederick F. and Thomas Teal, *The Loyalty Effect: The Hidden Force Behind Growth, Profits, and Lasting Value.* The Harvard Business School Press, Cambridge, Mass.,1996.
6. Keiningham, Timothy L. and Terry G. Vavra, *The Customer Delight Principle: Exceeding Customers' Expectations for Bottom-Line Success.* McGraw-Hill, New York, 2001.
7. Wheeler, Jay and Shaun Smith, *Managing the Customer Experience: Turning Customers into Advocates.* FT-Prentice-Hall, Upper Saddle River, New Jersey, 2002.

CHAPTER 4

# Diagnosing Your Practice—A Simple Guide to Effective Practice Assessment

Take a look at what you experience in your practice today, and you'll undoubtedly agree with Gregory Mertz of the Horizon Group Ltd.[1] Medical care costs are rising by double digits, benefit costs are contributing to employer backlash, practice overhead is continuing to increase, and physician reimbursement is failing to keep pace with inflation.

If your practice is like most and if you want to succeed, things must change. Obviously, you can no longer conduct business as you've done in the past. No successful practice can. And as lead physician or practice administrator with fiscal responsibility, you know this better than anyone.

So what should you do? What *can* you do?

First, on the operations side, you must monitor and control your practice's revenue cycle activities, utilize today's technology while investing in automation, and analyze the way you operate. You must find new ways to operate efficiently and effectively without compromising customer service.

As a manager, you should look at the roles of both clinical and nonclinical staff to ensure efficiency without compromising care. You also must find ways to schedule patients more efficiently, which may require you to make big decisions about hours of business and overhead. To meet your patients' needs, for example, you may have to schedule patients early in the morning, late into the evening, or even on weekends.

As you assess your practice, you need to look at how well you respond to the changing needs of your environment—both for what is coming and what exists in your community now. But before you begin your assessment, you have to look at the big picture.

One of the key issues is to understand the population around you. Who are they in terms of demographics, such as age, income, profession, health status, and other defining information? And if you have multiple offices, you have to realize that this demographic may differ from community to community.

Eighty percent of America's senior citizens, aged 65 and older, live with at least one chronic disease according to a report released earlier this year by the Centers for Disease Control and Prevention. According to the study, seven chronic diseases (diabetes, cancer, hypertension, stroke, heart disease, pulmonary conditions, and mental illness) have a total impact on the economy of $1.3 trillion annually.[2] In addition, according to a report from the Center on Budget and Policy Priorities, the number of uninsured Americans rose for the sixth consecutive year in 2006, to 47.0 million and the number of uninsured children rose for the second straight year, to 8.7 million, according to Census data released on August 28, 2007.[3] Let's face it, the US health care system soon will have to cope with the needs of aging low- and middle-income baby boomers, many of whom have increased health care issues, unstable health insurance coverage, high medical costs, and problems with debt.

When you take a look at the lay of the land—whether for your strategic plan, your business plan, or your marketing plan—you'll become aware of what concerns people about our health care system. Older workers and their spouses are worried about being able to afford health care insurance. A majority of mature consumers say they'd be interested in receiving Medicare before age 65. Even Americans with moderate incomes face high rates of unstable health care coverage.

A January 19, 2007, *Kansas City Business Journal* article quoted the January edition of *Physicians Practice* magazine,[4] which said that

> *The average physician reimbursement from commercial payers and Medicare collapsed in 2006, with payment levels averaging seventeen percent below that of 2002 and a staggering 37 percent below that of 2004.*

In June 2006, the Center for Studying Health System Change, a nonprofit research group in Washington, D.C., reported that the average physician's inflation-adjusted income declined 7 percent from 1995 to 2003, with primary care doctors taking a 10 percent cut during the same period.[5]

## ASSESSING YOUR PRACTICE

Earlier in this book, I said things have changed, yet they remain the same. Practice assessment is one of the areas in which things really have changed very little. That's primarily because patients' needs haven't changed a lot, with the exception of how powerful the Internet has become. This ubiquitous tool has given patients the ability to communicate with you almost instantly, either by e-mail or Website. Furthermore, they expect you to use these tools and respond in a timely manner.

You may be asking, "What can I do to make my practice succeed in today's situation?" "How can marketing help me?" "Where do I start?"

You also may ask, "What does a practice assessment have to do with medical marketing?" The simple answer is: everything. A practice assessment is the vital first step of any effective marketing plan. And it's the answer to the question of where to start. In a very practical sense, you must assess where you are before you can move forward.

So, how do you assess your practice?

Always begin your practice assessment with an eye toward finding ways to maintain and increase your market share. Start by examining your practice's strengths, weaknesses, opportunities, and threats—what we call SWOT—and defining your goals. Only after you understand these two elements (SWOT and goals) will you be able to prioritize your marketing challenges.

An effective practice assessment includes a review of both internal and external factors. When conducting an *internal managed care* assessment, look at your contracts, affiliations, fee schedules, payer mix, revenues, and procedural fees. Evaluate capitated contracts and their significance within your practice.

When you do an external managed care assessment, look at enrollment, products, major customers, new initiatives, market share, and your competitors.

As you assess your *community*, identify major employers and primary referrers. Also, list existing managed care plans and managed care plans that are entering the community, plus Medicaid and Medicare health maintenance organizations.

Always keep in mind that the relationships of the future are being built today. And with so many consolidations taking place, the person you work with at one organization today may very well be the same one you'll work with at a different organization tomorrow! Again, that circle of "yes, it's changed, yet it's still the same."

Your assessment also should identify your *customers* so you can develop and implement appropriate marketing strategies that will meet their needs. Keep in mind the marketing cornerstones, **The Four A's— Access, Availability, Accommodation,** and **Accountability.**

As you assess, obviously you must research what your *patients* want. As an example, the FACT organization, a byproduct of the Jackson Hole Group, learned this about patient desires. Patients want their physicians to:

- Honor their values and preferences.
- Respect them as persons.
- Communicate clearly.
- Give them power.
- Heal them as whole persons.
- Coordinate across complexity of care.
- Change the relationship from autocratic to partnering.

Having learned that, you should implement the following marketing strategies:

- Treat patients as guests.
- Use technology such as the Internet and electronic medical records.
- Conduct patient surveys.
- Create your practice's database for mailings.
- Provide patients with educational information.
- Call selected patients after their visits.
- Empower all staff to be personable, personal, and accountable.
- Address your patients with appropriate respect.

As you conduct your assessment, you also should identify the needs of *referral physicians*. These include

- Giving their patients quality care.
- Having patients referred back for care.
- Receiving prompt informative reports.
- Having referred patients scheduled promptly.
- Having your practice be accountable.

This allows you to implement the following strategies:

- Create a database of your referral physicians.
- Keep referrers informed and involved.
- Make it easy for referrers to reach you.
- Offer a dedicated referral phone line.
- Organize a think tank with referrers for difficult cases.
- Provide clinical newsletters or mailings.
- Develop measurable marketing activities.

Again, in your assessment, you should look at *managed care* needs. Among other things, these referral physicians want cost-effectiveness, geographic access, best-demonstrated practices, payer-friendly physicians, and your support at recredentialing time. See Exhibit 4.1 for sample practice assesssment guidelines.

To address these needs, your group might want to consider implementing the following marketing strategies:

- Share your utilization review outcomes.
- Call your managed care contacts at least four times per year.
- Communicate practice differentiation.
- Track patients and revenues.
- Communicate everything in writing.
- Share cost-reduction strategies.
- Get to know administrative personnel.
- Obtain direct marketing approval via your contract.

As you assess the wants and needs of *employers*, you'll learn that their top priorities are quality, access, and pricing. Value purchasing is also important to them, and, frequently, they're willing to develop relationships with providers.

> **EXHIBIT 4.1 ■ Practice Assessment Guidelines**
>
> As you begin your practice assessment, keep in mind these general guidelines. Understand that you must:
>
> - Know who you are.
> - Know what you want.
> - Know your customers.
> - Know what your customers want.
> - Know your group and its capabilities.
> - Have a plan.
> - Get it implemented on an ongoing basis.
> - Know what legal constraints there are on marketing and structure your plan accordingly.
> - Understand that marketing is an evolution of behaviors and layers.
> - Write down specific goals.
> - Develop basic communication tools.
> - Build your brand.
> - Hold a strategic retreat.
> - Support your internal staff and empower them.
> - Understand media relations and use the media as a resource.
> - Put yourself in a mindset to lead in your community.
> - Recognize the power of customer service.
> - Recognize that patients are number one and have a great deal of power.
> - Spend time to create a list that defines what differentiates your practice and provides value-added opportunities to all your customers.
> - Do what you do well, even if you can't do everything.

Having this knowledge will allow you to implement the following strategies:

- Make contact with current and new community employers.
- Keep employers updated.
- Get to know the benefits manager.
- Create a database for mailings.
- Write articles for company newsletters.

# DIAGNOSING YOUR PRACTICE

- Invite employers to lunch and to tour your practice.
- Correspond via physician letter or newsletter.

If you've previously conducted these assessments, it's a good idea to take another look at them periodically. When you do, be sure to step back and be objective. Evaluate your existing goals to be sure they're still current and that they address what you want for your future.

Examine your mission statement to determine if it's still valid and enumerate the value-added characteristics that differentiate your practice from your competitors. Make sure that your management information system (MIS) has adequate capability to handle the important operational issues that will arise as your practice matures. See Exhibit 4.2 for a sample practice assessment.

Finally, be consistently sensitive to customer service issues throughout all aspects of your assessment.

## YOUR AUDIT LIST

As you continue your practice assessment, you should look at the following list to determine your standing in regard to marketing materials and other elements of customer service.

- Practice brand-name identity
- Marketing plan or plan of action
- Communication tools
- Relationships
- Competition
- Marketing partners
- Group image
- Public relations
- Community relations
- Promotions for the group
- Mind-set of the group

## ASSESSING YOUR PRACTICE IDENTITY

Before implementing your marketing plan, it's also important to make sure your practice has the tools to easily differentiate your practice from those of your competitors and colleagues in the eyes of your community.

## EXHIBIT 4.2 ■ Sample Practice Assessment

As you assess your practice, you may want to consider some of the following typical characteristics of a subspecialty practice. Some or all may apply to your practice, but of course, you'll want to customize your assessment based on your current situation.

**STRENGTHS**

- Minimal competition (because of creative positioning)
- Good geographic locations
- Strong work ethic
- Willingness to change
- Practice subspecialization
- Strong practice administrator
- Strategic recruiting process
- Belief in marketing

**WEAKNESSES**

- Lack of a group mentality
- Lack of vision
- Group apathy
- Inability to make decisions
- Large size (causing a perception of a mill mentality)
- Lack of strong leadership
- Market share not keeping up with community growth
- Lack of marketing

**OPPORTUNITIES**

- Join or be a developmental leader in a specialty network
- Develop a physician panel to do provider relations with the local health care coalition
- Maximize on the health system's strategy to reenergize relations with their medical staff
- Develop an equity position in a specialty hospital or surgical center
- Contract to provide services in outlying areas via the use of technology
- Relocate an existing office with declining census to an area of high residential and commercial growth

- Review service strategies within the practice and make a commitment to enhance our service approach and implementation
- Update Website to add value for patients

**THREATS**

- Merger of other specialty groups within the region
- Exclusion from physician-developed networks
- Failure to develop management information system (MIS), which compromises ability to compete with other groups who have invested in MIS
- Patients are seeking treatment where they have access
- Patients perceived as giving up "quality" providers in exchange for **Availability** and **Accommodation** at other heath care outlets such as in grocery stores, drug store chains, and other venues

**VALUE-ADDED OR PRACTICE DIFFERENTIATION FACTORS**

- Physician credentials
- Specially credentialed staff
- Location or geographic distribution of office sites
- Operational systems
- MIS systems
- Practice capabilities
- Willingness to accept risk
- Global pricing
- Focus on building relationships with payers and employers
- Commitment to a service mentality for our customers

(See Exhibit 4.3.) Start by reviewing your most fundamental communication tools. Ask yourself the following:

- Do we have a memorable practice name?
- Do we have a graphic identity (logo) that represents what our practice stands for?

These two elements are as basic as it gets when it comes to projecting your desired practice image. And they couldn't be more important to establishing a successful practice identity. Keep in mind that the logo

### EXHIBIT 4.3 ■ How to Differentiate Your Practice

Sometimes physicians and managers tell me they really have a difficult time creating a differentiation list (the "value-added" elements that set their practice apart from others). Because they do the same things everyday, they often don't see their practice as being special or unique to the clients and patients they serve. But look around every time you go shopping. You'll see how easy it is to itemize special attributes.

When patients come to your office, it's very important that you fully and consistently educate them about your products and services. If you survey your patients, you'll probably be amazed to find out how little they're aware of all the products and services provided within your practice. It's especially true in certain specialties, such as orthopaedics, where patients often say they went to a podiatrist because they didn't know an orthopaedic group provided foot and ankle care. Or patients who went to a chiropractor because they didn't know their sports medicine doctor's group also took care of backs.

Take time to review your practice and think about all you offer. Write it down. Not only will it help focus your marketing, it will be of value during your negotiations with other physicians, hospitals, and managed care.

---

you create is for the ease of recognition for your patients and others who do business with your practice.

As you develop your corporate identity package, plan for the following basic items:

- Logo design
- Letterhead
- Customized #10 envelope
- Business cards
- Note card
- Note card envelope
- Self-stick mailing label
- Appointment card
- Fax cover sheet

Additional communication tools you will need in the future may include the following:

- Patient handbook
- Fact sheet template design
- Practice brochure
- Practice folder

It's very important to create a visual image that allows your patients and other clients to recognize your practice immediately. You want to stand out and differentiate your practice from all of the others who provide care in your specialty and community.

## ASSESSING YOUR LOGO

I believe the quality of your logo design can make a big difference in how potential and current patients look at your practice. The key to success in the marketplace can be that simple!

Trademarks and logos make up the most international language in the world. An excellent logo design can cross many barriers and provide your practice with a means of delivering to your patients an unequivocal and uniform message.

Every successful practice has its own "personality," and just as human personalities are complex, so too is your practice's personality. A successful logo is a means of condensing a complex reality into a single, simple statement, one that can be controlled, modified, developed, and matured over time. Your logo needs to be much more than just a distinguishing mark for your practice. It must be an indication of quality, value, and reliability.

When considering your logo, keep in mind that it is often your first opportunity to communicate an image for your organization and to create a predisposition in your favor. As you work with an artist or a graphic designer, communicate clearly what you wish to convey. Articulate which words best describe your organization. These are likely to include the following:

- Quality
- Integrity

- Attention to detail
- Professionalism
- Caring
- A practice that is:
  - Up-to-date
  - Efficient
  - Experienced
  - Knowledgeable
  - Conscientious
  - Innovative
  - Friendly, caring
  - Thorough
  - Reliable

Remember these characteristics, as well as the following guidelines, as you work with a designer to develop a logo that truly represents your practice. Your logo should:

- Differentiate your practice from competitors through a distinct identity that contains a minimum of elements.
- Be clear and readable in all sizes, from large (signage) to small (1 to 5 inches or smaller, if needs dictate).
- Be strong enough to stand alone, as required for signage, yet simple enough to have a distinctive presence when other information should stand out (as in print advertising).
- Copy and fax well.
- Reproduce well in color, as well as black and white, for both high-quality and budget printing projects.
- Utilize no more than two timeless print styles, based on classic principles of weight, balance, and proportion.

Group practice logo examples appear in Exhibit 4.4.

## ASSESSING YOUR STAFF

Let's talk about making the right hire at the right time. This will help you position for **Accommodation** and **Accountability,** the first two of **The Four A's.**

For insight into this area, I've called on Annetta Wilson, a certified professional behavioral analyst. Annetta has held management positions as a community affairs director and marketing director and is a certified trainer and member of the International Association of Coaches.[6] She is

**EXHIBIT 4.4** ■ **Sample Group Practice Logos**

Used with permission of Jewett Orthopaedic Clinic.

Used with permission of Partners in Women's Healthcare.

Used with permission of Vascular Surgery & Vein Care Center.

also an award-winning journalist, and has worked in the broadcast industry for three decades as a news anchor, reporter, producer, talk show host, and writer.

Here's what Annetta has to say about staff assessment: Who's working in your office or for your company? Who do people see when they walk in the door? How are patients and clients greeted? What does that say about your practice?

Your staff must be qualified. What may be neglected or overlooked is how those staff members come across to the people who pay you to take care of them. Wouldn't it be great if you had a crystal ball that could predict how your staff will behave *and* let you know how to best communicate with each of them?

That crystal ball exists. Although there are multiple products on the market, I prefer the DISC™ Assessment. DISC is an acronym for dominance, influence, steadiness, and compliance. Simply put, it virtually predicts how someone handles problems, people, and the pace of their environment, rules, and procedures.[7]

It's a neutral language that focuses on observable behavior, not individual personalities. The outcome is not based on culture, race, or gender. The DISC assessment can reveal an employee's individual strengths and possible limitations. It can be used to help develop an action plan for increasing productivity and making an organization more effective. Bottom line: it can save you tons of time, money, and wasted effort in hiring the wrong person for the job!

What's needed in your place of business? The first person a potential patient or client sees should not be someone who prefers to handle facts and figures and would rather not have to deal with people.

At the same time, the person who handles the money should not be focused primarily on meeting patients or clients and making sure they feel comfortable or at ease. Although it's important, is that what you hire a financial expert to do?

I think you get the picture. Although all of us at times adapt our behavior to the situation we're in, the DISC assessment can show you how someone behaves naturally *and* how his or her adapted behavior looks.

Natural behavior is who we really are: the person behind the "mask" we often wear in public. Adapted behavior shows up more often than not in the workplace—except when the person is under stress. Then his or her natural behavior kicks into high gear, sometimes with a vengeance.

Think of the employee that suddenly "loses it," doing something inappropriate or out of character that totally shocks everyone. Would it help to know that behavior is a possibility ahead of time? Conversely, imagine knowing the strengths a staff member brings to the table, although those strengths may not be readily apparent. Could that make it easier to know where to plug that person in to help your office or practice run like a well-oiled machine? How would that free you up to do what *you* need to do instead of spending time playing referee?

Knowing which behavioral styles work best together can help eliminate a great deal of potential friction. What do these behavioral styles look like? Here is a brief overview.[7]

**D—dominance:** adventuresome, competitive, daring, decisive, direct

**I—influence:** charming, confident, convincing, enthusiastic, inspiring

**S—steadiness:** amiable, team player, good listener, patient, steady

**C—compliance:** high standard, conscientious, diplomatic, analytical, accurate

In reviewing this, do you recognize the people with whom you work? Do you recognize yourself? Most of us are combinations of the styles, with one or two playing a dominant role in how we behave.

How do you make it all work? One of the ways is through a certified professional behavioral analyst who can provide a workshop called dynamic communication.[7] The goals are to help everyone in the room understand and recognize their own behavior, know how other behavioral styles operate within a team, and learn how to adapt for a better work environment.

Can a job have a style? Absolutely! There's a special DISC assessment designed to create the behavioral style of a particular job. There are many options available to you as a medical professional to help you stay at the top of your game. They all eventually lead back to being able to communicate with power.

As Annetta's words illustrate, a good hire makes life easier on patients, staff, and supervisors in a health care practice, just as it does at a television station, Walt Disney World, or any other company. If you're looking for an effective way to assess your staff, I suggest that you investigate the program Annetta recommends or one similar to it.

## REFERENCES

1. Mertz, Gregory J., *MGMA Connextion.* Medical Group Management Association, Englewood, Colo. 2006;6.

2. Senior Citizens Information and News. "Seven most common chronic diseases costing U.S. $1 trillion, headed to $6 trillion." October 3, 2007. Available online at www.seniorjournal.com/NEWS/Health/2007/7-10-03-SevenMostCommon.htm. Accessed October 24, 2007.

3. Center on Budget and Policy Priorities. "More Americans, including more children, now lack health insurance." Revised August 31, 2007. Available online at: www.cbpp.org/8-28-07health.htm. Accessed October 24, 2007.

4. Roberts, Rob, "Area doctors say reimbursement from insurers is fading fast." *Kansas City Business Journal.* January 19, 2007. Available online at: www.bizjournals.com/kansascity/stories/2007/01/22/story6.html. Accessed September 10, 2007.

5. Roberts, Rob, "Center for studying health system change: Tracking Reports: Losing ground: Physician Income, 1995-2003." Available online at *Kansas City Business Journal.* January 22, 2007. www.bizjournals.com/.

6. Wilson, Annetta, www.YourCoachforSuccess.com. Orlando, Fla.

7. Target Training International, Ltd., provides validated assessments to help pinpoint behaviors and actions of superior performers in many job classifications and in 26 languages. The company has 7,000 national and international distributor partners and serves more than 100,000 companies.

CHAPTER 5

# Developing Bulletproof Referral Relationships

As practice leader, one of your roles is to encourage physicians in your group to develop positive relationships with referring physicians and help develop comfortable ways to enhance those relationships.

You and your physicians will have many different levels of relations with referring physicians. Many of these relationships probably have changed as a result of the loss of the camaraderie that developed when physicians saw each other daily on hospital floors, in physicians' dining rooms, and at hospital meetings. As you know, this situation has altered significantly since the movement to outpatient medicine.

In today's new reality, it's more important than ever that your physicians focus on these relationships. The question is, can certain behaviors move these referral relationships along? Definitely!

Although it sounds very basic, it's no less important that these referrals often are based on personal relationships. That's why I've asked my friend and colleague, Bob Kodzis, to share his wisdom about the power of great relationships. A nationally acclaimed writer, marketer, and president of Flight of Ideas, Bob also contributed to *Ready-Set-Market!*[1]

I believe we all can benefit from his relationship theories, not just for developing relationships with referrers but also, as you'll see, with patients, staff, and others. The following are his insights and specific suggestions focused toward building referral relationships.

## BOB KODZIS: THE POWER OF GREAT RELATIONSHIPS

If I've learned anything during my 23 years in health care marketing, it is this: there is no marketing tool or promotion known to man more powerful than a good, sincere, and mutually beneficial relationship.

That's a bold statement. *And it may be the most important wisdom offered in this book or any other marketing book.* The prize of long-term success will go to the practice manager who can find a way to build great relationships with their patients, their employees, their doctors, their referral sources, and even their vendors.

Before we explore the full range of relationships that can propel your business to greater heights, let's talk about what makes a relationship great.

## *What is a Great Relationship?*

There are several common traits to all truly great relationships. These traits hold true for personal relationships and professional relationships. I often encourage my clients, when they are unsure how to proceed with a customer or other business relationship, to imagine their business relationships as personal relationships. Personal relationships are much more familiar to us as human beings. And aside from intimacy and physician contact, the basic premises of personal and business relationships are identical.

## *One-on-One*

The strongest relationships we experience as human beings are one-on-one relationships. In their groundbreaking book *The One to One Future*,[2] Don Peppers and Martha Rogers make an extraordinary case for bringing all customer relationships to a one-on-one level. Group relationships are an illusion. If the relationship is not person-to-person, it's not a real relationship. Businesses do not have relationships with businesses. Patients do not have relationships with your practice. Each patient has a relationship with someone in your practice, and more likely they have a series of relationships with several individuals in your office.

One-on-one is the only way to go when working to build great relationships.

## *Mutually Beneficial*

Mutual benefit is a critical element of any long-term relationship. Both parties must achieve a significant benefit from the relationship. These benefits do not need to be equal or even similar, but the perceived benefit derived by each side must outweigh the challenges associated with maintaining the relationship. A useful exercise is to create a "benefit inventory" for all of your critical relationships to assess which relationships are of greatest value and which relationships are at greatest risk.

## *Altruistic*

In great relationships, participants care about each other beyond the transaction. They look well beyond the question of "What's in it for me?" If you do not truly care about the other person and are not willing to help them beyond the boundaries of your own benefit, you are not in a great relationship. Consider your existing relationships and ask the basic questions "What's in it for them?" and "What can I do to increase the value that they get from this relationship?"

## *Communicative*

One of the cornerstones of every great relationship is communication. This involves sharing information, listening to the information shared, and using that information to further strengthen bonds. A former boss and mentor of mine once gave every member of my marketing staff a framed document to hang over the doors of our offices. It bore four very profound words, "Who needs to know?" It was a spark that helped to ensure that we kept people informed whenever we had information that could benefit or otherwise impact their lives. This handy reminder brought value to all of my professional relationships.

## *Based in Trust*

Trust is possibly the most important ingredient in any relationship. Building trust takes time, respect, consistency, honesty, integrity, and constant communication. In most cases, it must be earned, but once earned, it will clear the path for unlimited growth in the relationship. Different people have different thresholds and requirements before they will extend trust to another human being, but I've found that the best way to build trust is to be trustworthy.

## *Frequent Personal Contact*

Great relationships require regular, relevant, and useful contact. The care and nurturing of a solid relationship is much like the care of a houseplant. Both require consistency, frequent attention, and a watchful eye. Pay attention. Sometimes specific action needs to be taken to allow for growth (i.e., pruning). And beware. If you ignore your relationship for a significant amount of time, it will grow weak and sparse. Neglect it for too long and it will die.

## Great Relationships are Survivors

One of the amazing benefits of great relationships is that they are strong enough to survive short-term mistakes, lapses in service, and inconveniences. Weak or nonexistent relationships die the minute things go awry, sending your customers scurrying to find alternate sources to meet their needs. In great relationships, participants are much more willing to give each other the benefit of the doubt and forgive mistakes.

## Willingness to Change

People involved in great relationships are willing to change and to customize their approach to benefit the other people involved. They do so with an understanding that change is sometimes required to ensure the balance of the mutual benefit in the relationship. A relationship with a static person is like dancing around a maypole—and that will grow old very soon. A relationship with someone who is willing to change is more like dancing with a responsive partner and has endless possibilities.

## Lifetime Value of a Customer

This is a principle that was shared with me by a very smart man named George Maynard III. George was the president of a multimillion-dollar health care foundation associated with an enormous health system where I spent many years learning the intricacies of health care marketing.

Early in my career, Maynard often played the role of Yoda to my Luke Skywalker. During one mentoring session he offered these words of wisdom:

> *I'm not interested in 'hit-and-run' relationships with our hospitals' donors. I'm interested in the value that they can bring to our organization over the course of their entire lives. I'm interested in the long haul, and I'm willing to do what it takes to foster those long-term (lifetime) relationships.*

George's words ignited a 1,000-watt light bulb in my head. This principle was not restricted to philanthropy—it applied to every important relationship our business had. During the 20-plus years that followed, I have had the opportunity to prove the extraordinary value of this "lifetime value" idea again and again.

If you or your doctors take the short view on relationships with your key stakeholders, the effort needed to foster long-term relationships may seem to outweigh the benefits of making that effort. Before you reject the lifetime value approach to relationship development, consider these basic facts.

- It costs 10 times more to initiate new customer relationships than it does to build on existing relationships.
- Shallow customer relationships are more susceptible to the advances of your competitors.
- Weak relationships will crumble when mistakes are made or expectations are not met.
- People with whom you have strong relationships may eventually act as willing marketing advocates for you and your business at no cost to your practice. In the long-term, they inspire economies of promotion—allowing you to spend less on every new unit of business generated. Those who take the short view on relationships are destined to reinvent the marketing wheel every time they enter the market, and their overall marketing costs will undoubtedly rise because that is what marketing, printing, and media costs do over time ... they rise.

## NAVIGATING THE WIDE SPECTRUM OF RELATIONSHIPS

While working as the chief marketing officer for a large not-for-profit hospital corporation in Florida, I developed a business model (discussed in the previous paragraph) called The Relationship Continuum™, based on some research done by National Research Corporation and several years in the field (Exhibit 5.1).

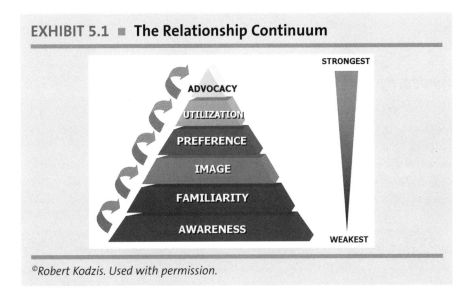

EXHIBIT 5.1 ■ The Relationship Continuum

©Robert Kodzis. Used with permission.

My goal in creating this model was to explain to the executives and the board of the corporation, the amount of time, the level of commitment, and the investment needed to build long-term relationships with stakeholders in the market: people who had the power to make or break our business.

The basic tenets of this model are simple.

- Relationships take time and attention.
- Relationships only grow stronger if we nurture them properly. This includes time, attention, responsiveness, and the constant sharing of information.
- The key to business success is building relationships with the right people and guiding them to a higher (stronger) level of vestment in the relationship.

When I share The Relationship Continuum model with my physician clients, my explanation goes something like this: "There are two groups of people in the world: those who know nothing about your practice and those who know something about your practice."

## *Awareness*

Those who are aware of your practice, obviously, are the largest subset of the group that knows something about your practice. *Awareness* is the "one-night stand" of relationship development. At this level, they know something about what you do, but not enough to have a well-formulated opinion about the way you do business or your approach to patient care. The most you can hope for at this level is interest in learning more.

## *Familiarity*

Those who choose to learn more (and are afforded the opportunity to learn more) about your practice and your doctors will climb to the *Familiarity* level of the relationship. These brave and curious souls will develop a stronger understanding of your practice, perhaps by visiting your Website or by talking to some of your patients. They will begin to get a greater sense of who you are and how you do what you do.

Because not everyone who is aware of your practice will seek to learn more, the number of people who elevate to the *Familiarity* level is smaller than the number of people in the *Awareness* level. This is a natural human dynamic. Consider all of the relationships in our lives. We each have far more acquaintances than we do people we adore.

The Relationship Continuum is no different. As the strength of the relationships gets stronger, the number of relationships decreases. It's a worthy trade-off when you consider the lifetime value of the people you serve.

Your longest and strongest customers are far less likely to leave your practice because of changes in the market, the advances of your competitors, or a bad experience in your office. They are also far more likely to demand that your practice and your doctors be included in health plans that they are considering for their families. This "pulling" power is priceless in today's seemingly random and fickle managed care market.

## *Image*

Some of those who are familiar with your practice will choose to do some more significant exploration and grow to understand the overall *Image* of your practice. They will know information about your doctors, the plans that you participate in, your locations, and maybe what you do better than any other practice in your specialty.

This is one of the most exciting stages in relationship development because we are approaching a decision point. It is also one of the most vulnerable points in relationship development because, in many cases, the customer is also exploring your competitors with a similar level of interest. It's a moment of truth; an inflection point. How the employees of your practice respond to customers at this point in the relationship will determine whether or not they (customers) prefer your practice to that of one of your competitors.

## *Preference*

If you share the right information, at the right time, in the right places, some of those who understand the *Image* of your practice will develop a *Preference* for your practice. They will be willing to give you a try. This is the highest point that marketing promotions and advertising tools can take your relationship. From this point forward, the strength of your relationship will depend entirely on the quality of care and level of customer service that you provide. After they develop a preference for your practice, the next logical step in the relationship is *Utilization*.

## Utilization

When a customer takes the step to make an appointment with your practice, they are making the ultimate leap of faith. This is a make or break moment for your practice. The actions of your doctors and your staff will determine whether they will laud or regret that decision. Everything else up to this point has been a promise.

At this point in the relationship, the patient will learn whether or not you keep your promises. If you fail to serve them to the level of expectation promised by your marketing and promotions, they will very likely leap off the existing relationship triangle to a parallel, but negative relationship triangle I refer to as the "Don't believe a word they say" triangle. If this happens, it is nearly impossible to win them back and they may become very vocal antagonists of your practice.

On the other hand, if you meet and exceed their expectations, some of them will progress to the next level in the relationship and become *Advocates* for your practice.

## Advocacy

This is exactly where we want our most important relationships to reside. Advocates are voluntary agents of your practice. They cannot help but promote your business because they have been served so well that they gush about their experience. Nothing we can put in print can match the sincere testimonial of a good advocate. A good advocate will leverage the strong relationships they have to bring more business to your practice.

## A Two-Way Street

Although much of the explanation of the Relationship Continuum model seemed to present customers climbing their way to stronger relationships with your practice, nothing could be further from the truth. In most cases, customers won't get on the triangle or progress to the next level of a relationship without specific and targeted action by you and members of your practice. The responsibility for building and coddling these relationships rests squarely on your shoulders and the shoulders of your doctors and other team members.

Your goal is to make the whole process and any resulting progressions easy. As the customer is gathering information about your practice, you also should be gathering information about the customer ... information that can prescribe the path to a stronger relationship.

You would do well to ask yourself, "What information do I need to be able to serve this customer better than any other practice in town?" Then find ways to gather that information in as unimposing a manner as possible. Start with questions such as "How did you learn about this practice?" and "What things are most important to you when you are trying to select a physician?" Continue with questions such as "Can I offer you any information about our practice?" and "Would you like to come for a tour of our office, see our environment, and meet some of the staff?"

## Proactively Choose Your Targets

Great practices are not created by fostering strong relationships with anyone who shows up at the door. Great practices are built by those who systematically target and make connections with stakeholders who can bring the greatest value to the practice.

Proactively select the kind of people and the quality of people you want to fill and surround your practice. This includes customers, employees, vendors, and future associates and partners. You cannot control every aspect of every relationship in your practice, but with diligent attention and persistence, you can steer your business to a much brighter future.

## The Value of Relationships Beyond Your Customers

The Relationship Continuum was described in terms of your customers, but it's important to note that their power and their value do not end with your customers. The quality and depth of your relationships have the power to drive every aspect of your business.

- Great relationships with your physicians can result in easier compliance with challenges such as dictation and documentation. It also will result in a greater willingness to consider your ideas as you work together to grow and refine the practice.
- Strong relationships with your employees will increase their willingness to go over and above the call of duty. It will reduce the tardiness, absence, and the waste of practice resources. It will reduce turnover and increase productivity.
- Great relationships with vendors can bring extraordinary resources and opportunities to your practice—from additional free samples to

free food and incentives for staff to inclusion in beta-site studies and new product trials.
- Strong relationships with referral sources can mean the difference between a struggling practice and a burgeoning one.

There is no marketing tool or promotion that is more powerful than a great relationship. Take the time to evaluate and take greater stock in your key relationships. The return on your investment of time and attention will be healthy growth, meaningful interactions, and the long-term success of your practice.

## FOSTERING POSITIVE REFERRAL RELATIONSHIPS

Now that you understand the value of relationships in general, thanks to Bob, let's talk about some specific behaviors that can foster positive referral relationships.

A good way to begin is to make sure your physicians are accessible and friendly to primary care physicians—in the medical staff lounge, at grand rounds, at committee meetings, and at social outings. Encourage them also to look for opportunities to provide in-service presentations regarding a new technique or service to the staff of primary care physicians in your area.

In many communities, physical growth impacts physicians' abilities to know colleagues as they did 20 years ago. Communities are more spread out geographically, as well as sometimes in medical practice towers. Nevertheless, it remains important to track referring physicians. And after you know who they are, you have a chance to acknowledge their referral patterns to you.

Studies show that referring physicians expect communication about the patients they refer to you, of course, but they also want to know you appreciate the referral. Communicating also helps to maintain your group's professional relationships. This is enhanced when you develop and implement a plan to keep in touch with them (Exhibits 5.2 and 5.3).

## EXHIBIT 5.2 ■ Referral Enhancement Behaviors for Physicians

**BE RESPECTFUL OF THE REFERRER**

If you find something questionable about the patient's treatment, take it up privately with the referring physician. Unless it's medically necessary, don't repeat tests already performed, because this drives up costs and can be offensive to the referring physician as well as the patient.

**USE BASIC MARKETING TECHNIQUES**

Print your cell phone and e-mail address on your business cards that will be used specifically for your referring physicians to make it easy to reach you and your practice. Provide referrers with brochures that will be of value to their patients. Be sure to include a brochure rack to keep the referrer's office neat.

**MONITOR YOUR REFERRAL PATTERNS**

Keep a log of who is referring and check it every month. If you discover that referrals from certain colleagues are declining, call to find out if you or your practice has offended them in some way.

**REMEMBER THOSE WHO SUPPORT YOUR PRACTICE**

It's not out of line to send a note or a gift certificate or to host referrers who have helped build your practice. You may send lunch to a referral physician's office, host a referrer's staff to a wine and cheese evening in your office, or make a contribution in honor of physicians in your community.

**RECOGNIZE THAT REFERRED PATIENTS ARE AMBASSADORS OF YOUR PRACTICE**

When patients return to the primary physician and are appreciative of the referral, it helps to build positive relations on your behalf. Create systems within your practice to see referred patients on time, treat them respectfully, and communicate appropriately with referring physicians.

# EXHIBIT 5.3 ■ Case Example: Referral Enhancement Program

Texas Retina Associates is a 40-year-old practice whose original office is in Dallas and who has expanded to 12 other offices around the state. They currently have 15 retina specialists in their group. Like many of you, they began their marketing by developing a sophisticated corporate identity.

General ophthalmologists and optometrists refer the majority of their patients. They concentrated their entire marketing plan in three areas.

1. Focus on meeting the needs of referring physicians
2. Measure and raise customer service in every Texas Retina Associates office
3. Enhance their brand identity

Their plan consisted of the following:

1. Create a physician referral newsletter and customize it, depending on the practice location. This means that the newsletter feature story for Lubbock, Texas, looked different than the feature story in the Waco issue (see Exhibits 5.5 and 5.6). That is a matter of coordination with the copywriting and the layout.
2. Create a clinical trial newsletter to go to all referring physicians (see Exhibit 5.9). This is a win/win for all. Texas Retina Associates needs lots of patients to fill their clinical trials. By communicating with referring physicians, it allows those physicians to be aware of the depth of the practice and find opportunities that are of value to their patients, and, finally, those patients participating in the trials receive retina health care at a discounted price.
3. Develop a consistent plan to introduce new physicians added to their practice, which includes a press release, a personal letter from the senior physician, an ad in the local paper (see Exhibits 5.4, 5.5, 5.7, and 5.8), and an introduction in the next referral newsletter.

*Used with permission of Texas Retina Associates.*

Here are some suggestions that will help you accomplish this.

- Spend time with referrers. Find out what's going on in their practices.
- Send brief periodic updates when your group adds locations, services, products, or new physicians.
- Hold an open house for referral physicians' staff.
- Partner with a hospital or local university to conduct a continuing medical education program.
- Send letters introducing new practice associates and areas of the subspecialization they bring to your practice (Exhibit 5.4).
- Partner with a referring physician group to present informational talks at community groups.
- Volunteer for medical staff committees.
- Serve on community advisory boards and task boards relating to health in your community.
- Develop patient education materials about subjects that reflect the skill, knowledge, and interest of your group and distribute them to health professionals.
- Be visible and available.
- Encourage every physician in your group to do one promotional activity per month (minimum), such as taking a referring physician to lunch or dinner.

In addition to these suggestions, there are other things you can do that will be of value to referring physicians. You should make it easy for them and their patients to use your services. If you joined a managed care panel after their booklet was printed, write a personal letter and let referrers know you're accessible and interested in their referrals. It's a perfect opportunity to let them know you set aside a few time slots every day for referred patients. Also let your top referrers know that you understand that when they need help, they need it now, not in two weeks.

At the same time, be sure to respect a referring physician's schedule. Rather than calling about a patient, you may want to consider other options. For example, information can be faxed or e-mailed, and both can be printed and added to the patient's chart as well.

**EXHIBIT 5.4** ■ **A Typical Letter to Referring Physicians About a New Associate Joining the Practice**

---

DR. NAME
PRACTICE NAME
STREET ADDRESS
CITY, STATE, ZIP

Dear Dr. NAME:

I want to take this opportunity to express our gratitude for your trust in referring your patients to us. As you know, our community continues to grow and so does the demand for our services. We are especially excited to share with you that a second physician, Stephen R. Smith, MD, will join our practice in August.

Dr. Smith comes to us highly recommended by his peers, with stellar credentials and a strong work history. He just finished his fellowship in vitreoretinal surgery at the Massachusetts Eye and Ear Infirmary in Boston. Prior to that, he completed his residency in ophthalmology at Northwestern University Feinberg School of Medicine in Chicago and a transitional internship at Tulane Medical School and Medical Center of Louisiana in New Orleans. Dr. Smith received his medical degree from Tulane Medical School in 2001. In addition, prior to pursuing his medical education, he worked as a management consultant for six years, including four years with Price Waterhouse.

Dr. Smith is mature, sharp, and well-rounded, yet down-to-earth, and we are delighted that he has chosen to join our practice and, in particular, the Lubbock community. Having him on board will allow us to extend our capacity and better serve the needs of you and your patients. We hope you have the opportunity to meet him soon and will extend to him a warm Lubbock welcome when you do.

As always, it is our honor and privilege to work with you. Please feel free to call us anytime with your questions, comments, or referrals: 806-792-0066.

Best Regards,

Senior Physician, MD

---

*Used with permission of Texas Retina Associates.*

Whether or not your physicians call a referring physician to report findings and recommendations, make sure they always send a prompt follow-up letter. And one important thing I've learned from conducting numerous referral surveys: referrers appreciate having an executive summary of findings with the report.

If your practice follows a patient for a long time, keep the referring physician informed about the patient's progress. If you find it necessary to refer the patient to another physician, let the primary practice know. Most referring physicians will be annoyed if they're not informed that one of their patients has had surgery or hospitalization. It can be very embarrassing if the patient's family calls the primary doctor and he/she has no idea what is taking place.

Referring physicians usually have spent years developing relationships with their patients. They know they'll be called to help the family sort through issues and complications. For that reason, always engage and partner with the referring physician to plan case management.

In addition to showing respect for the referring physician, find a way to say thank you for the continual interaction between your two practices. You can do this by writing a personal note of thanks, making a phone call to express your appreciation, or simply initiating a gesture that communicates your awareness of the relationship your practices share.

Whenever possible and appropriate, remind your physicians to be sensitive when talking to referred patients—frequently, what your physicians say will be repeated to the primary doctors. An off-hand remark or thoughtless statement may come back to haunt your practice.

Some specialists take the attitude that they're fixing a problem the primary care doctor can't solve. That certainly is not conducive to building positive referral relationships. Obviously, it's better for practice-building if the specialist realizes this and, instead, positions for a complementary relationship. Exhibits 5.5 through 5.10 show examples of how to start and continue these relationships:

- Exhibit 5.5  A Referral Physician Newsletter Introducing a New Associate
- Exhibit 5.6  The Same Referral Physician Newsletter Introducing Another Associate Customized for Another Community

- Exhibit 5.7  An Announcement Card for a New Associate
- Exhibit 5.8  Ad to Introduce a New Associate
- Exhibit 5.9  A Clincal Trial Newsletter
- Exhibit 5.10  Referral Pad and Thanksgiving Card Showing Communication with Referring Physician

Remember, everybody benefits when referring relationships are open, honest, and interactive.

**EXHIBIT 5.5** ■ **A Referral Physician Newsletter Introducing a New Associate**

# Making a Difference

A Newsletter from Texas Retina Associates — Fall 2006

### To our referring physicians:

*Thank you for continuing to entrust your patients to our care. As the communities we serve grow, we are expanding our capacity and services to meet the demand for vitreoretinal care. From offering more clinical trials and the latest treatment options to opening a new office and adding physicians to improve access to care, we remain committed to meeting your needs and those of your patients. Please take a few moments to read through this newsletter for the latest news about our practice. We also invite you to visit our Web site: **www.texasretina.com** to learn more. In addition, we encourage you to call any one of us directly at any time with questions, suggestions or concerns.*

### Clinical Trials

Our research program, now in its 20th year, is one of the largest in the country for a non-academic practice and could offer opportunities for your patients. We are currently involved in 20 national clinical trials testing promising new treatments for a number of retina conditions, including diabetic macular edema, drusen, age-related macular degeneration, uveitis, vein occlusion and posterior vitreous detachment. Please feel free to contact our research department at **214-692-6885, ext. 1** if you think you have a patient who may benefit from one of these studies.

## Stephen R. Smith, M.D. Joins Texas Retina Associates Lubbock Office

As the Lubbock community has continued to grow, so has the demand for our services. We are pleased to announce that ophthalmologist and retina specialist **Stephen R. Smith, M.D.** joined Texas Retina Associates on August 15, serving patients in our Lubbock office alongside **Michel J. Shami, M.D.** The addition of Dr. Smith provides the practice with a second physician, allowing us to expand our capacity to better serve you and your patients.

"With his stellar education and experience, we are delighted Dr. Smith has chosen to join our medical team and community," said Dr. Shami.

Dr. Smith came to Texas Retina from a vitreoretinal fellowship at Massachusetts Eye and Ear Infirmary in Boston. Prior to that, he spent three years in Chicago completing his residency in ophthalmology at Northwestern University Feinberg School of Medicine. He served a transitional internship at Tulane Medical School and Medical Center of Louisiana in New Orleans where he also received his medical degree.

Dr. Smith is excited about joining Texas Retina and serving the growing Lubbock community. "I was so impressed with the strength and quality of this physician team," said Dr. Smith. "They are all leaders in the field and remain committed to ongoing education and research. I look forward to working with them to provide the best retina care available to our patients."

### In This Issue

| | |
|---|---|
| Stephen R. Smith, M.D. Joins Texas Retina Associates Lubbock Office | 1 |
| To Our Referring Physicians | 1 |
| Clinical Trials | 1 |
| Texas Retina Provides Latest Treatment Options for Wet AMD | 2 |
| Physicians and Office Locations | 2 |

Page ①

*Used with permission of Texas Retina Associates.*

**EXHIBIT 5.6** ■ **The Same Referral Physician Newsletter Introducing Another Associate Customized for Another Community**

# Making a Difference

A Newsletter from Texas Retina Associates — Fall 2006

## Texas Retina Associates Welcomes James V. Campbell, M.D. and Establishes New Waco Office

### To our referring physicians:

*Thank you for continuing to entrust your patients to our care. As the communities we serve grow, we are expanding our capacity and services to meet the demand for vitreoretinal care. From offering more clinical trials and the latest treatment options to opening a new office and adding physicians to improve access to care, we remain committed to meeting your needs and those of your patients. Please take a few moments to read through this newsletter for the latest news about our practice. We also invite you to visit our Web site: www.texasretina.com to learn more. In addition, we encourage you to call any one of us directly at any time with questions, suggestions or concerns.*

### Clinical Trials

Our research program, now in its 20th year, is one of the largest in the country for a non-academic practice and could offer opportunities for your patients. We are currently involved in 20 national clinical trials testing promising new treatments for a number of retina conditions, including diabetic macular edema, drusen, age-related macular degeneration, uveitis, vein occlusion and posterior vitreous detachment. Please feel free to contact our research department at **214-692-6885, ext. 1** if you think you have a patient who may benefit from one of these studies.

We are pleased to announce that board-certified ophthalmologist and retina specialist **James V. Campbell, M.D.** has merged his Waco vitreoretinal practice with Texas Retina Associates as of August 1. This merger established Texas Retina's 12th office throughout the state.

Dr. Campbell has practiced in the Waco community for the past 17 years. He completed a vitreoretinal fellowship at Baylor College of Medicine in Houston in 1989 where he also served his residency in ophthalmology. Dr. Campbell earned his medical degree from Tulane University in 1973 and served as a family practice physician for several years before pursuing ophthalmology and vitreoretinal care. He is a member of the American Academy of Ophthalmology, the Texas Medical Association and the McLennan County Medical Society.

"Texas Retina Associates' experience, medical expertise and resources enhance the level of vitreoretinal care we can provide to the residents of Central Texas," said Dr. Campbell. "Over the years, they have earned a solid reputation for offering patients access to the latest technology and medical advances while remaining compassionate, personal and attentive. We share the same philosophy of care, and I am excited to now be a part of this medical team."

This merger has also allowed Dr. Campbell to improve access to care, providing patient coverage when he is away or personally unable to manage referrals. A fellow Texas Retina associate will be in the Waco office at times to see patients who need consultation when Dr. Campbell is out.

**New Waco Office**
7030 New Sanger Road, Suite 102
Waco, Texas 76712
Phone: **254.753.7007**
Fax: **254.753.5225**
Open Monday – Friday, 8 a.m. – 5 p.m.

### In This Issue

| | |
|---|---|
| Texas Retina Associates Welcomes James V. Campbell, M.D. and Establishes New Waco Office | 1 |
| To Our Referring Physicians | 1 |
| Clinical Trials | 1 |
| Texas Retina Provides Latest Treatment Options for Wet AMD | 2 |
| Physicians and Office Locations | 2 |

Page ①

*Used with permission of Texas Retina Associates.*

# EXHIBIT 5.7 ■ An Announcement Card for a New Associate

## TEXAS RETINA ASSOCIATES
*Office Locations*

**Dallas — Main**
7150 Greenville Avenue, Suite 400
Dallas, Texas 75231
214.692.6941 • 214.739.5797 fax

**Dallas — Baylor**
3600 Gaston Avenue, Suite 1055
Dallas, Texas 75246
214.821.4540 • 214.821.9073 fax

**Arlington**
1001 N. Waldrop Drive, Suite 512
Arlington, Texas 76012
817.261.9625 • 817.261.9586 fax

**Lubbock**
4517 98th Street
Lubbock, Texas 79424
806.792.0066 • 806.792.2446 fax

**Corsicana**
301 Hospital Drive
Corsicana, Texas 75110
903.872.4611 • 903.874.0701 fax

**Sherman**
2627 Masters Drive
Sherman, Texas 75090
903.893.8443 • 903.893.6468 fax

**Denton**
2210 San Jacinto Blvd., Suite 1
Denton, Texas 76205
800.695.6941 • 940.383.2608 fax

**Wichita Falls**
5800 Kell Blvd. Suite 100
Wichita Falls, Texas 76310
940.691.3232 • 940.691.5535 fax

**Paris**
575 DeShong, Suite B
Paris, Texas 75462
903.783.8321 • 903.783.1546 fax

**Plano**
1708 Coit Road, Suite 215
Plano, Texas 75075
972.596.9222 • 972.596.9225 fax

**Fort Worth**
800 5th Avenue, Suite 510
Fort Worth, Texas 76104
817.334.0882 • 817.334.0885 fax

**Waco — *Opening August 2006***
7030 New Sanger Road, Suite 102
Waco, Texas 76712
254.753.7077 • 254.753.5225 fax

Toll-free **800.695.6941**
www.texasretina.com
info@texasretina.com

TEXAS RETINA ASSOCIATES

*Announces the Association of*
**Stephen R. Smith, M.D.**
*To Our Practice*

4517 98th Street
Lubbock, Texas 79424
**806.792.0066**

| | |
|---|---|
| Albert Vaiser, M.D. | Rajiv Anand, M.D. |
| William B. Snyder, M.D. | Wayne A. Solley, M.D. |
| Dwain G. Fuller, M.D. | Michel J. Shami, M.D. |
| Gary Edd Fish, M.D. | Robert C. Wang, M.D. |
| Rand Spencer, M.D. | Lori E. Coors, M.D. |
| Bradley F. Jost, M.D. | James V. Campbell, M.D. |
| David Callanan, M.D. | Stephen R. Smith, M.D. |

---

*The physicians of Texas Retina Associates provide comprehensive services for medical and surgical treatment of diseases involving the vitreous, retina and choroid.*

STEPHEN R. SMITH, M.D.

**Current Clinical Trials of Texas Retina Associates**

☐ AREDS 2 –
  A Vitamin Supplement Study for Macular Degeneration

☐ Allergan Posurdex Implant Studies –
  Dexamethasone Implants for RVO, DME and Uveitis

☐ DRCR.net Diabetic Studies

☐ Eli Lilly PKC Inhibitor Studies for DME

☐ Bausch & Lomb Plasmin Injection Study for the Creation of a PVD

| | | |
|---|---|---|
| **Fellowship** | | Vitreoretinal Disease and Surgery |
| *2005-2006* | | Massachusetts Eye and Ear Infirmary |
| | | Harvard University |
| | | Boston, Massachusetts |
| **Ophthalmology Residency** | | Northwestern University |
| *2001-2005* | | Feinberg School of Medicine |
| | | Department of Ophthalmology |
| | | Chicago, Illinois |
| **Transitional Internship** | | Tulane Medical School and Medical Center |
| *2001-2002* | | of Louisiana New Orleans |
| | | New Orleans, Louisiana |
| **Medical School** | | Tulane Medical School |
| *1997-2001* | | New Orleans, Lousiana |

*Used with permission of Texas Retina Associates.*

EXHIBIT 5.8 ■ Ad to Introduce a New Associate

# EXPERT RETINA CARE ... RIGHT IN YOUR COMMUNITY

Michel J. Shami, M.D. and Texas Retina Associates

Warmly Welcome **Stephen R. Smith, M.D.**

- Board certified and expertly trained at Northwestern University and the Massachusetts Eye and Ear Infirmary at Harvard University
- Part of Texas' largest, most experienced ophthalmology practice focused specifically on the diagnosis, treatment and surgery of the retina and vitreous
- Provides care for retinal tears, retinal detachment, age-related macular degeneration and diabetic retinopathy
- Participates in national clinical trials, bringing you the newest retina and vitreous treatments

4517 98th Street ■ Lubbock, Texas 79424 ■ www.texasretina.com

Call **806.792.0066** for an appointment

TEXAS RETINA ASSOCIATES

Used with permission of Texas Retina Associates.

# DEVELOPING BULLETPROOF REFERRAL RELATIONSHIPS

**EXHIBIT 5.9** ■ **A Clinical Trial Newsletter**

# CLINICAL TRIALS UPDATE

*A Newsletter from Texas Retina Associates*  Volume 4 — April 2006

## Texas Retina Seeks Drusen Patients for New Study on AREDS Oral Supplement

Drusen, small yellow deposits under the macula, frequently occur in people over age 50 and are the earliest sign of age-related macular degeneration. The Age-Related Eye Disease Study II (AREDS II) is a multi-center, randomized trial to evaluate the effect of lutein/zeaxanthin and omega-3 long-chain polyunsaturated fatty acids (LCPUFAs) in high supplemental doses on the progression from drusen to advanced age-related macular degeneration.

Over the next 18 months, Texas Retina is seeking 150 patients with drusen in one or both eyes to participate in this clinical trial which will run for seven years. All patients will receive the original AREDS formula vitamins, and in addition, will receive one of four other groups: Lutein/zeaxanthin, Omega 3's, Lutein/zeaxanthin plus Omega 3's or a placebo. Patients must agree to stop any current vitamins they currently take that contain these elements. In addition, patients who take a regular multi-vitamin will be supplied Centrum Silver for the duration of the study.

Clinical trials such as this offer hope of slowing down and possibly preventing the progression of age-related macular degeneration. We hope you will encourage your eligible patients to participate in this important research.

**Upcoming Studies:**
DRCRnet Avastin Study – May 2006
Light Sciences Talaporfin Study – Fall 2006

### Dear Colleague,

At Texas Retina Associates, we remain committed to providing you and your patients with the best possible retina care both now and in the future. Clinical trials play a key role in helping us achieve this goal.

Our research program, now in its 20th year, is one of the largest in the country for a non-academic practice, and it continues to grow. We are currently involved in 17 national clinical trials such as the featured AREDS II study, testing promising new treatments for a number of retina conditions, including diabetic macular edema, drusen, age-related macular degeneration, uveitis, vein occlusion and posterior vitreous detachment.

Please take a moment to scan through this newsletter to determine if there is a study that might be of value to any of your patients. In addition, we are always seeking new trials and will keep you informed of these opportunities.

Thank you for continuing to entrust your patients to our care. As always, we encourage you to call any one of us directly at any time with questions, suggestions or concerns.

Sincerely,

*The Physicians of
Texas Retina Associates*

## In This Issue

| | |
|---|---|
| Texas Retina Seeks Drusen Patients for New Study on AREDS Oral Supplement | 1 |
| Dear Colleague | 1 |
| Future Clinical Trials | 1 |
| Clinical Trials | 2–11 |
| Physicians & Office Locations | 12 |

---

| | |
|---|---|
| | res, study drug vs. placebo |
| Placebo Control: | Yes |
| Main Inclusion Criteria: | Mild to moderate diabetic macular edema with good vision (20/40 or better) |
| Main Exclusion Criteria: | Previous laser treatment<br>HgA1c > 11 |
| Cost to Patient: | No |
| Contact Person: | Jean Arnwine/Dallas<br>214-692-6885 x 1<br>Fax 214-265-0935<br>jarnwine@texasretina.com    Cheryl Lee/ Arlington<br>817-794-0180<br>Fax 817-261-9165<br>clee@texasretina.com |

Page 2

*Used with permission of Texas Retina Associates.*

**EXHIBIT 5.10** ■ **Referral Pad and Thanksgiving Card Showing Communication with Referring Physicians**

# E Y E

## PHYSICIANS
of Central Florida

Leaders in Pediatric
and Adult Eye Care

Michael S. Zamore, M.D.
*1952-2000*

Robert S. Gold, M.D.
David B. Auerbach, D.O.
Louis C. Blumenfeld, M.D.
Larry S. Lewis, O.D.
Julie A. Galbreath, O.D.

225 West State Road 434
Suite 111
Longwood, FL 32750
**407-767-6411** p
**407-767-8160** f

249 Moray Lane
Winter Park, FL 32792
**407-645-4350** p
**407-645-0337** f

www.eyephy.com

_____ Patient

_____ Referring Doctor

_____ Diagnosis/Reason for Referral

_____ Appointment

DATE _____ TIME _____

*Used with permission of Eye Physicians of Central Florida.*

Dear Friends,

Your confidence in us and our commitment to quality and compassionate eye care is a source of great inspiration every day.

Thank you, and our warmest wishes for the happiest of Thanksgivings.

Robert Gold, M.D., David Auerbach, D.O.
Louis Blumenfeld, M.D., and Larry Lewis O.D.

*Robert S. Gold, M.D.*

*David B. Auerbach, D.O.*

*Louis C. Blumenfeld, M.D.*

*Larry Lewis, O.D.*

Please feel free to call upon us or send family and friends when an eye problem arises at either Winter Park, 407-645-4350 or Longwood, 407-767-6411.

*Used with permission of Eye Physicians of Central Florida.*

## REFERENCES

1. Eliscu, Andrea T., *Ready-Set-Market!* Medical Group Management Association, Englewood, Colo. 1999.
2. Peppers, Don and Martha Rogers, *The One to One Future: Building Relationships One Customer at a Time.* Doubleday and Company, New York, 1996.

CHAPTER 6

# Putting Our Heads Together— A Guide to Practice Retreats

As I've said earlier in the book, a practice retreat can serve an important role in an effective marketing program. However, not all practices can (or will) commit to the time and financial investment required for a full-fledged marketing retreat, although some do include a marketing section in their business retreats. Fortunately, you don't need a retreat to move forward or to solve specific issues within your practice.

## TO RETREAT OR NOT TO RETREAT?

So how do you know when it's time to hold a retreat to think strategically about the future of your practice?

Here are some key indicators to help you decide if the time is right.

- You're working harder and making less money than you used to.
- Your colleagues are opting for early retirement or changing careers or considering career alternatives. (Haven't you always wanted to run a bookstore?)
- You're losing patients.
- You aren't getting your share of new patients in the marketplace.
- You're spending more time on paperwork than patient care—or at least it seems that way.
- You're experiencing high turnover in staff and spending more and more time on recruiting, training, and retraining.
- You're thinking about reorganizing your practice.
- It just isn't fun anymore.

That the world is changing comes as no surprise, but the speed at which it's changing is mind-boggling. This is evidenced by the fact that what you did last year doesn't seem to work anymore. When a business imperative pushes you to think, "We have to do some things differently or we won't be here 5 years from now," it's definitely time to reflect on your future.

So what do you do? How can you reflect when your work is consuming so much of your time? What about getting away from your practice—with others—to spend time considering how to position your practice to develop and sustain a competitive advantage in spite of the never-ending changes?

Think you can't afford the time and expense? You actually can't afford *not* to invest if you want to be content in your business in 5 years. The best option is to set aside at least a day or two for strategic thinking and planning, followed by at least quarterly updates to review how you're doing. That is what I mean when I recommend a retreat.

What benefits can you expect from your efforts to plan strategically for the future? You'll have the opportunity to do the following:

- Examine what works well and what doesn't.
- Gain insights from your customers (patients, staff, referring physicians, hospital administrators, managed care, the doctors in your group).
- Identify emerging trends and marketplace needs and decide which of these your group is best suited to take advantage of now and in the future.
- Talk openly about the threats to your ongoing success and what you need to do to meet the seemingly ever-growing challenges.
- Bring your group into clear alignment around what your purpose should be, what you want to create together for the future, the kind of values you want to integrate into all parts of your operation, and the three to five key strategies on which your group needs to focus its energy and resources in order to make the biggest difference.

In other words, a retreat will get everyone associated with your group on the same page—working toward the same goals and the same future. It also will enable you to establish clear accountabilities and timeframes. The old adage that "people support what they create" is true. Given a clear direction and the opportunity to see where they can contribute, people in an organization usually will pull together to make it happen.

After you've decided to schedule a strategic planning retreat, the following steps should help you avoid pitfalls and help you achieve the outcomes you want.

## Who Should Attend a Retreat?

When thinking about who should be involved, I recommend that you err on the side of inclusiveness without making the group so large that serious conversation and strategic thinking become unwieldy.

Consider whose thinking you would want to help forge your group's future. Also think about who will be significantly impacted by changes in the way you operate and do business. If someone could significantly dampen your possibilities of success if he or she doesn't support the changes, it's a good chance that person should be a part of the strategic planning process.

## Survey Your Customers in Advance

Because the changing industry brings new players to the table, you may need to spend some time thinking about who your customers really are. Knowing what key customers think about your practice and the future of health care before the retreat can help guide your thinking during the retreat.

## Review Current Literature Related to Your Practice and Health Care Trends

So much is happening in health care, it's hard to stay on top of it all. Nevertheless, it's important to know what's happening and where the health care profession seems to be headed. If you can't do it all yourself, ask others to help and divide up professional magazines, news magazines, an Internet search, and other sources that may speculate about the future of health care in the United States. Before the retreat, circulate the best as prereading to help stimulate thinking.

## Identify a Location

Pick a place away from the hubbub that will be conducive to reflective thought. The location needs to be away from phones, televisions, and pagers. That may seem impossible but, in reality, no one is irreplaceable for a day or so. Do whatever it takes to cover your practice so you and other retreat participants will be disturbed only in a true emergency that no one else can handle.

## Determine the Length of Time

As mentioned previously, plan at least one or two days, preferably two. Reflective thinking is enhanced if enough time is allowed for thorough discussion of complete ideas and group consensus on decisions. Consider beginning on a Friday afternoon, carrying on into the evening, and continuing on Saturday. Recognize that strategic planning is a journey, not an event, and you may need more than one session. If so, plan the sessions close together so you don't lose momentum.

## Consider an Outside Facilitator

Hiring a facilitator who is a process expert with strategic planning experience enables everyone who attends the retreat to stay focused and participate in rethinking the group's practice to meet changing demands and expectations. The facilitator should do the following:

- Help the retreat planners identify the outcomes hoped for as a result of the strategic planning retreat, as well as who should attend.
- Advise the retreat planner of room arrangements and equipment needs.
- Learn as much as possible about your practice before the retreat.
- Help you identify perceived trends that are likely to impact your operation.
- Conduct confidential interviews with all retreat participants to gain their insights into the practice as it exists now and where they see the challenges and opportunities for the future.
- Conduct similar confidential interviews with other key stakeholders such as patients, affiliated hospitals, referral sources, and other employees.

## Internal Staff Retreat

Following are two examples of what you can accomplish with a staff retreat. If either of these types of retreats seems appropriate for your practice, I hope you'll consider conducting one. You'll learn a lot and, although it may seem like a major investment of time and dollars, it can be an effective tool for practice success.

First is a sample of the interview questions and the planning that occurred for a mature obstetrics and gynecology practice with a vision to grow and add physicians, along with a third full-time office. They were concerned that their infrastructure was not solid enough to handle all the proposed ideas for change. They also had some issues among the physicians that required facilitation to resolve (Exhibit 6.1).

I share this case study with the group's permission so that you may see situations and issues that are similar to those in your own practice. This group waited almost a year to implement the items identified at the retreat. That said, their retreat did help them accomplish several important goals. They enhanced their sense of teamwork, focused on branding, raised their customer service quotient, added a fifth physician, and opened a third, full-time office.

Another example of a practice retreat we facilitated, along with Bob Kodzis of Flight of Ideas, was for Eye Physicians of Central Florida, a visionary five-person group eager to market and participate in their community. They've created a new logo, rebranded the practice, focused on serving their referral physicians, selected promotional items, and begun to do limited advertising in small community publications, not the large citywide newspaper.

In this case, the physicians decided to hold a retreat for only the staff—no physicians attended. This was a very big step for the group because it was held on a traditional patient day, meaning that no patients were scheduled. The staff was impressed that the doctors cared enough about the practice and fixing the dysfunction within the practice to invest resources to hold the retreat and to give up a half-day of patient billing. See Exhibit 6.2 for the retreat agenda and Exhibit 6.3 for the survey each staff member was asked to fill out in preparation as an investment for the retreat.

Exhibit 6.4 shows the post-retreat summary report, which identified to the physicians how their staff members were feeling.

The group worked on many of the issues and later held another half-day retreat. Exhibit 6.5 shows the outcome from the second staff retreat.

I thank the Eye Physicians of Central Florida for sharing this and some of their other marketing endeavors with you. (See Chapter 9 for an example of how to market the opening of a new office.)

**EXHIBIT 6.1** ■ **Strategic Planning Facilitation and Consultation Proposal**

### STRATEGIC PLANNING FACILITATION AND CONSULTATION PROPOSAL FOR WYMORE OB/GYN

*Purpose of Proposal*

The purpose of this proposal is to assist the partners of Wymore OB/Gyn to develop a cohesive plan of action that will guide the direction and growth of their practice during the next 3 years.

*The Process*

The following are the major elements of this project:

- Interview of partners and practice management team.
- During this phase of the process, Bob Kodzis will gather some initial information from each of the partners and key practice administrators.
- Each interview will last 45–60 minutes, and resulting information will be incorporated into the planning retreat.

*Full-Day Planning Retreat—Focus on the Future*

Once the initial information has been gathered, an agenda will be created to address the specific issues and opportunities that are most critical to the success of Wymore OB/Gyn. It's important that all key stakeholders participate in this phase of the process. A key stakeholder is anyone who has the power to make or break your business. The agenda for the day will be designed in phases to allow for discussions on three levels:

- Partners only
- Partners and associates
- All stakeholders

Although the interviews will provide specific direction for our agenda, some possible areas of focus include:

- Identifying our critical success factors
- Selecting our top priorities for action
- Structuring our practice for greater success
- Clarification of roles, responsibilities, and expectations
- Summary report and recommendations

All of the interview information and retreat output will be transcribed and formatted into a professional report, with recommendations within seven days of the planning retreat. This report is the foundation of a strategic plan that will guide the future growth and direction of Wymore OB/Gyn.

*Timeline*

All of the steps above can be accomplished within a three-week period. The estimated timeline to accomplish all of the steps outlined in this proposal is as follows:

- Interviews:      1 week
- Retreat:         1.5 business days (with setup/breakdown)
- Summary report:  1 week

This timeline is contingent upon the availability of key stakeholders for interviews and the retreat.

*Caveats and Requirements*

Andrea Eliscu and Bob Kodzis will be given access to the practice audit report that will be generated by JP Griffin. Although it's not a requirement, we strongly recommend that the planning retreat be held offsite. During the last 20 years, we've learned that a different environment is a good first step toward a fresh way of thinking.

**ACTIONS AS A RESULT OF THE RETREAT**

*The Essence of Our Mission*

To empower women and their families in their own well-being by providing the best possible care, service, and education. Other words that we chose regarding why this practice exists:

- Empower women by educating them
- Be the best OB/Gyn practice in the area in care and service
- Provide good medical care
- Take pride in what we create
- Leadership
- The practice that people want to come to
- Satisfied patients
- Nice mix of healthy and surgical patients
- Collegiality
- Special!
- Personal growth and development

*(continued)*

## EXHIBIT 6.1 ■ Strategic Planning Facilitation and Consultation Proposal
*(Continued)*

### Elements of our Vision

Each physician was asked to share his or her vision for a future Wymore OB/Gyn practice. The goal of this exercise is to allow the partners and future partners to hear each other's goals for the future and find the areas in which all physicians can help to move the practice forward. Several areas of alignment were identified. The following are the individual physician's visions and desires for the future:

*Response from MD #1*

- In 5 years I want a stable practice.
- I see us growing to six physicians.
- Our location will be determined and stable.
- We will be known as the leaders in OB/Gyn.
- Our referrals and resulting patient load will be maximized.
- We will have more control over our level of reimbursement.
- Our offices will be modernized with a computer in every office and electronic medical records.
- We will cleanse the practice of old hassles.
- Eventually, want to have kids, a family—take less call, have more time off.

*Response from MD #2*

- Let's drive a Lexus, not a Pinto.
- Long-term: we will provide extra products and services—retail and fee-based—of interest to women.
- Vitamins.
- Skin care.
- We will offer more organized patient education—for a price.
- Our doctors will have the freedom to practice medicine.
- I envision a call schedule of six doctors.
- We will have filled scheduling for all doctors.
- We will market the practice to people who can impact our referrals.
- Eventually, I'd like to go to a 4-day work week.
- I want a seamless and smooth-running practice.
- I want to feel happiness when I come to work.
- Marriage and kids??? Maybe.
- Business in development: vitamins.

*Response from MD #3*

- My big dream is to create a premier multidisciplinary women's center with one-stop shopping for a woman's health care needs.
- I envision six doctors in our practice.
- I want more time off and less exhaustion.
- I want to be able to have a dog!
- I want less call...no call...no weekends.
- I'd like 3 days in the office, 1 day on call, and 3 days off.

*Response from MD #4*

- How do you balance your dreams and desires with the frustrations of practicing medicine?
- I want a stable, cohesive practice. Not just a bunch of doctors sharing call. I want camaraderie, support, and help from my partners.
- I want us to have common goals.
- I don't want to grow too big, but I want the practice to become like a Swiss watch—to run very well consistently.
- I want an atmosphere that feels good for our employees and our patients.
- It should be a place I enjoy coming to work.
- Fairness, compensation, and recognition of all kinds of work being done to build and support the practice. This includes administrative work and marketing.
- We all should be able to have balanced lives and time with our families.
- In the future, I want to do 85% of what I do now.
- I want some space to grow personally.

Most of the elements of these visions are quite aligned. Issues like desire to become renowned for the quality, service, and range of services provided and desire to have a cohesive partnership permeate these concepts. However, everyone agrees that the desire for more time off among all physicians will require a long-term solution.

**WHAT IS MOST CRITICAL TO OUR SUCCESS?**

It's important to remember that ALL of the following Critical Success Factors are vital to the success of the practice. Although they have been prioritized, none of these vital

*(continued)*

**EXHIBIT 6.1** ■ **Strategic Planning Facilitation and Consultation Proposal**
*(Continued)*

---

signs can be ignored. They have been listed in order of perceived performance (best performance to worst) as judged by the practice leadership group. The number of X marks indicates the number of people who think Wymore OB/Gyn performs weakly in a particular area. The number of ✔ marks indicates the number of people who think Wymore OB/Gyn performs strongly in a particular area.

- Quality of staff ✔✔✔✔✔
  - Volume & stability
- Quality of care ✔✔✔✔✔
- Customer satisfaction ✔✔✔
- Accountability ✔✔✔
- Revenue 0
- A/R & reimbursement ✔ X
- Role clarity X X X
- Entrepreneurialism X X X X
- Teamwork X X X X
- Marketing & branding X X X X X

*Our Major Goals*

Of the critical success factors, the mission, and the other discussions held throughout the day, the following were the tangible goals that the group agreed were most important:

- Formalize the role of Office Manager—write a position description and standards of performance.
  - Responsible: Ms. L with help from consultant and approval from Board
  - Develop mechanism to allow staff input into evaluation of Office Manager (360-degree review) on annual basis.
  - Responsible: TBD
- Quarterly performance review of Office Manager—including recommended path for skill and knowledge development.
  - Responsible: TBD
- Create an Ad Hoc "Direct Access" Committee of the Board, which will allow employees to address issues not appropriate to be addressed with the Office

Manager. Create a set of clear guidelines for employees explaining the very limited reasons one would choose to address this committee.
- Responsible: Partners and Doctors
- Create a Marketing Plan for Wymore OB/Gyn. Plan will address recommendations on branding, building referral relationships, and building the image of our practice.
  - Responsible: Y.K. (Dr. K will bring updates to the physicians as needed to ensure that they can support the directions being explored.)
- TEAMWORK: Seek guidance from our employees to help us develop a plan to improve communication and teamwork throughout the practice.
  - Responsible: K.F.
- Role Clarity—this area of focus is being addressed in two of the following goals and in the sections entitled "The Role of a Partner," and "Formalizing the Role of Office Manager." With all of these efforts, Wymore OB/Gyn will have a more defined, directed, and accountable leadership team, but only if the leadership of the practice regularly measures performance against set standards and coaches employees to the needed levels of performance and expertise. Follow-up on recruitment of solid short-term MD Associate candidates.
  - Responsible: Y. K.
- Share information about qualified Midwives for partner consideration.
  - Responsible: Consultant, Physicians, and Ms. L
- Better integrate Ms. I. into the clinical environment before announcing her promotion.
  - Responsible: Ms. I, Ms. L, and Doctors
- Develop a position description and standards of performance for the Clinical Coordinator Role.
  - Responsible: Ms. I, with help and support from Ms. L and Doctors

***Other Goals to be Explored and Addressed***

- Explore possibility of extended hours as a means of easing weekly workload burden.
- Two days of extended hours could eliminate one day in the office each week.
- Staff must be willing to have more flexible hours, too.

*(continued)*

**EXHIBIT 6.1** ■ **Strategic Planning Facilitation and Consultation Proposal**
*(Continued)*

*The IDEAL Future Location for Wymore OB/Gyn*

The following are elements of the ideal next location for the practice. These should be used as criteria for assessing potential locations:

- Closer to Arnold Palmer Hospital
- Access to main road/highway (I-4, East-West Expressway)
- Needs to have good demographics and socioeconomics for OB and Gyn care
- Needs to have more space than the existing office (which is 3,500 square feet)
- We need to explore APH's plans for the next 5 years seeking opportunities to build relationships and align efforts
- Refer to "satellite" offices as "neighborhood offices" or "community offices".

*For Doctors Only:*

Any of the following information may be shared with all staff at the time agreed upon by the physician leadership team.

*The Role of Partner*

- Show a vested interest in the progress of the practice.
- Come up with (and share) ideas to improve the practice.
- Be proactive.
- Help to create cohesion in the office among partners and staff.
- Increase revenue to the practice.
- Fiscal responsibility.
- "Big picture" and long-term thinking.
- Be objective.
- Keep other doctors aware of any developments that impact the practice.
- Cover each other's backs—help each other out without having to be asked.
- Promote and uphold the good name of the practice.
- Show solidarity when it comes to decisions and policies.
- Provide leadership in helping new doctors to find their way/get oriented.
- Set the example for our entire staff.
- Accept functional responsibility to run the practice (one or more categories of responsibility—e.g., marketing, recruitment, billing).
- Ease transition during times of change.
- Address individual and private issues directly.

- We should develop a partner evaluation process to measure fulfillment of expectations, agreements, and needed workload.
- We must keep each other informed of all significant developments that could impact our practice.
- Monthly meetings should include ad hoc issues and future focus. Every partner meeting should include some focus on the future.

### *Clarification*

*Dr. A*

- I want to know that our life matters to our partners.
- I will not have us (NB and I) live half of our life on call.
- We are willing to do 7–10 days of call a month between the two of us.

*Dr. B*

- I am not willing to stop delivering babies.
- I need less call (less money is OK) within 6 months.
- I want to share call with NA (7–10 calls per month for both of us).

*Dr. F*

- I am not willing to enter into a 2-for-1 call system for two of our partners indefinitely.
- I am willing to take more call for more compensation for up to 2–3 years, but no more. It must have a defined end.
- We must find a long-term solution to our call challenges.

*Dr. K*

- I'm not willing to do Q3 beyond 6 months. I won't do Q3 unless compensated.
- We must expand our call to allow NA and NB to have a life together.

**ADDENDUM: PRE-SESSION INTERVIEW SUMMARY**

### *Why Does Wymore OB/Gyn Exist?*

- Good patient care
- Good patient care is our motto. We provide services that other offices don't. We treat them like family.

*(continued)*

**EXHIBIT 6.1** ■ **Strategic Planning Facilitation and Consultation Proposal**
*(Continued)*

- To make money—no Medicaid, no patient education
- We are doctors with similar ideas practicing medicine together
- Serving the community
- Not sure

*Critical Success Factors*

- **** Revenue and collection—accounts receivable
- ***** Quality of patient care
- ***** Customer service/customer satisfaction
- **** Marketing
- **** Internal communication/teamwork
- *** Reimbursement
- *** Volume of patients
- ** Insurance contracts
- ** Role clarity
- Other:
  - Quality
  - Organization
  - Constant call coverage
  - Contingency planning
  - Checks and balances in our systems
  - Community perception
  - Relationships
  - Staff—volume, quality, stability
  - A forum for clinical discussion
  - Accountability
  - Solidarity among physicians after decisions have been made
  - Happiness of the physicians

*Strongest Factors*

- Quality of care
- Service
- A/R
- Employee retention
- Our physicians

- Structures and processes are currently working well
- Highly reliable, wonderful employees

**Weakest Factors**
- Insurance contracts—no process for getting new contracts
- Organization—needs to be better
- Teamwork
- Communication
- Clinicals
- Personnel issues—employee riffs, nursing issues, no teamwork
- Leaving too much to Office Manager
- "Old-school" perception of some of our doctors

**"Take-Away" from the Retreat/Common Goals—Five-year Vision**
- \*\*\* A plan for the future
- \*\*\* Addressing growth—to grow or not to grow
- \*\* Role clarification
- \*\* Building trust and teamwork—between levels and within levels
  - (It's a 5 right now on a scale of 10)
- \*\* Marketing of practice
- Addressing the roles of physicians and employees
- Addressing employee friendships with doctors
- How do we grow the practice and keep a personal touch?
- Reimbursement strategy
- What will we do with our brand?
- Are we moving?
- A successful practice
- A reasonable amount of work
- Job description for practice manager
- Achieving the right atmosphere

**Obstacles to the Success of the Practice**
- Reimbursement—no ability to negotiate
- Communication—within departments and throughout the practice
- Cliques—lack of teamwork

*(continued)*

## EXHIBIT 6.1 ■ Strategic Planning Facilitation and Consultation Proposal
*(Continued)*

- The system is not working well. Things are slipping through the cracks (mainly in OB).
- Nonclinical (admin) participants in the clinical process.
- Management by intimidation
- Documentation issues and follow-up issues
- Over-reliance on Dr. A for administrative tasks
- We don't pay enough attention to the happiness of the staff.
- Doctors don't know the employees well—leave everything to Office Manager.

*Staff (Non-management) Comments*

- ***** I love working with these doctors—they are terrific!
- ***** Issues with triage CMA's attitude, team approach, and relationship with Dr. K
- ****We all have to get along—be a team
- *** Too much work
- ** Need to upgrade phone system and computer system
- Ms. I untouchable?
- Ms. I talks down to me.
- No call back from triage nurse
- Does not treat me with respect
- Ms. I. does not help out the other nurses.
- Not all doctors get the same amount of respect.
- Good teamwork within parts of the practice
- Girls at front desk step over boundaries of what is appropriate sometimes.
- I like my job.
- I like doing what I do.
- Too many unnecessary calls (hitting 0) in the phone system
- Too many cliques
- Low trust
- Too much daily chaos in this practice
- Need some job descriptions
- Senior people treat junior people badly here.
- Confusion because of individual physicians' treatment protocols

*Used with permission of Wymore OB/Gyn.*

## EXHIBIT 6.2 ▪ Staff Retreat and Brainstorming Session

**EYE PHYSICIANS OF CENTRAL FLORIDA**
**AGENDA FOR STAFF RETREAT AND BRAINSTORMING SESSION**

**12:00** Why we have arranged this day for our staff...

Doctors say a few words to kick off the experience.

**12:15** Lunch – Welcome – Introductions – Ground Rules

**12:45** Mission Possible

Defining every team member's role in bringing the practice mission to life—(This will help each team member to assess their role in terms of the big picture, it will also allow each employee to learn more about the value that each team member brings to the table—individual or small functional groups).

**1:30** Start. Stop. Change.

This exercise puts each participant in the role of CEO. In the process they will be asked to define the things we need to start doing, the things we need to stop doing, and the things we need to change in order to make this the best practice possible. I will distill the key messages and common points for action. It's a real eye-opener!

**2:30** Break

**2:45** Designing the Perfect Eye Doctor

**3:15** Improving Employee and Patient Satisfaction

In this small group brainstorming exercise, participants will generate ideas to improve employee satisfaction and patient satisfaction. The two "satisfactions" are inextricably intertwined—So we'll hit both in one exercise. The result will be a series of great ideas to buoy the practice and the people within.

**4:15** Values, Principles to Make Us a Stronger Team

End on a promising and empowering note—they will establish guidelines to govern their behavior and activities—and in the process take responsibility for holding up their end of the practice.

**5:00** Go Home

*Used with permission of Eye Physicians of Central Florida.*

## EXHIBIT 6.3 ■ Staff Retreat Survey

This survey is confidential. Nobody will see your individual responses except our retreat facilitator. The results of this short survey will be used to help us address some of the biggest issues facing our practice. Please be very honest and tell us what you really think.

1. What is the single biggest issue/challenge affecting the success of our practice?

   _____

   _____

   _____

   _____

2. I would be happier working here if only somebody would:

   _____

   _____

   _____

   _____

3. The one thing that makes it hardest for me to do the best job I can for our patients is:

   _____

   _____

   _____

   _____

*Used with permission of Eye Physicians of Central Florida.*

# EXHIBIT 6.4 ■ Staff Retreat Summary Report

**START. STOP. CHANGE.**

We started with the tough questions right off the bat. The team responded with terrific candor, and a few themes emerged quickly. The items at the top of the list are the most popular themes (several people feel this way). These are always good starting places to institute change if you want to impact morale and employee satisfaction.

***START—What Do We Need to START Doing that We Don't Do Right Now?***

- Teamwork
- Communication—talking/listening
- Orientation/training new employees properly
- Treat each other with respect.
- More consistency between offices
- Direct deposit
- Get organized.
- Employee appreciation
- Pay/benefits issues
  - Pay more
  - Raises
  - Bonuses
  - PTO program
- Be more professional.
- Doctors and managers should listen to staff before making judgments based on feedback from patients.
- Patient dilation room
- Restocking patient rooms daily
- Organize specific time to answer phone calls.
- Finish what you start.
- Motivation
- Use flags to identify who (including the technician) is in the exam room.
- Initial the schedule to see who saw whom.
- Clean up after yourself in the staff bathroom.
- Automatic lensometers
- Acknowledge patients as soon as they come in.

*(continued)*

**EXHIBIT 6.4 ■ Staff Retreat Summary Report** *(Continued)*

- Treat our established patients with more respect.
- Start expressing how you feel—honestly.
- Pull charts when patients call with questions.
- Laugh more together.

*STOP—What Things Do We Need to STOP Doing Around Here?*

*Note: There was amazing consistency in this category, which accounts for the limited number of issues.*

- GOSSIP (mentioned by 17 of 20 participants)
- Rudeness toward each other—especially in front of patients
- Making patients go through the "6-month" information update process
- Tattling
- Yelling (all of us, including the doctors)
- Friday paydays (change to different day)
- Vacation accrual policy
- Dr. G—Type A response; stop getting involved with office minutia
- Making patients wait
- Talking over patients
- Calling out my name when you step out of an exam room
- Dr. A—Abbreviating names, nicknames
  - Throwing too much at the staff at once
  - Moving too fast for our patients—take the time
- Favoritism
- Changing the rules on us
- Management participation in gossip, talking behind people's backs
- Temporary charts
- Allowing interruptions in patient care (e.g., cell phone calls)

*CHANGE—What Else Do We Need to CHANGE?*

- Payday
- PTO policy
- Vacation accrual policy
- Patient information update
- Have one tech follow one doctor
- Uniforms—Thursday scrubs

- Front desk meetings—they are all complaints and putting out fires—not positive at all
- One person assigned to phones
- Office managers
- 90-day evaluation period, nonpaid forced holidays
- Copiers need to be replaced
- Printers need to be replaced
- Stop placing so much emphasis on business and start emphasizing care
- Mrs. D
  - Listen to the staff before making judgments
  - When filling in, do the whole job, don't delegate it
  - Pick up the phone like the rest of us

**PRACTICE MAKES PERFECT**

Three groups participated in this visioning exercise. The exercise was simple. All the problems are resolved, and the practice is being recognized nationally in an interview with Oprah. Their challenge was to answer Oprah's questions about how they achieved such unprecedented success. There was a great deal of consistency between groups and all seemed to have fun with this creative exercise.

Here are the questions and their answers.

1. If you could identify the top three things that contributed to the success of your practice and the happiness of your employees, what three things would you identify?
    - Quality care
      - Educated, highly trained staff
      - One-on-one interaction
    - Excellent benefits including incentives and bonuses
    - An outstanding training program
    - Teamwork and respect
    - Patient respect
      - Sensitive to their needs
      - Listen to their needs
      - Make them feel at home
    - Advanced technology—state-of-the-art equipment and fully computerized

*(continued)*

# EXHIBIT 6.4 ■ Staff Retreat Summary Report *(Continued)*

2. Describe how the employees at this perfect practice treat each other—Physician-to-staff, staff-to-staff, and staff-to-management
   - Physicians treat the staff like family
     - Professional and friendly
     - Our doctors actually listen to us.
   - Staff treat each other like best friends.
     - Teamwork and respect
     - Laughter
     - Tell jokes
     - Every Friday is "Health Spa Day"—with Friday afternoon off.
   - Managers mentor the staff.
     - Approachability and trust
     - Door always open
     - Management listens to our needs.
3. What makes the new and improved Eye Physicians of Central Florida different from every other medical or surgical practice out there?
   - We are extremely technologically advanced.
   - We respect the patient's time.
   - There is excellent communication between the doctors, the staff, and the patients.
   - Quality care
   - Doctor and staff fully accessible
   - Customer service—caring and happy staff
   - Greet people with a smile
   - All of our employees are well educated and highly paid, including expenses and travel.
   - Understanding
4. What things DON'T you do at this practice (what bad habits and irritating little things are missing)?
   - We eliminated negativity.
     - Bickering and gossiping
   - We eliminated patient backlog.
   - All records are kept onsite—no temporary charts.
   - Excessive patient paperwork

- No doctor screaming
- No ugly uniforms
- No doctor answering cell phone during patient time/visit

**THE GOOD STUFF**

We asked the staff to identify a few things that they like about working at Eye Physicians of Central Florida…the things they don't want to change:

- Our physicians are truly kind, and they interact very well with the staff.
- The doctors (and the staff) really care about their patients.
- Dr. Z's personality lives on in the practice.
- My time with patients
- Approachability of our doctors
- Doctors: don't stop teaching us
- Don't move billing department offsite—like it onsite
- We like how punctual our doctors are.
- Keep it a fun place to work

Despite some of the issues raised in this report, when asked if it is a fun place to work, the group responded with a resounding YES.

### *New Way to Update Patient Information*

In an effort to walk away with something actionable, the group chose to take on the issue of changing the way they update patient information. The goal was to decrease the hassle and frustration that so often accompanies the current process.

The group recommended that the front desk crew take on responsibility for asking patients if any of their vital information has changed. If yes, then the front desk will print out a "short form" for the patient to complete and return.

Laura will explore the details of this process and present the details of the recommended approach to the doctors and managers.

### *Principles to Guide Us*

We ended the day with a few principles to help guide all of us toward a happier and more productive future together. The group was asked if they could commit to these guidelines and hold themselves and each other accountable. Further, we asked if

*(continued)*

# EXHIBIT 6.4 ■ Staff Retreat Summary Report *(Continued)*

anybody could not or would not abide by these principles. Nobody indicated that they couldn't or wouldn't. Here are the principles that the group recommended and approved.

- We will not gossip or listen to gossip.
- We will be consistent in all of our offices—policies and training.
- We will go the extra mile to help each other out and back each other up.
- We will never say "It's not my job."
- We will get rid of the petty stuff.
- We will each fulfill our own responsibilities at the highest level possible.
- We won't yell at (or to) each other.
- We will each take responsibility for our own words and actions.
- What goes on in our administrator's office stays in our administrator's office.

**Coolest Motto . . . Florida Ophthalmology Caregivers United in Service**

### Caveat to Doctor

The only way that you can take away from the progress that has been made with this retreat is to do nothing or do everything behind closed doors.

A fast, open, active response to these issues will help you take this process to the next level. Everyone we worked with seemed responsive and held genuine care and affection for the patients and doctors of this practice. I have great hope for the future success and happiness of your group.

Act now—even if your action includes telling the staff what you cannot or will not do. They need to know where they stand. They took great courage to share their honest concerns and ideas. The greatest reward and reassurance you can give them (and yourselves) is to create a plan that combines their input and your vision.

And no matter what, have fun.

*Used with permission of Eye Physicians of Central Florida.*

# EXHIBIT 6.5 ■ Staff Follow-up Retreat

**MATRIX OF AVERAGES**

We surveyed all of the staff on how the practice had evolved since our retreat in the spring. This information was compiled in a spreadsheet. Any issue that earned an average importance of eight or higher and a performance of six or lower is considered to be a key issue requiring attention and action.

Those issues included:

- Honesty
- Organization
- Pulling charts
- Gossip and tattling
- Talking over patients
- Consistency between offices
- Training
- Front desk meetings

The following were the group's answers to the two open-ended questions on each survey sheet. The number of asterisks following any item indicates the number of people who offered that response.

What I've done to make the work environment better:

- Less gossip ****
- More laughter ***
- Become more organized **
- More teamwork in the office now**
- Avoid problems that don't pertain to me
- We are working harder to get along
- I extend myself to everyone and anyone
- Reorganized dilating waiting area to cut patient pile up in half

What the doctors and managers have done to make the work environment better:

- Direct deposit ****
- They have improved in a lot of ways **
- They have been more friendly**

*(continued)*

**EXHIBIT 6.5** ■ **Staff Follow-up Retreat** *(Continued)*

- I can see that they have tried making things better by meeting some of our needs and wants from the original retreat.
- They have allowed me to work independently without so much rubbernecking.
- Not as much yelling
- Started more frequent training and learning sessions
- Agreed to allow a new waiting area

Many of the survey questions were discussed at length. The following sections summarize some of the key points that were discussed.

## MAJOR ISSUES

### Training

- Need more orientation and mentoring
- There is a lot of pressure placed on the trainer to train and do her job at the same time—this dilutes impact of both.
- Need more formal training regarding teamwork
- Training right now is a big information dump.
  - Computer program is tough to learn—need more one-on-one training.
  - "They teach you the system and then throw you in the fire."
  - Mrs. D is very specific about how she wants things done.

### Respect

- Some MD respect issues remain—name yelling and interruptions
  - The group acknowledged significant improvement and effort on the part of the doctors.

## THE CHALLENGES OF WORKING AT THE NORTH OFFICE

- We are big, and we are new.
- We have all new people.
- We have very high turnover.
- We operate at a faster pace.
- The "daily list" is impossible to complete in one day (front desk).

### Professionalism

- Are we too loud?
- Do we laugh and play too much in front of patients?

- People not being taken care of right away.
- We need to separate the personal and the professional.

### *Organization*
- The drawers are disgusting.
- We need to prepare the workspace for the next person coming in.
- Clutter
- Challenges completing daily list
- Doctors sometimes assume that a room is not stocked when they cannot find what they are looking for (often it is actually in the room).

### *Organize Time for Phone Calls*
- Surgery scheduler needs space with a phone and support to do her job.

### *Motivation*
- More negative reinforcement than positive coming from management
- Some employees are less motivated than others.
- Mrs. D is definitely working to improve her leadership skills

### *Bathrooms*
- We need a better method of odor control.
- We need to self-check and clean up after ourselves.
- Is it possible to create a bathroom that's not in the break room—bad combination?

### *Honesty*
- Some staff feel that there is retribution from management for honesty (complaining).

### *Pulling Charts*
- Non-urgent calls can go to voicemail.
- Front desk should be familiar with what's going on in the back.

### *Employee Appreciation*
- There have been improvements.
- Dr. A's letter to the staff was very appreciated.
- Dr. G is yelling less.

*(continued)*

## EXHIBIT 6.5 ■ Staff Follow-up Retreat *(Continued)*

- We need more positive communication.
- We'd like more recognition for filling the gaps (vacancies, vacations, sick time).
- Appreciation means saying thank you for specific things and notes like the one left by Dr. A.

*Consistency*

- As we add patients, we develop communication issues.
- There is conflict between the North and the East office. East keeps pointing out our errors rather than helping us with them
- There seems to be less patience by the doctors in the North office.
- We've been referred to as North Hell.
- We need to distinguish between the East and North office's charts.
- Inconsistencies between the practice manager and her assistant regarding what's acceptable and what's not (PTO/vacation)
- Differences between promises made at hire and reality—90-day raise

*New Phone System*

- Decreased efficiency with the new phone system
- We changed our phone system, but we didn't change our system for answering them.
- Is there a software update available for this system?
- Mrs. D: Don't yell for help with the phones—help us—answer the phone.
- Should we have two schedulers?
- Too much too fast
- Front desk team cannot move from their space.

*Staff Meetings*

- Mrs. D's meeting is too long, same list of stuff, too redundant.
- Need to get to the point—hit main points
- Good to rotate leadership of the meeting consistently and be fair

*Other*

- We need updated ICD-9 books.
- Would like more cross training and job shadowing.
- Front desk is the hub and needs extra support.
- Billing department: more cross training so that all can do all functions, not just a few
- Optical business versus ophthalmology business—issues of closing the office (OPH) and cutting off the optical customers. Need more flexibility—need to negotiate with staff to ensure coverage. Carol will explore opportunities to address this issue.

**"NOTES FROM THE PARKING LOT"**

*These are issues raised by employees during the retreat follow-up.*

- New Tardy Rule—bothers several of the staff. Feel it is too severe and it's not fair in light of the flexibility that is expected of them at the end of the day. They want the practice to be consistent and not to force both ends of the day. Allow for reasonable exceptions.
- Policies need to pertain to every employee. Direct Deposit—when payday falls on a holiday, people who don't have bank accounts can't get their checks until Monday. Why be punished for not having a bank account?
- We need new printers.
- Issue of not accruing vacation time
- Problem with new waiting area—none of the doctors and few of the staff utilize it.

Finally, as a gesture of appreciation, each staff person was given a wrapped gift at the end of the follow-up retreat. Inside was a notepad that had been personalized with each staff's person name. The staff loved seeing their names imprinted on a stationery pad. More than 60 percent of the staff wrote personal thank-you notes to the physicians for the gift and for making the investment in their work environment.

*Used with permission of Eye Physicians of Central Florida.*

CHAPTER 7

# Telling Your Story—Practical Approaches to Managing Your Media Message

When I mention media opportunities, you probably think of the traditional press releases you're comfortable creating on behalf of your practice. Those opportunities still exist, of course. But in this chapter, I want to address your opportunities to serve as a valuable resource to the media—to work effectively with radio and television stations—as well as how to craft your message exactly as you want it through the use of print advertising.

The media is one segment of the marketplace that has changed tremendously over the past decade. Today, electronic media outlets face extreme competition for viewers in most markets, and I encourage you to take advantage of that competition. Use it to your practice's advantage—the ball is in your court!

A press release may or may not get picked up by television, print, or radio outlets in your market. No matter how important you believe your message is to the community, it's often lost in the shuffle of news stories that cross the news directors' or reporters' desks. That's not to say that communicating through releases isn't still an important part of your marketing effort. However, the only way to be assured of expressing your specific message is through paid advertising. That's the only way you have total control of your message.

I've asked my colleague, Annetta Wilson, to offer her expertise in this arena. Annetta, whom we originally met in Chapter 4, is a certified professional behavioral analyst and president of Annetta Wilson Media Training & Success Coaching. She is a business strategist specializing in media training, presentation, and communication skills coaching. She's a successful talent coach for on-air journalists at CNN and has coached for Walt Disney World's Ambassador Program.

## ANNETTA WILSON: MEDIA MESSAGES

You handle emergencies almost routinely—you probably can deal with a crisis with your eyes shut. But if a television news crew would show up at your door because a patient or lawyer called and *suggested* that you did something wrong, you'd suddenly have that "deer in the headlights" look, your throat would be as dry as the Sahara, your mouth would feel like it was stuffed with cotton, and you'd be looking for the nearest exit to head for the hills!

Having a game plan for such a crisis is crucial. Having the *right* people to execute that plan is imperative. You must answer three questions:

1. "What's your message?"
2. "Who's doing the talking?"
3. "Who's minding the door?"

In planning for media relations, you need to know *who* is meeting everyone who comes through your door as well as how to talk to the media. And you need to know it *before* a crisis occurs. Unfortunately, it's a fact of life in today's lawsuit-happy society that medical professionals must be among the first to cover their flanks. Some of your colleagues may have closed their doors because of malpractice suits and rising insurance rates, so no one has to tell you that a little "Media 101" preventive medicine is mandatory for the health of your business.

Before you throw up your hands and determine that there's no way you can win against people who buy videotape by the case and ink by the barrel, let me assure you that there is a way to navigate through the media minefield. Let's start with the basics.

For most group practices, this will pertain to sending press releases about a "special" patient story involving staff, introducing a new physician, being "first" to do a procedure in your community, or leading a community relations effort tied to preventive health care.

There's an old saying that if you respect the law and also like sausage, you should never watch either being made. The same holds true for the process of how the stories you watch on television news programs get selected. I'm going to tell you how it happens.

Every morning and every afternoon in newsrooms across the country, there's a game of "show and tell." Reporters, newsroom managers, and news producers hold "editorial" meetings. Reporters must come to those meetings armed with ideas for news stories. In a game of round robin, reporters must quickly convince everyone in the room that their ideas would make an interesting, titillating, blow-everyone-out-of-the-water news story. If they can't sell the idea to the people in that room, you don't see it on the news that evening.

If a story is to ever see the light of day and make it into your living room, the reporter must make a compelling argument. He or she must be ready to provide information, such as statistics; trends; who is, was, or will be affected; and why the story is important. Their case carries more weight if they can come up with an "expert" (that's your practice) to back up the information (or dispute it) and someone who's been affected by whatever the issue or topic happens to be (perhaps one of your patients).

It's a simple fact that a news story needs an official or expert voice to give the story credibility. In the best instances, news stories have more than one expert (usually voicing opposite views) to ensure a sense of balance. We're not talking about editorials, opinion columns, or talk shows, but legitimate news stories.

That's where you come in. If there is a buzz in your industry about a medical breakthrough, a new or emerging trend, a rise or drop in statistical data, a famous person who's benefited from (or died from) something that one of your physicians has extensive knowledge about or expertise in, he or she is now poised to become an expert in a news story!

How do the media find you? They don't. *You find them.* And you find them before the hot topic comes up. You have to play detective. Fortunately, this is not a difficult task. If you live in a large city with more than one television station, it's very likely that each station has a reporter who covers health issues almost exclusively. If your town is smaller, reporters will likely cover a variety of areas or beats. Some radio stations also have news programs that may include health news reports.

What you must do is pick up the phone, call the television station (or newspaper), and find out who covers medical or health-related issues. When you've got a name, call that person and introduce yourself. Tell him or her about your practice's area of expertise and who your physicians are. Offer to send information in case they ever need background for a story. Then make sure you send it.

Voilà! Your practice has just become a resource for a reporter's story. When you send the information, be sure to include your business card, phone number, e-mail address, Website, and any other method that can be used to get in touch with you. That's the minimum amount of effort necessary to get on a reporter's radar screen without hiring a public relations agency to do it for you.

What happens when the reporter calls? You've got to be ready to talk, and you've got to keep it short, simple, and to the point. No industry jargon or medical lingo. You and your physicians must master the art of speaking in sound bytes. In simplest terms, a sound byte is a 6- to 10-second statement. That's it: 6 to 10 seconds!

Why such a short amount of time? Because the average television news story is between 45 seconds and 1.5 minutes long (radio stories are even shorter). Furthermore, that time must include background and current information, an interview (in most cases), and a conclusion (called a wrap-up). The good news is that keeping your answers short reduces the likelihood that what you say will be edited!

Although speaking in sound bytes is not difficult, it does take practice and it's easier to grasp with the help of an experienced media trainer. Ideally, you should choose one who has been a reporter.

It's always easier to be interviewed when there's good news or something positive to talk about. But what do you do when all heck breaks loose?

That's when you put your game plan into action. If you're going to speak to a reporter, you must do three things:

1. Acknowledge what happened (DON'T LIE).
2. Respond quickly (the phrase "no comment" rarely stops a story from being reported).
3. Be prepared to talk about the actions that need to take place to remedy the situation.

*Here is a huge caveat:* This information includes only the basics. Each incident calls for a unique response. There are as many variables as there are situations. I do not advise you to start randomly spouting information unless you've had media training. And remember, there may be situations when you need to consult with an attorney in addition to media training.

If you do find yourself at the end of a microphone, remember that it cannot suck words out of your head! Take your time and think before you answer questions. Most important, answer only what you're asked. Saying too much can open a can of worms that you may want to keep closed!

In a crisis, the best defense is a good offense. Prepare a statement ahead of time and create a fact sheet with important information that will help the reporter tell a balanced story. The emphasis is on the word *fact*. Speculation is simply your opinion. Opinions are best when they're labeled as such.

If you're asked for your "opinion," preface your comments by saying that it's your opinion. If you're asked a question and you don't know the answer, offer to get back in touch with the reporter after you've gathered more information. Remember that reporters have deadlines, so find out when that deadline is and make sure you call back by then!

Analyzing the situation that caused the crisis can help you create the best crisis response. The most effective media training is interactive and provides you with several options and opportunities to do just that.

You may never have to deal with the media, but you almost certainly will have to talk to people in the course of your work. How you present yourself can get you what you want, send people running for the door, or bore them to death. The prevailing wisdom is that 55 percent of communication is nonverbal (body language), 38 percent is tone of voice, and only 7 percent are the words we use.

Being an expert in your field does not translate automatically into being a great public speaker or presenter. Very often, it does not. Speaking in front of a group of people can be more terrifying than facing a news reporter. In fact, some surveys show that the fear of speaking in public outranks the fear of dying!

But with the help of presentation skills coaching, you can use the secrets public speakers rely on to command a response from an audience, learn a simple technique to calm your nerves, and never be caught with nothing to say if you're asked to speak (even if you're not prepared).

These media training techniques have been used successfully by businesses in the health care industry, including the presidents of hospitals;

the chief operating officers of hospitals, the public relations managers of regional health care systems, vice presidents of human resources for health care systems, and directors of ancillary services acting as spokespersons.

The same techniques can be used for medical practices when physicians are interviewed in response to health care issues of importance to the community, such as when a president's wife has skin cancer, a television star has a stroke, a national figure is in a car crash with traumatic injuries, or a new laser aids in cataract surgery. Other national stories that can have a local angle include Medicare reductions that impact radiologists and cardiologists, medical malpractice skyrocketing costs that cause obstetric and gynecologic physicians to leave a community, and the always-popular cosmetic surgery stories.

## REAL-LIFE CASE

I follow Annetta's expert advice with an example of a story that received wide coverage in the Central Florida community in print, as well as on the CBS and NBC television affiliates. As it happened, the patient was wonderfully charismatic and in telling his story, a dramatic one at that, waxed on about how wonderful his orthopedic surgeon was in helping him reach his goal.

The patient, Ken Mitchell, searched for a relationship with a joint replacement surgeon who would "really listen, hear me" so he could reach his goal to climb Mt. Everest with two artificial knees. That surgeon was Richard Konsens, MD, knee replacement specialist at the Jewett Orthopaedic Clinic, in Winter Park, Florida.

The news release we distributed, along with the feature article that appeared 3 months later in the *Orlando Sentinel*, are provided in Exhibits 7.1 and 7.2. I use this model to demonstrate that the media eventually picked up the press release that was sent to bring visibility to Dr. Konsens and the Jewett Orthopaedic Clinic. We touched base with our media contacts every 3 weeks or so until finally they let us know their editors wanted them to do the story. It was a story about Ken Mitchell and his amazing family. Dr. Konsens was mentioned near the end of the story.

One of the items important to realize when creating a press release is that in large city newspapers reporters write the stories and another department writes the headlines. At times, one may seem to have little to do with the other.

## EXHIBIT 7.1 ■ News Release

**FOR IMMEDIATE RELEASE:**
MEDIA CONTACT: Andrea Eliscu
407-629-0062/mmiandrea@sprintmail.com

*JEWETT ORTHOPAEDIC CLINIC PATIENT CLIMBS MOUNT EVEREST AFTER KNEE REPLACEMENT SURGERY*

WINTER PARK, Fla. — Orlando resident and former Atlanta Falcons linebacker Ken Mitchell recently climbed Mount Everest four years after having his left knee replaced by Richard M. Konsens, MD, of the Jewett Orthopaedic Clinic.

In this, his first attempt, Mitchell scaled 24,000 feet on the northern or Tibetan side of the mountain over the course of several weeks in April and May to reach Camp Four. Severe weather conditions kept him from continuing to the 29,035-foot summit, but he plans to return in two years to reach the peak.

"Climbing Everest has always been a goal of mine," said Mitchell. "I have three children who suffer from Tourette's Syndrome and have always encouraged them that they can achieve whatever they set their mind to. After my knee surgery, we had our weekly family meeting, and they challenged me to still pursue my dream. As hard as it was, my knees worked great. I can honestly say that I have never seen or felt anything so beautiful. I will continue to train and can't wait to go back and stand atop the peak."

Currently an asset manager for Primerica Financial Services and a father of nine, Mitchell, age 57, had enjoyed a lifetime of athletic pursuits that took a toll on his body, especially his knees. He played high school basketball and baseball in California, spent a short time as a catcher with the California Angels organization, served in the Marine Corps special services and then attended the University of Nevada Las Vegas (UNLV) on a basketball and baseball scholarship. His junior year at UNLV, he decided to try football as a walk-on, made the team and played linebacker for two years. While he was not drafted, he pursued pro football and played for the Atlanta Falcons from 1972-1975. After football, he stayed active by participating in Ironman triathlons and mountain climbing. Eventually the pain became too much. He had his right knee replaced in 2000 and his left knee replaced in April 2002.

Knee replacement surgery involves removing the worn cartilage and bone and replacing it with metal and plastic joint surfaces that relieve pain and restore alignment and function. Approximately 500,000 of these procedures are performed in the United States each year.

*(continued)*

## EXHIBIT 7.1 ■ **News Release** *(Continued)*

"When I went to check on Ken after his surgery, he told me of his plans to continue mountain climbing. I was thinking he might start with Mt. Dora. I never imagined he would scale Everest," said Dr. Konsens.

True to form, Mitchell pushed through his recovery and therapy. He quickly gave up the cane and all medications. He began swimming and climbing stairs. Six months after the surgery, he was riding his bike 50-100 miles at a time. Over the next few years, he continued to build up his strength, flexibility and stamina, climbing Mt. Rainier before tackling Everest.

"This was an unbelievable feat of determination and endurance," said Dr. Konsens. "Every patient who has a joint replacement has specific goals and needs. While Ken's were extreme and rare, it proves just how far the knee replacements have progressed. We are allowing people to get back to truly living and accomplishing their goals, no matter how lofty. People like Ken are challenging us to raise our expectations when we do these surgeries."

Mitchell is far from done pursuing his athletic dreams. In addition to climbing Everest again, he plans to scale the Matterhorn and Switzerland's Mt. Eiger as well as enter the Hawaiian Ironman Triathlon and swim the English Channel.

"I have always felt that I am just an average athlete who works extra hard. I am so grateful to have my new knees and still have a lot I want to accomplish," he said.

Voted one of Orlando's Top Doctors in 2002, 2003 and 2004 in Orlando Magazine, Dr. Konsens has practiced in Winter Park since 1990 and has served as a team physician for the Orlando Magic and UCF basketball teams. He graduated from Dartmouth College and received his medical degree from the Mt. Sinai School of Medicine in New York City. Dr. Konsens completed his residency at Case Western Reserve in Cleveland and a fellowship in joint replacement at Oxford University in England.

Founded in 1936 by Eugene L. Jewett, MD, the Jewett Orthopaedic Clinic has been recognized internationally as a pioneer and leader in orthopaedic care for more than 70 years. Jewett doctors performed some of the first total knee replacements in the state of Florida and some of the first arthroscopic knee surgeries in the Southeast. They have also designed and developed several innovative joint replacement systems used worldwide. The Clinic's 23 board-certified/board-eligible, fellowship-trained physicians, ten physician assistants and team of health care professionals provide a full range of orthopaedic care, specializing in sports medicine, joint replacement, foot and ankle care, surgery and rehabilitation of the hand, and care for spinal injuries and conditions. Jewett serves as the team physicians for the Orlando Magic, the University of Central Florida, Rollins College, the Orlando Predators, the Orlando Ballet and Cirque du Soleil. The practice has seven offices throughout Central Florida.

*Reprinted with permission of Jewett Orthopaedic Clinic.*

EXHIBIT 7.2 ■ Article from *Orlando Sentinel*, October 2006

### PASSION FOR SPORTS HELPS ORLANDO FAMILY DEAL WITH TOURETTE'S SYNDROME

By Andrea Adelson

*Sentinel* Staff Writer

Ken Mitchell inched his way up Mount Everest with his broken body. His knees ached. His hands throbbed. His shoulders could barely carry the weight of the 50 pounds he carried in his backpack, full of oxygen canisters, rope, clothes and extra equipment.

He hardly ate. He never slept. It took hours to move a few precious yards toward the glorious summit. When it felt as if he could go no further, he thought back to his family in Orlando.

His wife and nine kids urged him to climb Everest, knowing how much he loved the rush of conquering the unexpected. He made the UNLV football team that way in 1970 as a walk-on. He did the same with the Atlanta Falcons, harassing them into a tryout, and then making the team. He completed two Ironman triathlons on knees so swollen he was unable to walk afterward.

His kids became mini-Kens, each one playing sports. When three of them were diagnosed with Tourette's syndrome, Ken told them to keep playing, to face their own challenges the way that he faced his. Now it was time for the kids to encourage their father.

So Mitchell pressed on, slowly marching toward the summit last May. When he reached 24,000 feet, a massive storm moved in, making it impossible to go another step. He turned back, more than 5,000 feet short of reaching the top.

*Reprinted with permission. Copyright © 2006, Orlando Sentinel.*

*(continued)*

## EXHIBIT 7.2 ■ Article from *Orlando Sentinel, October 2006 (Continued)*

On the long trek down, Mitchell, 57, tried to remember the last time he failed to finish a challenge. But it hardly mattered. Making it to Everest was enough. "It's not about summiting to me," Mitchell says. "The kids said, 'Dad, you need to do this.' My wife said she wanted me to do it. I just had a wonderful trip." His journey embodies everything Mitchell has taught his children.

Missi, at 27 the oldest child, remembers how Ken would drop her and sister Mandi off at Red Bug Park to play pickup basketball against grown men when they were 13. "We were these two little blonde girls with ponytails who were like, 'We got next!' The guys were like, 'Yeah, right!' But I would be boxing them out and taking rebounds. It was funny," Missi said.

Matt, 16, once blocked a shot from Larry Bird's son during an AAU game two years ago. "I blocked it right into Larry Bird's lap!" Matt says. "Then I said, 'Guess your son doesn't take after you!'" Everyone plays. Missi was the first to play sports, starting in gymnastics at the age of 2, and then playing basketball, volleyball, Powder Puff football, softball and baseball. Mandi, 25, played every sport Missi played.

On and on it goes. Monte, 23, played basketball. The three oldest kids, who are Ken's from a previous marriage, no longer live at home. The six who do keep Ken and his wife, Candy, on their toes. Matt, at 6 feet 6, plays basketball and offensive line on the Winter Park High varsity team. Michelle, 15, plays on the Orlando Christian Prep basketball team, which recently was rocked when Coach Buck Lanham was charged with possession of child pornography and possession of marijuana.

Mike, 12, plays basketball and football. So does Mickey, 11, who is already 5-foot-8 in the fourth grade. The youngest boys, McKinley, 9, and Morgan, 6, also play hoops. "Sports is in our blood," says Missi, who has a 7-month-old son named Caden. "I can't wait for my son to get started playing," she added. "I was trying to figure out what's the first thing a little boy can do. I guess karate?"

### *Devastating Diagnosis*

Watching everyone interact, it is impossible to tell that Matt, Mike and McKinley have Tourette's syndrome. Matt was the first one diagnosed when he was 7. He was constantly twitching, but Ken knew something was wrong when he saw Matt's arm and head jerk back simultaneously in one long, reckless motion. He took Matt to the doctor. They got the diagnosis. The family was devastated.

"There have been many times tears come out of our eyes, they can't sleep, they can't study or maybe somebody was making fun of them on the court," Ken said. "There's just tremendous pain because the tics are so severe."

There are 200,000 people in the United States known to suffer from the neurological disorder, which causes involuntary tics and movements. But Ken refused to let Matt, Mike and McKinley feel sorry for themselves, and kept them in sports. In fact, sports have helped them focus, make friends and learn the value of hard work and discipline.

### Tough Times for All

Still, there have been tough times for everyone. Candy remembered a time standing at the checkout line in Publix (a local grocery store). Matt was making all sorts of grunts and noises. The woman behind them started backing away. "So Matt turns around and says, 'I'm not contagious. I have Tourette's syndrome," Candy says. "Well, the cashiers all knew me there, so they looked at me and gave me a huge smile."

One Sunday at church, all three boys sat next to each other in a pew, grunting and twitching. A new member of the congregation approached after the service and said to Ken, "You need to teach your kids some social graces." Ken explained. Her face turned white. She apologized.

The three boys have gotten technical fouls during games because their twitches are misconstrued as showing off. At one game, two boys were making fun of Matt in the stands, mimicking his twitching. Missi walked over and confronted them. They quickly stopped. Now that he is older, Matt is more in control of his Tourette's than his brothers. But he never let it bother him.

"I never really got embarrassed about anything," Matt says. "A lot of my friends, if I wouldn't have told them, they wouldn't know I had it." Ditto for his coaches and teammates at Winter Park. Though he started playing football this year, Matt has earned significant playing time. "Once he started you could see he had the natural instincts to be a football player," Winter Park Coach Larry Gergley says. When asked whether Tourette's has been a problem, Gergley said, "It hasn't even been a factor."

Matt wanted to play football because of Ken. Though Ken started out playing basketball and baseball—spending a short time in the Angels organization after high school—he wanted to give football a try his junior year at UNLV in 1970.

He begged for a spot on the team. Coach Bill Ireland said no, and then left to teach a class. When he returned three hours later, Mitchell was still sitting in his office. "I'm not leaving until you give me a uniform," Mitchell told him. Finally Ireland agreed, but warned Mitchell that the athletic department was running short on equipment. Mitchell was issued oversized pants with a hole in the rear. He got old, crusty shoes three sizes too big. He got a helmet so big that he was forced to look out of the ear

*(continued)*

## EXHIBIT 7.2 ■ Article from *Orlando Sentinel*, October 2006 *(Continued)*

hole half the time. Ken was mortified when he walked onto the field. "I have never seen so many people laugh so hard in all their life," Ken says.

But he used that as motivation and stuck around, playing offensive line in his first year, then linebacker in 1971. Though Mitchell went undrafted, he was desperate to play in the pros. He decided to phone every NFL team and offer his services. Mitchell was rebuffed each time. He finally decided to pester the Atlanta Falcons, hoping that might increase his chances of success.

Mitchell phoned the Falcons every hour on the hour every day for three weeks. Each time, the answer was no. Finally, he got lucky. Director of Player Personnel Tom Braatz happened to answer the phone because the switchboard operator stepped away. Mitchell once again begged for a tryout. Braatz relented.

### Finally a Falcon

"You'll have a tryout," Braatz told Mitchell. "But the deal is we're going to have an attorney present so when we cut you, you're going to sign an agreement saying you'll never call us again for the rest of your life." Mitchell blew them away at his workout, and earned a trip to training camp. He arrived three weeks early to start working out. Broke, he slept under the bleachers. Finally the first day arrived. Using the same work ethic that got him a spot at UNLV, Mitchell made the team.

He ended up playing with the Falcons from 1972–75. Mitchell stayed active in sports after he retired. He coached his kids in basketball and took up mountain climbing.

Ken Mitchell, of Orlando, Florida, the first person to climb Mt. Everest with two artificial knees (2006). Reprinted with permission. Copyright © 2006, Orlando Sentinel.

But eventually the pain in his knees became too intense. He had his right knee replaced in 2000, the left in 2002.

He refused to let that slow him down. Before he had his left knee done, he told his doctor, Richard Konsens, he planned on scaling Everest. The two have since developed a close relationship, and Mitchell has given talks with Konsens at different hospitals around the region.

"He's been an inspiration to me, to people he's come in contact with at the hospital and some of the patients I've introduced him to," Konsens said. "I'm sure he's an inspiration to his children, his friends and his family." There is no doubting that. Why else would his children be so crazy about sports?

*Successful, Too*

Missi played at Flagler College. Mandi played at Lynn University. Five of the kids won state youth basketball championships last year. Mickey won four himself, playing on two different AAU teams and two different Youth Basketball of America teams.

Garbage cans full of trophies line the garage. But those are not as important, given everything the Mitchells have gone through. "You learn from the tough things in life," Ken says. "It's the hard stuff that will give you the love of the fight. Winning is great, but you have to take pride in that journey."

The Mitchells know that better than anyone.

Adelson, Andrea, "Passion for Sports Helps Orlando Family Deal with Tourette's Syndrome," Orlando Sentinel, *Oct. 11, 2006, p C.1. Reprinted with permission. Copyright © 2006*, Orlando Sentinel.

Two television stations also picked up the story and involved Dr. Konsens in both the news story and the live interview on the 5 p.m. news program.

## MAKING TELEVISION WORK FOR YOUR PRACTICE

As a medical practice leader or group practice administrator, you (and your physicians) may have been reluctant to meet with radio, television, or print representatives. Traditionally, practices have the following concerns: the community will frown on them if they begin advertising; media reps will take advantage of them; they don't know how to buy media services; they don't have a real marketing plan or plan of action so they can't put so many resources toward an opportunity brought to them by radio, television, or print outlets.

To take the mystery out of how television advertising can work for you, I've called on my colleague, Tom Calato. Tom is an adjunct professor at the University of Central Florida, School of Communications, and recently retired general sales manager for WKMG-TV, Orlando. With extensive Internet marketing experience, he manages WKMG's local6.com, Central Florida's #1 television Web channel, as well as oversees the Miami, Jacksonville, Madison, and Milwaukee sites for the company.

## TOM CALATO: TELEVISION—USING THE MEDIUM WELL

Two million dollars! We hear it every year. A commercial in the Super Bowl costs $2 million (or more).

It's true, of course. But context is everything. A 30-second commercial reaching potentially every single viewer watching the big game across the entire nation at the same time does indeed carry that hefty price tag. But most practices that advertise are not trying to reach every viewer across the country. You usually only care about your local marketplace, the area of influence for your practice, and from which you draw your patients.

So how do you navigate this world of television advertising? Will it really cost you thousands of dollars to advertise? How can you best use this medium to your advantage to not only gain results in the long term, but also brand yourself and your practice as the experts in your field?

This need not be a daunting task. Simply understanding the landscape of the medium will shed enough light on the present and future of television advertising to help you make result-generating decisions and grow your practice.

### *How It Works*

We can dispense with the history lesson of the invention, development, and growth of television. Instead, let's look at how television stations are structured, programmed, and sold as an advertising medium. This chapter is meant to be a "how-to" guide to the world of *American Idol, Survivor,* network and local newscasts, and even the most popular syndicated shows such as *Oprah* and *Dr. Phil.*

First, though, we have to understand how a station works. Very simply, a television station is nothing more than a local business. Sure, the Federal Communications Commission granted the license, but that regulatory agency primarily oversees the technical use of the spectrum by television and radio stations.

## *Programming*

A station is granted a license to operate in the public interest within the community it serves. Programming is generated from one of three sources. The first are programs purchased from program providers, also known as syndicators. The syndicators sell the local television stations shows to air throughout the day and throughout the week. These range from "off-net" shows, also called reruns, and "first-run" shows, those produced specifically for television stations and which these program providers sell television market by television market to any station that wants to pay for them. Examples of off-net programs are *Seinfeld, Friends,* and *The Simpsons,* all shows that have been on in prime time and live out their lives as reruns.

First-run show examples are popular non–prime-time shows such as *Oprah, Dr. Phil,* and *Rachael Ray*—shows produced specifically for sale by syndicators on a market-to-market basis across the country. You can travel the United States and find *Oprah, Friends, Dr. Phil,* and *The Simpsons* on many different affiliated stations. That is, a mix of ABC, NBC, CBS, FOX, or even the CW may all carry these shows without any commonality or corporate ties.

The second and most well-known source of programming is the network affiliation. In the beginning, television brought news, entertainment, and sports into the home. But individual stations found it difficult and extremely expensive to create their own programming to broadcast to their city or region of license.

Enter the television networks. As ABC, CBS, and NBC grew, they were able to entice local stations with nearly limitless resources and an ever-growing national footprint. A network provided a central source for a local station to receive, and retransmit, the same news, entertainment, and sports programming it had been struggling to provide on its own. Until quite recently, all networks paid the local stations, sometimes as much as a few million dollars annually, just to put the national network label on their local station.

Life was good for the local station. A steady programming source for their morning, afternoon, and prime time lineup, and a nightly news show that brought the world to the local marketplace came their way at no cost. To top it off, they were paid a handsome sum just for adding the CBS eye, NBC peacock, or ABC logo to their own call letters. The networks covered all the costs of producing these shows and made them available to the local affiliate to air in prime time and other times of the day, such as the morning, daytime soap operas, and, of course, the national evening news.

Finally, and most important to a television station, is local origination programming. The most visible example of this is the local news. With early morning newscasts, local cut-ins during *Good Morning America,* the *CBS Morning Show,* and the *Today Show,* stations kick off their day of local programming. Many also program a noon newscast, some start evening newscasts as early as 4 p.m., and virtually every station has a late newscast at either 10 or 11 p.m.

With these three programming sources, stations can provide the platform for a television station's business model; that is, to purchase, receive from the network, or create its own programs, generating viewership and selling advertising throughout the day.

Syndicated shows are primarily a cash expense to the station. Each half-hour show provides the opportunity for 7 or so minutes an hour of local sales time. Shows from the network don't cost the station any cash outlay, but the network sells the majority of the commercial time across the country, while the local station may receive up to 1.5 minutes of time to sell in each half hour. Local origination shows are the most lucrative for the station. Each newscast is formatted for as many commercial minutes as a station wants to program and for which it believes will help it generate the highest possible ratings. With up to 6 hours of news each weekday and up to 8 hours on the weekend, stations see this area as their bread and butter.

This business model served local broadcasters well for more than 40 years. But the times they are a-changing. Whereas the 1950s offered viewers two or three television stations to choose from, independent (nonaffiliated) stations, new networks such as FOX, WB (now CW), and UPN (now My Network TV), have sprung up to provide additional competition.

That's not even scratching the surface when it comes to cable competition for the viewer's share of time. Over 100 cable stations, the advent of digital television, and the satellite delivery of programming have all combined to shrink the traditional broadcast viewing audience. Add in *YouTube, MySpace,* and personal viewing on iPods and personal video recorders and you have to wonder just how to reach the masses anymore. Can you still use television as a marketing tool?

The answer is yes! And the answer is localism. Just as television viewership has changed dramatically over the years, so have marketing opportunities. Advertising on television has evolved into much more than the basic 30-second unit that has pervaded our lives from *Dragnet* to *I Love Lucy* to *Father Knows Best* to *The Love Boat, Magnum PI, Dallas, Who Wants To Be A Millionaire?, Survivor,* and *American Idol.*

The days of ABC, NBC, and CBS ruling the network roost have come and gone. Instead of buying one ad on a top-rated affiliate, there are upstarts such as Fox, WB, and CW to consider. Add to this mix the multitude of cable channels with advertising to sell and you see why so many potential advertisers turn their back on television as a marketing medium. In some cases, it's simply too confusing to understand and to purchase.

## Localism

Enter the need for localism. This new concept has taken priority at every station in the country. The next few sections will give you some insight into just how you can take advantage of this desire to grow a television station at the grassroots, local level.

Local market focus groups have shown an overwhelming commonality across American markets. Without relationship to market size or geography, the top three focus group hot buttons are the same. Personal well-being, family well-being, and community safety rank at the top of this list. Television station news directors who pay tens of thousands of dollars per year for this research are responding in great numbers. Newscasts are structured to focus on those three areas of concern. Station promotion of those newscasts strike at the heart of those topics to generate tune-in for each and every newscast. Entire ratings sweeps during February, May, July, and November are planned well in advance with those three topics firmly on the mind of the news management team, led, of course, by the station's general manager.

How can you as a group practice administrator take advantage of these opportunities? One of the best ways, of course, is to become best friends with a station's general manager and get her or him to promote you in a variety of newscasts!

Far-fetched? Not really. General managers of local market stations are constantly on the lookout for market information, market research, and input from the grassroots level. Time and prior commitments permitting, they're willing to sit on your boards, communicate with you at Chamber of Commerce functions, participate in health-related fundraisers, and create local programming when it makes sense for their stations.

Meeting the general manager might take a little work, but the surest way to get on the radar screen is to show a willingness to spend money with the television station. Ascertainment of community needs used to be a formalized part of a station's licensing responsibility. Good broadcast managers still collect community input from community leaders. Believe me, your input is welcomed.

## *Getting on the Air*

Spending money with a station doesn't mean buying that multimillion dollar Super Bowl spot. In fact, although $2 million will get you a 30-second ad across the entire country, all you really may want is a 30-second ad in your community on your local television affiliate carrying the game. Local spots in the big game may be as low as $5,000 to just under $100,000. Still not cheap, but a far cry from the $1 million price tag it costs to cover the nation.

Spending money with a station may mean as little as a $5,000-per-month commitment to a campaign of spots in a variety of newscasts or high-profile, demographically targeted shows such as *Dr. Phil* or *Oprah*.

After a pattern of spending is established, your account executive from the station can begin the process of allowing you to expand your marketing plan. A good account executive will promote your willingness as an advertiser to "do more" with the station. This willingness starts with you. After your account executive brings your desires to the station's general sales manager, a good general sales manager will more often than not work with the general manager and the news director to facilitate a meeting between all parties to craft a well-thought-out promotional opportunity for you and one that will generate ratings for the station.

## *The News and Your Role*

This is where we take a break and analyze the needs of both parties. As stated, a television station is a business. It is not in the business of providing a free promotional platform to anyone. Everything must come together to either bring viewers to that specific channel or produce ratings in some other meaningful way. Countless great ideas have died from being nothing more than self-promotion by a business or service company without regard to how many viewers the segment will bring to a station.

Must the idea be sensationalistic? Not necessarily. Should it be interesting and thought-provoking, with the potential to make the station money in the long-term through higher ratings? Absolutely!

How do you promote that story, advancement, or breakthrough? How do you let people know about the safety of a new procedure? The local news seems like the best place. But with a half-hour newscast, sometimes having as much as 11 minutes of commercial time, 5 minutes devoted to weather, and 2 minutes for sports, the remaining 12 minutes are usually all accounted for by the breaking news of the day. This is, of course, subjective and the call of the news director and news producers. The free time you are looking for is rarely available.

The limited news time available combined with corporate downsizing at most television stations means that something has to take a back seat. Most often, one of those topics left on the cutting room floor may be of a medical nature. Although we all want our television stations to cover stories for the improvement of everyone in the community, the fact remains that there are often stories of a broader interest, stories that generate more local "buzz" and, yes, stories written, produced, and aired simply for the ratings "bump" the station receives, especially during the four times each year when ratings are collected.

How can you get the newscast time you're looking for? One way is to become a local news expert in your specialty. Offer the services of your physicians to the station as experts who can be the "go-to" resources for the news producer or reporter.

There are a variety of national news resources available to a station. These may come in prepackaged reports the station simply puts on the air with an introduction by the local anchors, giving the appearance that the report is from a local source. However, the emphasis on localism and often the cost of the prepackaged reports are steering news directors away from them.

If a local resource is available that gets to the heart of a particular topic, the station will much prefer that opportunity. That's where the local medical professional comes in. By having an existing relationship, it makes it easy for the reporter to simply call up the medical expert, get his or her take, and put the story on the air with someone in the local community. Often, simply offering up your services to the station will be all that's necessary.

The best time to make this offer, of course, is well in advance of any press releases you might send to the station. If station management sees you as an expert without an immediate marketing agenda, they will be much more likely to take you on. Some stations might pay their expert, whereas others simply have them on call when a particular topic comes up on which the reporter needs more information.

The news card, if played properly, can certainly get you on the air of a local television station, and consistency may provide the branding you need to be a success in this arena. But as mentioned previously, having a revenue-based relationship is the surest way to get your message across. And although it's one way to be selected as the medical expert on your local newscasts, it's no guarantee. If you're looking for a sure way to get airtime, the best way is to make an advertising buy.

## Advertising Buys

Although the phrase "advertising buy" has sent many practice managers running for the hills, the fact remains that the value of television as a marketing medium is tremendous. More than 98 percent of all US households own a television, and more than 81 percent of those own more than one set, making television much more pervasive than any other medium.

Additional statistics from the Television Bureau of Advertising show that the average household spends 8 hours, 11 minutes of viewing a day. Women average just more than 5 hours, whereas men average just more than 4.5 hours. That's a lot of time spent watching television and an excellent environment for your advertising message.

With cable and satellite viewing, of course, we live in a much different world today than at the inception of television. However, the fact remains that the over-the-air broadcast stations (ABC, CBS, NBC, and FOX) each reach more than 70 percent of the viewing audience in any given market each week. Although cable doesn't have any single cable channel reaching more than 40 percent of the weekly audience, it still can reach a targeted audience and, in some cases, it can play a significant role in a good marketing plan.

Local television fosters good community relations, and your presence as an advertiser on your local station shows your commitment to the community as well. Think about the major advertisers you see on television day in and day out. They've become part of the fabric of what your community is all about. Seeing your local car dealer, financial analyst, and, yes, your local attorney on television daily gives them breakthrough recognition. It's the unaided recall they're looking for.

When someone needs a car, they don't immediately go to the Yellow Pages. Their mind goes back to whom they've recently seen or become aware of through advertising. That dealer has broken through the clutter, not only with the type of commercial, but also with an ongoing, consistent presence.

Your practice can do the same, and although advertising expenditures can run into tens of thousands of dollars each month, an effective campaign can be done for much less. In fact, the best advertising campaigns are those that provide a strong return on investment.

Although it is relatively easy to make an ad purchase on television, few health care professionals have the expertise to make an effective buy. Many advertising agencies and public relations firms are well versed in the field of television ad buying, although it's not always necessary to hire one. Many businesses choose to go it alone, with someone in the office responsible, hiring an in-house marketing person, or, in some cases where time is not an issue, dabbling in it themselves.

## *Where to Start?*

That said, you should understand that a call to a well-respected ad agency or public relations firm with expertise in the health care field is the surest way to shorten the time between concept and execution. Internet resources or your local advertising or public relations federation can provide leads for you and give you a roster from which to start interviewing.

Look for those firms with the expertise you don't have and give them the opportunity to develop a long-term plan for you. Outline your expectations and monitor results on a regular basis. Not just with reports, but with face-to-face meetings.

A good ad or public relations firm will spend time analyzing your practice. Spending time with you and in your office observing and analyzing are critical, and you'll be surprised at how much you can learn about your operation from an outsider. Although they may not know the specifics of your practice, they often can provide you with valuable insights you may have overlooked or taken for granted.

After a plan of action has been put together, your agency will contact individual television stations and gather the information you need to roll out your plan. Then it's a matter of execution and monitoring for the long-term. A critical point to remember is that, just like driving from New York to Los Angeles requires a well thought-out route well in advance, it also requires constant checkpoints to make sure you are making progress. There may be detours along the way and an occasional flat tire, but starting your journey in New York and giving up in Des Moines means your mission may never be fulfilled.

## *Going It Alone*

If you have the time and choose to create your own plan, calling an account executive to visit your practice for an initial consultation is really quite simple. A phone call to the general or local sales manager of each television station in the market will soon lead to a 1-hour session in which you can meet with the sales professional. Although each will promote his or her own station and programming, your first meeting should be conversational, consultative, and open. You should be prepared to outline what you're hoping to accomplish, the demographic target you wish to reach, your timeline expectations, and some sort of budget range.

Your account executive will then prepare a plan using in-depth market research. Ratings information on individual shows is helpful, but a strategic plan of attack using a combination of the local Nielsen ratings, as well as lifestyle statistics from such respected companies as Scarborough or Simmons, will provide the information you need to get the most out of your ad dollar.

For example, you can find out which newscast in your market has the highest percentage of women older than age 50 who live in a household earning more than $100,000 per year, drive a BMW, have health insurance, and vacation in Hawaii. If that's your audience, great. If not, your account executive can find out just where that audience is, even if it's on a competitor's program.

After your account executive returns with a plan, you'll need to decide how many and which stations you'll work with. Often, the personality, professionalism, and expertise of the account executive will help you decide. Just as your patients choose you for your expertise and their trust in you, deciding whom you'll work with is just as important. Your comfort level with your ad buy has a lot to do with your account executive.

Should the station and its programming be the one you want to work with, but the account executive not to your liking, feel free to call the general or local sales manager, explain your concern and ask for a different account executive.

Advertising buys are based on a number of factors. Of course, one is the programming environment you'll place your commercial in. News, entertainment, or sports programming are just a few of those options. Your decision is made easier when the account executive provides you with research to show the demographic composition of each show.

Choosing an older-skewing show such as *60 Minutes* over the younger-geared *The Rachel Ray Show* will be a call you make based on your practice. Choosing a male environment such as NCAA basketball or NFL on Sunday might be the right direction for a practice dominated by male patients.

Your next step is to compare rates among competitors. Station account executives can provide a comparison by taking their individual rates, showing you the ratings for each show, and leveling the playing field so you can compare one station's rates and ratings with another. You'll then be able to use this information in deciding which station or combination of stations you'll use.

## Making a Commercial

After you've made your ad buy with the stations, you'll need to meet with the creative director to discuss how your ad will look, what you'll say, and the general branding plan you have in mind for your practice. If you're working with an ad agency or public relations firm, you should still be involved in the creative process, but with professional agency assistance.

In many cases, you'll also find at least one television station in your market that specializes in local production. The station will meet with you, analyze your needs creatively, and work through much the same process as you did in planning the ad buy. You'll meet with a producer along with your account executive and discuss creative direction. Another topic of conversation will be the production timeline. Though it may be accelerated in some cases, you can usually expect a 3- to 4-week window to get your finished product from the station's production team.

Costs are always a concern regarding the production of a spot. Depending on the market, your 30-second spot produced directly by a station may be included with your ad buy at no charge or it may cost you from $3,000 to $10,000. Of course, animation, graphics, music, talent fees, and complex editing can increase your cost well beyond those estimates, but you will control that with your direction.

As with working through an ad agency, monitoring of your on-air schedules is critical. Regular updates from your account executive, attention to detail, and making sure your commercials air in the programs you purchased are just as important as putting together the initial buy. A growing number of advertisers have the account executive's assistant at the station call their office daily with the exact times their ad will air that day. For some interested in a more immediate and direct response, this can be an excellent monitoring tool. These "call now for more information" spots can be monitored readily with someone in your office monitoring the phone or the hiring of an outside answering service.

It all comes down to making sure you get an appropriate return on the investment of your advertising dollar.

## The Credit Process

No matter which route you choose, buying television time will require submitting a credit application to the station and an initial expectation of cash in advance for the first schedule unless and until credit is established. After your credit is accepted, you can expect to be billed monthly with payment within 30 days as the industry norm. You may be able to work out different terms, but that can be done after you've established your initial relationship with the account executive and the station.

Your local account executives can be your best friends at the station. They are, after all, paid on commission, and it is to their benefit to champion your cause regarding all aspects of your station dealings. If you need special handling of your account or extra attention from management, use your account executive to get what you feel you deserve. And if the account executive is not responsive to your needs, the general sales manager will want to know.

Now that we've covered the news angle and the straight purchase of airtime methods of promoting yourself or your practice, let's take a look at some other, nontraditional ways of getting on the air

## *Eight Elite Opportunities*

### 1. Creating a Franchise

A franchise is your ownership of something the station produces on a regular basis. This can be as simple as a local medical update, created within the newscast and aired daily or once per week at the same time. Don't be afraid to ask the station to help you create this franchise. You may get pushback in the event the station doesn't have a medical reporter or chooses not to cover medical topics regularly.

In that case, there's nothing wrong with producing this franchise yourself, buying the time, and asking for it to be placed at a specific time. The revenue you generate for the station will get you the attention you need to get your message across. If the station places your update as the first element in a commercial break, it may even come across as a news story.

### 2. Buying a Promotional Event

All stations have community or promotional events they become involved with on a local level. By sponsoring of one of these events, you will become known for your community involvement and the recognition of your sponsorship within the station family. Buying time within a promotional event will also have the station management behind you, which can give your message an extra push throughout the duration of the promotional event.

### 3. Owning a Show

Rather than buying commercial time within a show in 30-second increments, it's possible to buy out an entire show. Perhaps a 2-hour movie on the weekend is a good time for you to advertise your practice or a specific procedure. By owning all of the commercial time during the movie, you're able to give a "telethon" feel to the movie with each and every commercial break containing nothing but a long-form message for your practice. In many instances, you even may have input on which movie the station will air.

Looking for an older demographic? Perhaps the station can air *On Golden Pond*. Looking for a younger demographic? A Harry Potter movie might work just as well. *Thelma and Louise, Die Hard,* and *Fried Green Tomatoes* all have distinct audiences and demographic groups you might want to reach. When you own all the time, your message will certainly be seen.

### 4. Talent Recognition

Being your own spokesperson can add personality to your message. Whether it's smooth and professional or has a somewhat less than polished appearance, you might be able to use talent recognition as a tool to break through the advertising clutter. You may also want to hire a local professional sports star, a local celebrity, or simply run a talent search for one of your own. Make sure your talent won't leave you after you spend a lot of resources promoting them. It may be a chance you have to take.

### 5. Added Value

A significant expenditure on a television station in your market can often lead to perks known as "added value." Added value is simply that—"something extra" the station provides as a thank-you for your business. Although this is most often in the form of additional spots at no charge, added value may take on many different forms. Inclusion in promotional events, having your logo and name added to a station event, sporting event tickets, or event dinner, golf, or entertainment gift certificates are all examples of the something extra you may receive.

### 6. Direct Response

Having a message that can spur the viewer to action by picking up the phone and calling you immediately is known as direct response. The station often runs these commercials during times when you have personnel ready and able to answer phone calls. A catchy phone number can break through the noise of so many ads in the marketplace and remind the viewer to give a special phone number a call for a special offer or opportunity. These rates are often very low and can provide a big payoff for very little investment. Stations publish direct rate cards at rates substantially below regular advertisers.

## 7. Pre-emptible

Buying a commercial at a rate that is well below or not on a station's rate card is known as buying pre-emptible time. Say you'd like to buy a spot in *American Idol*. A station's rate card may call for $5,000 per local commercial. You have the opportunity to make the station an offer, say $2,000. Should the station not be able to sell out their time at the $5,000 level, or have a last-minute cancellation, you have the chance of having your commercial air.

It should be noted, however, that a last-minute sale of a spot at the $5,000 level to another advertiser could get your commercial preempted or bumped from airing. You will not have to pay for the commercial, of course, but remember, you won't have aired your message either.

## 8. Ancillary Opportunities

Special newspaper publications, television station Internet sites, You Tube, audio and video local production, and a host of other opportunities exist within the television station world. A station's Website can provide you with links to your own site or even give you the chance to produce video that the station airs only on cable. This can be a long-form or short-form spot. With Internet sites reaching as many at 2 million people in mid-size markets, developing your content and airing it within the world of the local station's Website is another excellent marketing tool for you.

A station also might produce a direct mail piece or other station promotional device. By adding your logo, message, or sponsorship, you can increase the reach of your message and add your brand to the local station's community involvement efforts. You may even be able to have the station produce a local wellness guide newspaper in which the station uses its resources to develop, write, and mail a very topical piece targeted to those interested in new medical practices, breakthroughs, or basic wellness information.

Remember that each time the station includes you in something they're doing, there's an implied endorsement of you.

## SUMMARY

Using the resources of a local market television station as part of your marketing mix may be just what you need to brand your practice. The tremendous audience television reaches on a national level can be used to your advantage on a local level now more than ever. Television stations are desperate for localism, and you can be part of that in a number of ways. Call your local station today. Operators are standing by!

### *Real-Life Promotion*

What Tom has shared is a lot to take in, but is not that difficult to act on. The following is an example of a television promotion that delivered television ad time, print, radio, and Internet as one promotional package for a number of forward-thinking practices.

An account representative from WKMG-TV, a CBS affiliate, met with us to share a multipronged package they thought would be of interest to some of our clients. Up to this time, not many of our clients used television as a medium because of budgetary issues and because they did not have an advertising spot to use even if the opportunity seemed to be a fit. This promotion was so intriguing we encouraged five of our clients to participate.

The station's plan was to create a *Wellness Guide* newspaper to be distributed between December and February with a corporate partner, the local YMCAs in Central Florida's multicounty area. Two hundred thousand copies were to be printed and distributed to the local YMCAs with promotion on the station taking place during the news hour, driving the viewing audience to pick up their copy of the *Guide* and to look for the *Guide* on the station's Website. The *Wellness Guide* covered articles on cancer screening, cosmetic surgery, dental health, diet, exercise, eye care, flu vaccinations, infant care, physical therapy, substance abuse/rehabilitation, and total joint replacement.

In addition, there also was a physician's reference guide in the publication, plus advertisements. Although there were multiple packages available, the ones that our clients found of value are shown in Exhibit 7.3.

I share these campaigns with you to provide exposure to what a proposal from the television station may look like when it is presented to you by your account representative. That said, you still should have reasonable negotiating power within the package that you're offered. Our

# EXHIBIT 7.3 ■ Sample Ads

## Package A

- 1/4 Page, Four-Color Ad
- $4000 bank of television advertising time for a customized package to air on WKMG between December 2006 and March 2007*
- Advertising on Local6.com (2 mos. X 100,000 = 200,000 impressions)
- Advertisement on exclusive "Today's Local 6" web page
- Production of Television Commercial**

**Investment: $5,000**

Accepted by:.............................................
Date:........................................................

$5000 Package

\* Program rate are prevailing rate at time of schedule placement
\*\* Production consisting of 1 hour shoot and 2 hours editing. Additional time for production will be billed at an prevailing hourly rate

## Print-Internet Only Package

| | |
|---|---|
| 1/8 Page, Four-Color Ad | $2500 |
| 1/4 Page, Four-Color Ad | $3500 |
| 1/2 Page, Four-Color Ad | $4500 |
| Full Page, Four-Color Ad | $5500 |

- Advertising on Local6.com
  (2 mos. X 100,000 = 200,000 impressions)

*(continued)*

**EXHIBIT 7.3** ■ **Sample Ads** *(Continued)*

1/8 page ad used by Eye Physicians of Central Florida in the *Wellness Guide*

Robert S. Gold, M.D., F.A.A.P.
David B. Auerbach, D.O.
Louis C. Blumenfeld, M.D., F.A.A.P.
Victor B. Thomas, M.D.
Larry S. Lewis, O.D.

Longwood
(407) 767-6411

Winter Park
(407) 645-4350

MetroWest
(407) 398-7730

EYE PHYSICIANS of Central Florida
Leaders in Pediatric and Adult Eye Care

1/8 page ad used by Partners in Women's Healthcare in the *Wellness Guide*

## *Women's healthcare for all generations.*

PARTNERS IN WOMEN'S HEALTHCARE
OBSTETRICS-GYNECOLOGY GROUP

Orlando • Oviedo • MetroWest
www.partnersinwomenshealthcare.com

*Nicholas Abrudescu, M.D.*
*Nancy L. Brown, M.D.*
*Kai Fu, M.D.*
*Yasmine N. Kareem, M.D.*
*Leigh C. White, M.D., Ph.D.*

**(407) 898-9922**
*It's how women's healthcare should be.*

Ads used with permission of Local6, WKMG-TV Orlando; Eye Physicians of Central Florida; and Partners in Women's Healthcare.

account rep at the time, Dick Katz, was fantastic in being creative and helpful in how to maximize our opportunities with this project. He helped us negotiate with the station to create and tape the commercial spots at no fee to our clients.

Both Eye Physicians of Central Florida and the Jewett Orthopaedic Convenient Care Center opted to go with $5,000 Package A, which included television spots. After this was agreed on, we met with the station's creative department to provide talking points so they could create scripts for the television commercials. The clients opted to go with two 15-second spots rather than one 30-second spot to achieve more frequency and reach.

The talking points (Exhibit 7.4) were developed to help the producer, who needed them to write copy for the television spots. This is something you must do—it gives the station a starting place for what is of value to you, the message you want to impart. From these talking points, scripts for the television spots were created, sent to the clients for approval, and then used with the video footage.

The two clients who bought the $5,000 television package received the following: $4,000 worth of 15-second spots that aired on morning news, noon news, *Dr. Phil,* and *Rachael Ray* until their budget was used. In addition, the two groups who bought Package A received radio exposure because the television station airs its entire programming on 87.7 FM all day long, meaning when the group's television spots ran, the audio portion was heard on the radio as well.

Of course, there was the *Wellness Guide,* which was distributed in the groups' offices, as well at the local YMCAs. And there was the television's station's 6-week *Wellness Guide* promotion to drive viewers to their Website. The groups were promised 200,000 impressions on the station's Website.

That means that a viewer could log on to Channel 6's Website, click on *Wellness Guide,* and go to the physician lists that were organized by specialty. All of the clients as advertisers were listed on the Website, whether or not they bought the television or print package.

After going to the Channel6TV.com Website, viewers could click on the health care specialties of orthopedics, ophthalmology, cardiology, internal medicine, or obstetrics/gynecology (the clients we had involved in this project), then they could click on a specific group. If they then

## EXHIBIT 7.4 ■ Sample Talking Points

**EYE PHYSICIANS OF CENTRAL FLORIDA—WKMG-TV**

*General Talking Points/Ideas*

- Five board-certified eye physicians, including two fellowship-trained pediatric ophthalmologists
- Providing care for children and adults of all ages
- Three conveniently located offices—Longwood, Winter Park, and MetroWest
- Comprehensive family eye care close to home
- Provide a full range of care—from routine exams to treatment for the most complicated pediatric and adult eye conditions
- The eye care you need from physicians you can trust
- The highest level of eye care available and a level of caring to match it
- Believe in treating each patient like family
- Full-service eye care center—everything from routine eye examinations and glasses to the latest treatments and surgery for both common and rare eye problems/conditions
- Specialize in pediatric ophthalmology, adult eye muscle disorders, cataract and laser surgery, neuro-ophthalmology, and oculoplastic, reconstructive, and cosmetic eyelid surgery
- Leaders in pediatric and adult eye care for 25 years
- Meeting our community's family eye care needs since 1981 (or for 25 years)

*Pediatric Points*

- Specializing in children's unique eye care needs—from common conditions to rare and difficult-to-diagnose disorders
- Two of Central Florida's only board-certified, fellowship-trained pediatric ophthalmologists

*Adult Points*

- Among the first in the United States to use the ReSTOR lens for cataract patients, allowing many to see clearly at all distances without bifocals or reading glasses

*Used with permission of Eye Physicians of Central Florida.*

**JEWETT ORTHOPAEDIC CONVENIENT CARE CENTER WKMG-TV CAMPAIGN**

*Goals*

- Create awareness of this new center/service
- Secure brand name identity for the Jewett Orthopaedic Convenient Care Center
- Position in consumers' minds as the "first stop" when you experience an unexpected injury
- Attract new patients with acute orthopaedic injuries to Jewett through the OCCC

*Target Audiences*

- Parents (moms)
- Weekend warriors
- Referral sources: employers, physicians (PCP, pediatricians), athletic trainers/coaches

*Challenge*

This is not a service consumers and referral sources will necessarily use immediately upon learning about it. We must continually create awareness so it becomes second nature, "top of mind" for when they do need it.

*Key Messages*

- No appointment necessary
- Reduces overall cost of care and treatment; provides cost-effective, efficient alternative to ER and urgent care centers; improves quality of care for patient; improves patient satisfaction; improves access to timely treatment; reduces unnecessary medical tests and procedures/duplication of services that often occur in the ER and urgent care centers
- Need to make sure consumers and existing Jewett patients know this is for new, urgent acute injuries and not an alternative to receive care for existing problems/follow-up
- Save time, save money, improve access, improve quality of care, and reduce unnecessary tests and expenses
- Open Monday through Saturday

*Used with permission of Jewett Orthopaedic Clinic.*

clicked on Jewett Orthopaedic Convenient Care Center or Eye Physicians, they would be automatically linked to that particular practice's Website.

Finally, when a viewer went to the Internet *Wellness Guide,* there were rotating banners for all the advertisers in the *Wellness Guide.* If the viewer clicked on a banner, he or she was immediately linked to that practice's Website.

This one project provided a matrix of opportunities for multiple marketing venues.

The goal of each practice was to raise its brand and present an appearance of **Access** and **Availability** to the practice. That said, it's important to remember that it takes a few months to realize the success of this type of campaign, and it also requires a way to monitor how patients became familiar with the practices. In this case, we knew that awareness was raised, but until there is a health care need, viewers and readers have no reason to use the groups.

Regardless, this was a terrific multilevel marketing opportunity for an unusually low fee. Another bonus is that the groups are now perceived as being engaged in the community with other power players, both the television station and the YMCA.

CHAPTER 8

# Reaching Out—A Guide To Community Relations

When we discuss the cornerstones of marketing, **The Four A's— Access, Availability, Accountability,** and **Accommondation,** we're not only talking about the coexistence a patient has with your practice. In addition to the connection a patient has with a direct referral from another physician, family, or friend, you can position your practice and physicians as leaders by your integration into your community.

It's fun and rewarding, plus it builds your brand and brings pride to your staff. It's also some of the best positioning you can do. Sharing her insight on this topic is Kristin Weissman, director of public relations for Full Sail Real World Education, an award-winning entertainment media college outside Orlando, Florida.

Kristin directs both press and community relations and helps to develop the brand and image of the organization. Throughout her experience in this role, Kristin has worked with such well-known events as the 2006 Sundance Film Festival and the 48th Annual Grammy Awards as well as groups like the National Association of Broadcasters. She also previously worked with the Miss America Pageant and Donald Trump Casinos.

Kristin's career achievements have been nationally recognized and she has received many honors, including the Manchester Executive and Professional Women in Central Florida Award, 2004; the Manchester Who's Who of Empowering Executives and Professionals Award, 2003; the Mobius Advertising Award, 2003; and Distinguished Alumni Student for Arcadia University/Beaver College in 2004, 2005, and 2006.

In addition, she has been nominated for the Margaret LeClair Interdisciplinary Writing Award, the Philadelphia Advertising Award, the New Charter Chapter Business Women's Association Award, and the America's Young Professionals Award. She also is a board member for OTRONICON, an interactive video gaming/multimedia event in partnership with the Orlando Science Center; a board member for the 2007 Florida Film Festival; and a board member on the Orlando Chamber of Commerce Trustee Committee.

## KRISTIN WEISSMAN: CRAFTING THE MESSAGE

English poet Alfred Tennyson once said *"I am a part of all that I have met."* This is a statement and a belief that all business owners, marketing professionals, and each individual embarking on a mission to reach his or her own community should adopt. The single most important concept in the field of public or community relations is that you are your community, and building a relationship with your public is key to your success. To take that one step further, the art of public or community relations is simple—knowing what your community wants is powerful; meeting that desire is everything.

The first initiative in meeting the demand is to acknowledge that your business is your brand. It is a brand that needs to be shaped, created and identified, and then shared through the benefits of public and community relations. You begin by investing in a solid public relations (PR) strategy.

Far too often, business owners make the mistake of sinking their entire marketing budget into an advertising campaign alone. Although advertising, such as commercials, print ads, and direct mail promotions, are valuable, they should work hand-in-hand with a strong and effective PR program.

The duty of PR is to build relationships—with your community, your target audience, and most important, with the media. The media is responsible for molding your message into the package that's best and most frequently received. One simple placement created by the work of PR—whether it's an article covered in a local or national newspaper or magazine or a TV spot that talks about your business—is valued at much more than 10 times what you would have spent paying to place an advertisement of any kind. Those victorious in the art of PR quickly identify the power of the press and how to use that power to their advantage as their greatest weapon to aid in the battle of successful business practice.

After you determine your audience and the media you will pursue, you must then develop your message. Sit down and think about what it is you want to convey about your business to the public. Is it your exceptional service, your location and convenience, or perhaps the quality of your care and facilities? Maybe it's all of the above.

After you form your message, you must craft your release. A press release is the primary tool in public or community relations. It is the nationally accepted method used to reach the media and pique their interest in your business. However, talking about your services is not enough. You also must identify the human story.

The human story is that aspect of your business that makes you unique. Maybe *you* are the story—your practice's history and changes for the future of medicine, background, how your business came to be, or a physician who has special training. Maybe it's your building, one of your patients, or a new type of medicine or treatment you're pioneering. Whatever makes you and your practice special, tell that story.

It's the human component that will drive the media to cover a story. You need to effectively articulate what it is that makes you or your practice so compelling that you instantly create a need and an urgency of how your story will impact, save, help, inspire, or improve the lives of media viewers, readers, and communities. You are in control of the message.

After you have your message crafted into a press release and you've identified key media that will cover your story, you must then look at your total branding package. Public and community relations are effective not because you're initiating one method of action. Rather, it's because you're building valuable relationships that will create a network in which to share your message through many different avenues.

Also, if you're completing any of the PR or marketing efforts on your own without the help of an in-house or freelance team, be aware that there are many books available or resources online to show you step-by-step how to compose a release and make your efforts successful. If you're searching to employ help, call your local PR chapter or visit their Website online through www.prsa.org to find a professional who might be a strong fit for you and your business.

## Community Relations 101

After you have an understanding of public relations, you'll find that community relations is quite similar. However, it deals strictly with your local community surroundings.

Generally, the best way to reach this mainstream audience is to hold an event. Draw attention to your practice through a grand opening, anniversary of the practice, children's health fair, senior salute, or other special occasion to welcome the community, local government officials, and press to see your facility, meet your staff, and learn more about what you have to offer. It's during this time when you'll also begin to more closely see the benefits of forging the connection between your marketing and PR teams.

So how do you conduct effective community relations and why should you do it? It's quite simple. By reaching out to your local community, you're not only marketing and advertising your services and making your neighborhood aware, but you're also building invaluable equity in your community "bank account."

Think of the last community event you attended—a fundraiser, charity walk-a-thon, or business networking function. Did you notice any of the other businesses or medical groups that were present? What did you think when you saw their sponsorship banner, walked by their trade show booth, reviewed their promotional materials, or even saw their name listed in a program?

Most likely, you may have found that business to be more credible for being associated with the event you enjoyed. You had a more favorable opinion of them because of their sponsorship efforts, or perhaps you even decided to use their services because you became aware of them or, subconsciously, you wanted to align yourself with a corporation or service that supported a cause you admired. *That's the power of community relations.*

But how do you find the right community event to sponsor?

In the medical community, there's an abundance of events to choose from, and it should be quite easy to find a community initiative that's right for you. Look online, in your local newspaper, even on bulletin boards in the supermarket. There are worthwhile community events all around you.

It's also very powerful to garner the support of local community officials. As you open your new clinic or medical practice, invite the media and the mayor of your town or a county official to cut the ribbon in a ribbon-cutting ceremony. Or hold a VIP event in your new facility to showcase your services and, again, invite the mayor or city commissioners to be a part, take a look around, and use that as an opportunity to put your cause in front of them.

Also, make sure to do your research. If you know that a certain commissioner or elected official shares your passion for cancer research, then make sure to target him or her specifically. The key is to find where you fit into the community picture and strategically place yourself there. It will add support to your service or newfound business and enhance a level of credibility and recognition that cannot be compared.

As you plan your community event or strategy, it's also essential that your marketing team designs a clear and easy-to-understand brochure to highlight your services and create a personal Website for your business. PR should oversee all content to make sure that the copy presented is consistent with the messaging created for your PR mission. By protecting the integrity of your brand, each of these elements should work in unison within your newfound brand identity.

Each of these ideas begins to formulate your PR techniques and starts the flow of your ideas to put into words the feeling and the heart of your new one-of-a-kind medical practice.

The most critical element to acknowledge is that the art of public and community relations is an ever-changing, daily, and consistent effort that makes a winning impact over time. Your content and message must remain fresh and maintain a steady stream of contact to keep your practice and your message top-of-mind. Similar to building a lasting friendship, public and community relations is a relationship that requires trust, dynamic interaction, and a feeling that both parties are needed to flourish and to grow. You are a part of everyone you meet. Now, tell them your story.

## CASE STUDIES

The following are examples of community relations case studies that demonstrate how these efforts were used to create success stories. The information was taken from the organizations' Websites in 2006. Check the Websites for further information or updates on these case studies.

### The Nissan Quest for Safety Program

As reported on www.nissanusa.com/about/corporate-info/community-relations.htm.

Nissan is committed to the overall safety of the general public and child seat safety is one of its highest priorities. In 1998, Nissan launched its award-winning Quest for Safety program. This program utilizes a strategic approach to inform caregivers in communities with below-average child seat usage rates about child seat safety and the proper installation and use of child safety seats and booster seats.

Under the Quest for Safety program, Nissan has formed strategic partnerships with the YWCA, Puente Learning Center, Crystal Stairs, and Los Angeles County Office of Education to offer free community child passenger safety educational seminars in Los Angeles communities. The 2005 education seminars conducted in Southern California focused on California's new child passenger safety law requiring children to be placed in child safety seats or boosters until age 6 or 60 pounds and provided caregivers with a hands-on demonstration on how to properly install a child safety seat or booster seat.

As part of this program, Nissan distributes its Child Passenger Safety Card. This easy referral card uses illustrations to depict how to properly install a child safety seat or booster. The card is sized to fit in the glove compartment to provide easy and simple reference for caregivers.

### University of Victoria (UVic)

As reported on www.coag.uvic.ca/cdsmp/cdsmp_program.htm.

Since 2000, UVic has helped Vancouver Island residents manage the everyday challenges of chronic illness through the Centre on Aging's Chronic Disease Self-Management Program (CDSMP).

The program trains volunteers living with chronic conditions to help people cope with illnesses such as diabetes, arthritis, heart disease, and more. To date, the CDSMP has trained 233 leaders on Vancouver Island who have gone on to deliver the course to 1,067 people.

"It works because it's a program that builds community capacity," says UVic's Dr. Patrick McGowan, who oversees the program. "These volunteer leaders live in the community and they use their training and experience with chronic illness to help and empower others."

*(continued)*

Nanaimo resident Pam Edgar, who originally turned to CDSMP to help manage her multiple sclerosis, decided to become a volunteer leader 2 years ago. "It's the best thing that could have happened in my life," she says. "What I've gotten back from delivering this program has been amazing."

"We focus on the problems, the symptoms they cause, and how to deal with them, rather than the specific diseases," says Edgar. "People leave with the tools to cope and a very positive frame of mind."

### Stony Brook Medical Center

As reported on www.stonybrookmedicalcenter.org.

*Speakers Bureau*

Provides "free" health lectures for community groups. Health care professionals present the latest information on a wide range of topics covering health and wellness, disease prevention, current treatment methods, the latest research, and accessing medical services.

*Health Fairs*

Stony Brook University Medical Center health care professionals participate in community health fairs and provide health information and perform health screenings.

*Smith Haven Mall Walkers Club*

Sponsored by Stony Brook University Medical Center, the mall walkers club meets the last Wednesday of every month at the Food Court in the Smith Haven Mall. Members receive a complimentary snack and blood pressure screening starting at 8 a.m., and hear an informative lecture at 9 a.m.

*Walk for Beauty-Walk for Life*

Held in October, this 4K/6K walk through scenic, historic areas of Stony Brook raises funds for breast and prostate cancer research at Stony Brook University.

*Health Initiative for Underserved Communities*

The Initiative provides community health education programs and screenings and works closely with grassroots organizations to improve access to care and support efforts to meet the needs of people living in underserved communities.

## Author's Case Study

In Chapter 4, I presented information about a retreat conducted by a four-doctor group named Wymore OB/Gyn. It took a year to implement recommendations from the retreat, but, as a result, the group expanded to five physicians and changed their name to Partners in Women's Healthcare to better reflect their mission. They also built a new full-time community office.

Part of their motivation for the change was their desire for a higher quality of personal life without giving up obstetrics. Although many physicians in the legally contentious and difficult state of Florida were giving up obstetrics, this practice wanted to make two points to their community:

1. They were taking new obstetric patients and in fact wanted more.
2. They wanted to be considered partners with their patients throughout a woman's lifespan—maternity to menopause.

Of course, they had to do the basic fundamentals—develop a new name, logo, and corporate identity package; communicate to their patients about the changes; select a promotional item to assert the new name and logo; and find ways to quickly engage with exiting patients and attract new ones.

One of their offices was geographically near Orlando's densely populated Asian community. As the group's marketing plan was developed, they looked at many community opportunities to spread their message. In addition to using public relations, they realized that advertising would be necessary to achieve their goals.

We will look at their plan, some of the initiatives to actualize the plan, and the tools that were created to achieve their goals (Exhibits 8.1–8.10).

Exhibit 8.1 describes the overall 24-month marketing and public relations plan. The grid shown in Exhibit 8.2 is a planning guide.

Exhibit 8.3 shows the new logo and letterhead to reinforce the Partners in Women's Healthcare corporate identity.

Exhibit 8.4 is a copy of a letter that was printed on the letterhead and mailed to all patients who had been to the practice within the past 24 months. The letter worked well to stimulate women to make appointments that they had "meant to" but hadn't realized how much time had passed since their last appointment. (Do you see the marketing cornerstone **Four A's** in this letter?)

As the practice was actively working to implement the tangible strategies and tactics of their plan, it was important to stay focused on the community relations opportunities in the plan. Exhibt 8.5 shows a few we suggested.

Exhibit 8.6 is the plan we came up with to thank the nurses who are part of their hospital community. Exhibit 8.7 indicated what steps the office manager should take to implement the plan.

We recommended an ad campaign to attract new patients. Exhibit 8.8 lists talking points on why to adverstise, and Exhibit 8.9 shows some of the ads targeted for specific groups in the multiple communities in which the practice engages.

Because the adverstising was such a big commitment to the practice's budget, the group decided to ask patients if they had seen any of the ads. Exhibit 8.10 is the survery that was used.

In everything they do, this practice embodies **The Four A's—Access, Accountability, Availability,** and **Accommodation.**

# EXHIBIT 8.1 ■ Marketing and Public Relations Plan (24 months)

**PARTNERS IN WOMEN'S HEALTHCARE 24-MONTH MARKETING & PUBLIC RELATIONS PLAN**

*Current Situation*

Partners in Women's Healthcare just re-named the practice from Wymore OB/Gyn and also developed a new logo to begin creating a new brand identity. The practice currently has four physician partners and trained support staff. They plan to add an additional physician in August.

The practice currently has three offices. The main office is located in the Kids Docs' building at the corner of Princeton and Bedford near Florida Hospital (open Mon.–Thurs., 8:30 a.m.–4 p.m. and Fri., 9 a.m.–3 p.m.). A second neighborhood office is located in Oviedo (open Mon., 1–7 p.m., Tues, 8:30 a.m.–3 p.m., Wed., 7 a.m.–1 p.m., and Friday, 9:30 a.m.–3 p.m.) and another neighborhood office is currently located in Southwest Orlando on Vineland Rd. (open Thurs., 7 a.m.–1 p.m.).

Partners in Women's Healthcare hopes to open a new office in MetroWest within the next six months that would be open four–five days a week and would replace the Vineland office. In addition, they would eventually like to move the main office closer to Arnold Palmer Hospital where they deliver all of their OB patients.

Partners in Women's Healthcare is a full-service OB/Gyn practice. They recently ventured into retail sales by offering Ameriscience multi-vitamins, and they are considering offering additional retail products, as well as a new laser service.

Most patients self-refer to the practice or are referred by a friend, family, or managed care plan. However, they do receive some referrals from primary care physicians (primarily FP, GP, and IM).

*Organizational Strengths and Weaknesses*

*Strengths*

- They are currently accepting new OB patients. Many other practices in the area are not.
- Customer/patient service—the practice is large enough to meet their patients' needs but small enough to know their patients and provide a higher level of personal service than many of the larger practices.

- Patient exams are handled by MDs only (no nurse practitioners).
- The physicians reported in personal self evaluation that they provide high-quality care. The physicians have been trained in the latest techniques and methods.
- Excellent staff—low turnover, many have been with the practice for several years.
- The physicians represent diverse cultures and backgrounds.
- The practice's main office is convenient to downtown Orlando. The two neighborhood offices are strategically located in rapidly growing communities.
- The practice offers convenient hours at its neighborhood offices—open early some days and late others.
- They participate in most major insurance plans.
- Physicians are fluent in several languages: French, Arabic, Chinese, and Romanian. Semi-fluent in German, Italian, and Spanish.

*Weaknesses*

- The practice does not have a usable database to use for communication with current patients and to track referrals/source of new patients.
- The practice lacks the standard collaterals and tools to market effectively.
- There is no current system for evaluating patient satisfaction and collecting suggestions for improvement.
- The practice has no established practice brand.
- The current location of the main office offers very little street visibility.

*Goals*

- Build brand name awareness of Partners in Women's Healthcare.
- Attract new patients to the practice, especially OB. Target: 50 percent increase in patient load per physician.
- Capture new market share (MetroWest) and build current market share (Orlando, Oviedo).
- Provide the highest level of patient/customer service in the market.
- Introduce new physician to the community.
- Successfully open new neighborhood office in MetroWest.

*(continued)*

## EXHIBIT 8.1 ■ Marketing and Public Relations Plan (24 months)
*(Continued)*

*Objectives*

- Create an easily usable database so we can implement marketing strategies to existing patients, referring physicians, and new patients and community contacts.
- Find the most effective method to attract patients to the practice.
- Create the brand.
- Communicate the brand to target audiences.
- Position the physicians as "experts" and resources among key community groups.
- Strengthen the practice's reputation for excellent customer service, and "wow" patients every step of the way.
- Expand retail offerings to better serve patients and build additional revenue streams.

*Positioning Statement*

"Big enough to meet your needs, small enough to know your name."

*Other Key Messages*

- "Accepting new OB patients" (can usually get in next day).
- "Where personal, compassionate, quality care is also convenient." (Extended hours, lunchtime appointments available.)
- "The quality care you expect, the personal attention you deserve."
- "The shared skills of a medical team, the expert care of your own personal physician."
- "Offices close to home or close to work."
- "Deliver at Arnold Palmer Hospital (Level III facility)."

*Target Audiences*

- Women who live or work near one of the three offices
  - OB patients (age 20–40)

- Working women (proximity to downtown)
- Gynecology patients
■ Potential referral sources
- Current patients
- Arnold Palmer Hospital (leadership, patient education, floor nurses, media relations)
- Primary care physicians
- Local employers

*Tracking*

■ The practice needs to develop a system for tracking the source of new patients (i.e., how they heard about you/why they came):
- Physician referral (need to track these by physician name and specialty)
- Friend or family member
- Arnold Palmer Hospital
- Advertising
- Direct mail
- Heard doctor speak/present
- Website
- Other

■ Also need to track patient volume to gauge overall increase (break into OB vs. Gyn?)
- Determine current volume of OB and Gyn to establish a benchmark
- Benchmark at 6 months, 12, and 18 months

*Note:* This was a very ambitious plan, and the physicians did not implement all of it. Examples of some of the projects they committed to are shared following the plan outline.

*Used with permission of Partners in Women's Healthcare.*

## EXHIBIT 8.2 ■ Action Plan

**OVERALL GOAL: 50 PERCENT INCREASE IN PATIENT LOAD PER PHYSICIAN**

Objective 1   Create the brand.

Objective 2   Communicate the brand.

Objective 3   Strengthen the practice's reputation for excellent customer service and "wow" patients every step of the way.

Objective 4   Introduce new physician.

Objective 5   Position the physicians as "experts" and resources among key community groups.

Objective 6   Successfully open new neighborhood office in MetroWest.

Objective 7   Expand retail offerings to better serve patients and build additional revenue streams.

*Initial 6-Month Plan*

| Objective | Strategy | Notes |
| --- | --- | --- |
| Create/communicate the brand to target audiences. | *Develop Corporate Identity Package with new name and logo—Letterhead and Envelopes, Business Cards, Appointment Cards, Note Card with Envelopes, Brochure, Website. | Steps:<br>1. Layout/design<br>2. Approvals<br>3. Printing |
| Communicate the brand to target audiences. | *Need to establish effective patient database to track referrals/source of new patients and maintain communication with current patients. | Medical Manager is unable to do this so you will need to set this up in Excel, Act, or some other user-friendly database. Will require an investment in data entry to set this up with all current patient info. |

*These strategies must be executed in order to build the infrastructure for future efforts.*

| Objective | Strategy | Notes |
|---|---|---|
| Communicate the brand to target audiences. Advertising by direct mail. | *Letter/direct mail postcard to current patients to:<br>▪ Announce the new name/look<br>▪ Educate about new products/services (i.e., vitamins)<br>▪ Highlight enhanced services (hours, etc.)<br>▪ Remind that accepting new patients/encourage referrals<br>▪ Solicit e-mail address to keep in touch<br>▪ Announce new physician starting in August? | Need usable patient database that can produce mailing labels.<br>Establish e-mailbox or phone extension for patients to respond and provide e-mail address.<br>Could design piece to look like a birth announcement.<br>Steps:<br>1. Set up patient database.<br>2. Develop/approve copy.<br>3. Mail merge.<br>4. Mail. |
| Communicate the brand to target audiences. | *Collect patient e-mail addresses. | Solicit through direct mail above and also develop in-office system to collect these when patients sign in. |
| Communicate the brand to target audiences. | *Develop practice Website. | Should be more than just a brochure but match the brochure in look and feel. Include directions to all three offices, links to women's health information/sites, list of community resources/support groups, new practice news/updates, etc.<br>Must be updated regularly.<br>Steps:<br>1. Determine content.<br>2. Identify web designer.<br>3. Create page.<br>4. Approve/revise as needed.<br>5. Update. |

*These strategies must be executed in order to build the infrastructure for future efforts.

*(continued)*

EXHIBIT 8.2 ■ **Action Plan** *(Continued)*

| Objective | Strategy | Notes |
|---|---|---|
| Communicate the brand to target audiences. | *Create and run print ad in targeted community publications:<br>■ *Winter Park/College Park News*<br>■ *Our Town*<br>■ *Jewish Heritage News*<br>■ *Tre–Asian Magazine* | Steps:<br>1. Develop/approve copy.<br>2. Creation/layout/design<br>3. Placement.<br>Alter ad as needed/appropriate to introduce new physician. |
| Communicate the brand to target audiences. | *Revise/update yellow pages ads and listings. | |
| Communicate the brand to target audiences/ introduce new physician.<br>Advertising by direct mail. | *Develop targeted direct mail piece to women in neighboring communities to position new brand (similar message to patient direct mail and can use same birth announcement format). | Focus on OB only?<br>Target women, age 20–40, household income $100,000+ in zip codes 32803, 32804, 32801, 32789 for Orlando office; 32765 for Oviedo. Hold off on Vineland until ready to open MW office.<br>In addition, focus on buying professional women's list to include but not be limited to female physicians, dentists, veterinarians, accountants, and lawyers.<br>Steps:<br>1. Finalize target audience/establish parameters.<br>2. Rent mail list.<br>3. Develop/approve copy.<br>4. Layout/design<br>5. Print.<br>6. Mail (mail house fee + postage). |

*These strategies must be executed in order to build the infrastructure for future efforts.

| Objective | Strategy | Notes |
|---|---|---|
| Communicate the brand to target audiences. | Produce magnet with new practice name, physicians' names, logo, hours, "Accepting new patients," etc. to include with patient and community direct mail piece. | Can also give to patients in the office.<br>Steps:<br>1. Layout/design<br>2. Production<br>3. Distribution |
| Communicate the brand to target audiences. | *Ensure managed care companies are updated with new name/current info. | Also make sure that they know you are accepting new patients. |
| Communicate the brand to target audiences. Strengthen the practice's reputation for excellent customer service, and "wow" patients every step of the way. | Create a patient handbook, including information on the practice, what to expect at a visit, contact procedures, payment policy, physician photos and bios, and other relevant data. Also consider developing an overall Q & A sheet with the most commonly asked questions. | Make this warm and friendly.<br>Steps:<br>1. Develop copy/compile materials and information.<br>2. Layout/design<br>3. Print.<br>4. Distribute. |
| Communicate the brand to target audiences. | Create practice fact sheet with information on services, hours, locations, etc. and brief bios on each physician. | For use as background for presentations, media, etc.<br>Steps:<br>1. Develop/approve copy.<br>2. Layout/design<br>3. Print. |
| Communicate the brand to target audiences. | Announce "birthing of new name," for current patients. Ideas:<br>• Create "birth announcement" poster that coordinates with direct mail image and place in all three offices for one year.<br>• Practice can develop additional in-office activities as desired. | Steps:<br>1. Develop/approve copy.<br>2. Layout/design<br>3. Print. |

*These strategies must be executed in order to build the infrastructure for future efforts.

*(continued)*

## EXHIBIT 8.2 ■ Action Plan *(Continued)*

| Objective | Strategy | Notes |
|---|---|---|
| Communicate the brand to target audiences. | Produce and run 30-second radio ad flight on targeted station(s). | Key messages include accepting OB patients and convenient quality care.<br><br>Steps:<br>1. Determine budget/ad schedule.<br>2. Make media buy.<br>3. Write ad copy.<br>4. Produce ad.<br>5. Run ad. |
| Communicate the brand to target audiences. | Research potential for better outdoor signage at main office. If not an option, start including directional with all communication: i.e., located in the Kids Docs building. | The objective is to both increase way finding as well as "top of mind" awareness by capitalizing on the heavy traffic along Princeton Ave. |
| Position the physicians as "experts" and resources among key community groups. | *Build relationships with Arnold Palmer Hospital and offer to serve as resources:<br>■ Administration<br>■ Patient education—Preconception Seminar, "Healthy Women" newsletter<br>■ Floor Nurses—show your appreciation for all they do; provide bagels or pizza for shifts twice a year; provide business cards with new logo | Physicians can serve as speakers, authors for articles, etc.<br><br>Steps:<br>1. Make initial contact/introductions.<br>2. Position as resource.<br>3. Follow up as needed. |
| Communicate the brand/Position new physician. | News release to announce new physician. | Steps:<br>1. Develop/approve copy.<br>2. Distribute.<br>3. Follow up as needed. |
| Communicate the brand/Position new physician. | New physician to make personal introductions/visits as appropriate to targeted referral sources (i.e., APH, key referring physicians, etc.). | |

*These strategies must be executed in order to build the infrastructure for future efforts.

| Objective | Strategy | Notes |
|---|---|---|
| Communicate the brand/Position new physician. | Determine if we should develop and send an announcement card, introducing the new physician to referring physicians and other key community referral sources. Need to determine if this is necessary based on volume of physician referrals. | Steps:<br>1. Finalize target audience.<br>2. Rent list if necessary.<br>3. Develop/approve copy.<br>4. Layout/design<br>5. Print<br>6. Mail (mail house fee + postage) |
| Create the brand. | Conduct small focus group with select current patients ("Patient Council") to:<br>- Solicit ideas to better serve patients, including working women<br>- Have them describe the practice.<br>- What do they want?<br>- What is important to them (of value)?<br>- Why do they come here?<br>- Why don't they go to your competition?<br>- How do they want you to communicate with them (mail, e-mail, etc.)?<br>- What topics are of interest to them?<br>- Would they attend patient education seminars/classes at PWHC? (For a fee?) | Need to provide dinner for focus group.<br>Steps:<br>1. Identify patients.<br>2. Contact/invite to focus group.<br>3. Prepare questions.<br>4. Conduct focus group session.<br>5. Compile report. |
| Create the brand. | Determine feasibility and implement patient suggestions/ recommendations for improvement (from focus group) that reinforce the practice's mission and vision, and facilitate excellent patient care (i.e., extended hours, etc.). | Idea: Can you create economies of scale by scheduling all annual exams on a specific day(s) of the week knowing they take about 20 minutes/patient? This would allow you to always be on time for these patients, which is impressive to them. Patients do not have to know that's how you schedule (transparent to them). |

*(continued)*

## EXHIBIT 8.2 ■ Action Plan *(Continued)*

| Objective | Strategy | Notes |
|---|---|---|
| Successfully open new neighborhood office in MetroWest. | Develop specific marketing strategies/plan for opening of new MetroWest office. | These strategies will need to be developed and executed when final site/targeted move-in date determined. |

### Additional Year 1 Strategies

| Objective | Strategy | Notes |
|---|---|---|
| Create/communicate the brand. Strengthen the practice's reputation for excellent customer service, and "wow" patients every step of the way. | Ensure that the office reflects the new brand:<br>■ Stencil name in waiting room.<br>■ Names/photos of staff in waiting room (make them personal/different from your typical headshot).<br>■ Provide computer to allow patients to check their e-mail.<br>■ Create special area for children waiting (toys, TV on Disney channel, etc.).<br>■ Update patient educational material.<br>■ Consider rotating monthly information board in waiting rooms (highlight different topics). | Create soothing, healing, patient-friendly environment.<br>Steps:<br>1. Discuss ideas.<br>2. Implement as appropriate.<br>3. Educate/involve staff. |
| Strengthen the practice's reputation for excellent customer service, and "wow" patients every step of the way. | Evaluate/refine/develop thank-you protocol for referring physicians. | Steps:<br>1. Determine/discuss current efforts.<br>2. Make suggestions/changes to strengthen communication and relationships. |
| Strengthen the practice's reputation for excellent customer service, and "wow" patients every step of the way. | Evaluate/refine/develop thank-you protocol for patients who refer. | Need to keep HIPAA guidelines in mind; must be generic.<br>Steps:<br>1. Determine/discuss current efforts.<br>2. Make suggestions/changes to strengthen communication and relationships. |

| Objective | Strategy | Notes |
|---|---|---|
| Strengthen the practice's reputation for excellent customer service, and "wow" patients every step of the way. | Provide latest health information to patients through articles, e-mail, and/or Website, etc. | Keep an eye out for "hot," timely women's health issues or topics and share the latest information/your position and recommendations with patients. |
| Position the physicians as "experts" and resources among key community groups. | Position Dr. Brown and Dr. Abrudescu as resources to women in the Jewish community. Need to research opportunities through the JCC, etc. | Steps:<br>1. Make initial contact.<br>2. Position as resource.<br>3. Explore opportunities.<br>4. Follow up as needed. |
| Position the physicians as "experts" and resources among key community groups. | Establish connection with Women's Resource Center. | Steps:<br>1. Make initial contact.<br>2. Position as resource.<br>3. Explore opportunities.<br>4. Follow up as needed. |
| Communicate the brand/position the physicians as "experts" and resources among key community groups. | Develop seminar/presentation on "Pregnancy Later in Life" and research opportunities to present it (libraries, workplaces, APH, etc.) | Trend/issue that is currently not addressed in local programs.<br>Are there any other unique and timely topics for community presentations?<br>Steps:<br>1. Make initial contact.<br>2. Position as resource.<br>3. Explore opportunities.<br>4. Follow up as needed. |

*(continued)*

## EXHIBIT 8.2 ■ **Action Plan** (Continued)

| Objective | Strategy | Notes |
|---|---|---|
| Strengthen the practice's reputation for excellent customer service, and "wow" patients every step of the way. | Create "To Do" list(s) or other creative and appropriate handout(s) for patients/distribution at presentations. May create custom version for "working moms." | Ideas: Include reminders about disability insurance, signing up for parent education, other necessary paperwork, hospital registration, infant CPR, breast pumps, lactation consulting, etc.<br>Steps:<br>1. Develop/approve copy.<br>2. Layout/design<br>3. Print as needed. |
| Communicate the brand/Position the physicians as "experts" and resources among key community groups. | Research other opportunities to reach/position the practice as a convenient, "expert" resource for "working women":<br>Women of Magic Awards (Magic 107.7 and *Orlando Sentinel*)<br>*Orlando Business Journal*: Women Who Mean Business<br>Bizwomen.com<br>Executive Women's Golf Association<br>WOW<br>Other executive women's groups | Steps:<br>1. Make initial contact.<br>2. Explore opportunities.<br>3. Present/discuss with partners.<br>4. Follow up as needed. |
| Communicate the brand/Position the physicians as "experts" and resources among key community groups. | Research other potential sponsorship opportunities to reach women in our target market:<br>Races (Track Shack)<br>Orlando Museum of Art "First Thursdays" – special women's art exhibits? | Steps:<br>1. Make initial contact.<br>2. Explore opportunities.<br>3. Present/discuss with partners.<br>4. Follow up as needed. |

| Objective | Strategy | Notes |
|---|---|---|
| Communicate the brand/position the physicians as "experts" and resources among key community groups. | Research opportunities to reach the Asian market (relatively untapped by other local OB/Gyns) through outlets such as the *Tre* magazine (Vietnamese). | Consider employing receptionist who is bilingual.<br>Steps:<br>1. Make initial contact.<br>2. Explore opportunities.<br>3. Present/discuss with partners.<br>4. Follow up as needed. |
| Strengthen the practice's reputation for excellent customer service, and "wow" patients every step of the way. | Identify all of your patient "Touchpoints" or "Moments of Truth" and develop/research new ways to "over-deliver." Examples:<br>Be prompt with patient paperwork requests (i.e., disability insurance).<br>Streamline paperwork/process for obtaining patient info/updates.<br>Provide "personal" attention—greet patient by name, track and "remember"/mention something about each patient—hobby, children, etc.—something they may have shared at their last visit.<br>Send a "congratulations" card home after a delivery.<br>Call patients a few days to a week after a delivery or surgery to follow up and check on them.<br>When running late, allow patient time/place to make a phone call (to office, babysitter, etc.).<br>If running late, offer coffee or water, or during lunch hour appointments, offer to order lunch "to go" for patient from previously identified nearby café/deli (keep menu on hand).<br>Provide stickers and/or coloring sheet/book for siblings who are waiting (can purchase cheaply in bulk or at Dollar Store, etc.) | Examples of "Touchpoints": calling the office, scheduling an appointment, meeting the receptionist, waiting in the waiting room, waiting in an exam room, meeting the nurse, meeting the physician, obtaining test results, calling with a question, receiving a bill, etc.)<br>Steps:<br>1. Identify all current "Touchpoints."<br>2. Work with staff to determine current approach.<br>3. Develop creative ideas to "over-deliver" on each one.<br>4. Compile suggestions and present to physician partners.<br>5. Implement as appropriate. |

*(continued)*

EXHIBIT 8.2 ■ **Action Plan** (Continued)

| Objective | Strategy | Notes |
|---|---|---|
| Create/Communicate the brand. | Develop internal reference for commonly asked questions so all staff members provide the same information. | Steps:<br>1. Work with staff to determine most common questions and appropriate responses.<br>2. Compile into reference sheet.<br>3. Distribute and educate staff about its use. |
| Strengthen the practice's reputation for excellent customer service, and "wow" patients every step of the way. | Develop/revise/update fact sheets on various health information topics that are distributed to patients. | Create common template or printed shells. Include practice name/logo. Determine whether or not to include physicians' names and office locations (could change).<br>Steps:<br>1. Inventory current topics.<br>2. Determine if all are relevant and if any key topics are missing.<br>3. Design template/shell.<br>4. Print all info sheets on template/shells. |
| *Year 2 Strategies* | | |
| Strengthen the practice's reputation for excellent customer service, and "wow" patients every step of the way. | Conduct focus group with women who are in target market but not current patients to:<br>■ Gauge their perceptions/knowledge of the practice as well as of your key competitors.<br>■ Evaluate awareness of your marketing activities as well as that of your competitors. What do they like/dislike?<br>■ Better understand what they are looking for in an OB/Gyn practice.<br>■ How/why do they choose their physician? | May need to pay participants. Need outside expert facilitator.<br>Steps:<br>1. Identify participants/target group.<br>2. Contact/invite to focus group.<br>3. Prepare questions.<br>4. Conduct focus group session.<br>5. Compile report. |

| Objective | Strategy | Notes |
|---|---|---|
| | ▪ Solicit ideas to improve level of service, especially to working women.<br>▪ What topics are of interest to them?<br>▪ Would they attend patient education seminars/classes at their physician office? (For a fee?) | |
| Communicate the brand/ Strengthen the practice's reputation for excellent customer service, and "wow" patients every step of the way. | Determine need/feasibility of offering monthly patient education seminar/class. | Needs to be something new and different from what is offered elsewhere in the community. May be more cost effective to work through APH or other existing venue.<br>Steps:<br>1. Determine topic(s).<br>2. Develop presentation(s).<br>3. Determine fees/cost.<br>4. Market program.<br>5. Refine and update as needed. |
| Communicate the brand to target audiences. | Create flyer to promote practice in the community and highlight key message points (i.e., accepting new patients). Distribute as appropriate throughout the community—maternity stores, athletic clubs, health food stores, etc. | Need to determine if targeted distribution points will accept and post flyer.<br>Steps:<br>1. Research potential distribution points.<br>2. Develop/approve copy.<br>3. Layout/design.<br>4. Print. |
| Position the physicians as "experts" and resources among key community groups. | Research opportunities through community women's health fairs (i.e., Orange County Medical Society). | Need to have appropriate display, materials, etc.<br>Steps:<br>1. Make initial contact.<br>2. Position as resource.<br>3. Explore opportunities.<br>4. Follow up as needed. |

*(continued)*

## EXHIBIT 8.2 ■ Action Plan *(Continued)*

| Objective | Strategy | Notes |
|---|---|---|
| Communicate the brand/ Strengthen the practice's reputation for excellent customer service, and "wow" patients every step of the way. | Produce water bottle, with practice name, logo, and healthy tips (i.e., for pregnancy). | Need to determine if just for OB patients or for all current patients. The idea is that women often keep or use these at work (on desks, meetings, etc.), and it could spark conversation. Steps: 1. Set budget. 2. Review options. 3. Select product. 4. Develop necessary artwork. 5. Produce/order. |
| Communicate the brand. | Create strategy to reach newcomers to neighborhoods surrounding offices: ■ Direct mail piece ■ Publications ■ Realtors ■ Downtown condos | The objective here is to reach women when they first move to the area before they have selected their OB/Gyn. Research *Orlando Style Magazine*—targets young newcomers to downtown. Steps: 1. Call and research options and associated costs. 2. Determine best approach and present to physician partners. 3. Evaluate and implement if approved. |
| Communicate the brand/ Strengthen the practice's reputation for excellent customer service, and "wow" patients every step of the way. | Research cost of producing creative baby t-shirt, bib, pacifier, or other "gift" to present patients in the hospital or upon their follow-up visit after delivering their babies. | Steps: 1. Set budget. 2. Determine quantity needed. 3. Review options. 4. Select product. 5. Develop necessary artwork. 6. Produce/order. |

| Objective | Strategy | Notes |
|---|---|---|
| Communicate the brand/position the physicians as "experts" and resources among key community groups. | Based on research of community positioning opportunities (Year 1 above), determine and schedule participation. | Develop schedule/implementation plan. |
| Communicate the brand. | Explore/develop opportunities to reach working women through workplace programs (i.e., seminars, health fairs). | Healthcare Coalition could serve as a resource.<br>Contact HR depts. at major employers with large number of female employees—Disney, Darden, Universal, ORHS, Lockheed, Orange County Public Schools, etc. for maximum impact.<br>Steps:<br>1. Make initial contact.<br>2. Position as a resource.<br>3. Explore opportunities.<br>4. Present/discuss with partners.<br>5. Follow up as needed. |
| Strengthen the practice's reputation for excellent customer service, and "wow" patients every step of the way. | Consider offering online scheduling or ability to e-mail for an appointment, general question. | Need to research. |

*Used with permission of Partners in Women's Healthcare.*

EXHIBIT 8.3 ■ **New Logo and Letterhead/Their Corporate Identity**

**PARTNERS IN WOMEN'S HEALTHCARE**
*OBSTETRICS-GYNECOLOGY GROUP*

Nicholas Abrudescu, M.D.
Nancy L. Brown, M.D.
Kai Fu, M.D.
Yasmine N. Kareem, M.D.
Leigh C. White, M.D., Ph.D.

ORLANDO OFFICE: 615 E. Princeton Street, Suite 101 • Orlando, FL 32803 • PHONE 407-898-9922 • FAX 407-898-9944
OVIEDO OFFICE: 1410 W. Broadway, Suite 202 • Oviedo, FL 32765 • PHONE 407-366-9195 • FAX 407-898-9944
METROWEST OFFICE: 6601 Vineland Road, Suite 109 • Orlando, FL 32819 • PHONE 407-898-9922 • FAX 407-898-9944
*www.partnersinwomenshealthcare.com*

*Used with permission of Partners in Women's Healthcare.*

## EXHIBIT 8.4 ■ Patient Letter

Dear Patient,

In an effort to better reflect our practice and philosophy of care, we are excited to announce our new name and look—***Partners in Women's Healthcare.*** We chose this name after careful thought, review, and discussion about who we are and the role we want to play in improving women's healthcare in our community. We believe this new name better represents our desire to work in close partnership with you to provide the latest medical information and treatment options to keep you and your family healthy while also ensuring you play an active role in making decisions about your care.

We also wanted to take this opportunity to share some news about our office:

- We are pleased to introduce **Leigh C. White, MD, PhD,** who will join Partners in Women's Healthcare on August 1. A resident of our community for four years, Dr. White recently completed her residency at Arnold Palmer Hospital for Children and Women. We have worked with her at APH over the past several years and are most impressed by her skills and the one-on-one care she provides her patients. We know she will make a fine addition to our team.
- As our community continues to grow, we want to be sure you know that we have **three convenient offices** to serve you—**Downtown Orlando, Oviedo, and Southwest Orlando/Vineland.**
- Because we know it can sometimes be difficult to take time off for an appointment during work hours, we also offer **extended hours.** Our Oviedo office is open until **7 p.m.** on Mondays and opens at **7 a.m.** on Wednesdays, and our Vineland office is open at **7 a.m.** on Thursdays. We also offer lunchtime appointments.
- Many of our patients ask for us to recommend a prenatal vitamin or daily multi-vitamin. In response and after comprehensive research of those on the market, we now offer **Ameriscience prenatal and multi-vitamins.** Please feel free to call us or ask us about these vitamins at your next visit.
- Our new Website, www.partnersinwomenshealthcare.com, is currently under construction. Look for more information about this exciting development soon.
- Finally, we want to make sure you know that we are **still accepting new patients, including OB patients.** While many practices in the area are reacting to the increased pressures and challenges of providing healthcare today by limiting their practices, we remain open and welcome your referrals of friends, family members, and colleagues.

While our name may have just changed, we want you to know that the people and philosophy are the same. Over the years, we have carefully grown our practice so that we are big enough to meet your needs, but stay small enough to really know you and offer the highest level of service. We remain committed to providing personal, convenient, compassionate, and quality care when and where you need it most. As such, we would also like to kindly request that you provide us your e-mail address so that we can send you timely and informative updates on both our practice and the latest medical advances in women's healthcare. You can do this at your next visit or by calling us at **407-898-9922.** In addition, we always welcome your feedback and suggestions, so feel free to call us anytime with ideas or concerns.

Thank you for trusting us with your healthcare needs. It is truly our honor and privilege to serve you.

Cordially,

Signed by All Physicians

*Used with permission of Partners in Women's Healthcare.*

## EXHIBIT 8.5 ■ Additional Opportunities

- Arnold Palmer Hospital—If you haven't already, we suggest you touch base with the patient education department to determine what opportunities they may have for you to fit into their programming (i.e., provide presentations, articles) and then position yourselves as able and willing resources.

- Focus on thanking the hospital staff and let them know you appreciate working with them

- Presentations—Once we have the information from #1 above, we recommend that you develop a list of five topics that any one of you could cover in a twenty-minute community presentation. Once the presentations are developed, we can look for opportunities in the community for you to present.

- New Patient Letter—Do you currently send a generic follow-up letter to new patients after their first visit? We think this would be a nice touch to thank them for choosing you, begin building the "partnership" relationship, reinforce their decision, etc. While it can certainly be a form letter, it would need to be manually signed to be effective.

*Used with permission of Partners in Women's Healthcare.*

## EXHIBIT 8.6 ■ Thank-You for Nurses

**Partners in Women's Healthcare**
**APH Nurse Thank-You**
**November 2005**

### BACKGROUND

We want to deliver food from a restaurant near ORH to some of the nurses/staff at APH to thank them for all that they do.

We want to deliver to the following areas:

| Area | # Day Shift | # Night Shift |
|---|---|---|
| Labor & Delivery | 40 | 40 |
| ASCU | 13 | 13 |
| Mother/Baby Units (Towers 3, 4, and 5) | 45 | 40 |
| Triage | 12 | 8 |
| **TOTAL** | **110** | **101** |

We need to **coordinate one delivery around 1 pm for the day shift** and the **other at 11 pm for the night shift.** For each delivery/shift, the food will need to be boxed separately/labeled for each area/floor. I have already coordinated with APH so that you will have **one point of contact there for the day delivery and one for the night delivery.** That person will then make sure the food gets to all of the appropriate areas on that shift.

**THANK-YOU NOTES:** You need to coordinate with the physicians to draft a personal thank-you note to each of the floors/areas for each shift:

1. Labor & Delivery—1 note for day shift and 1 note for night shift
2. ASCU—1 note for day shift and 1 note for night shift
3. Mother/Baby Units—Need 3 notes for each shift—one for each floor (3, 4, and 5) for a total of 6 notes
4. Triage—1 note for day shift and 1 note for night shift

Total # of notes needed is 12. We recommend that each physician take 2–3. If this is not possible, one of the physicians can do it on behalf of all of them. Another nice touch would be for all of the pysicians to sign each note. You need to be sure the envelope for each note card is clearly labeled with the area name and shift so the restaurant can attach it to the food box for that area.

**CONTACTS/PROCEDURE: Day shift contact** at APH is **Pam Moreland (321-841-6924).** She is the secretary to the L&D nurse manager Linda Deforest. The delivery person will need to come to Guest Service Check-in and have them call Pam. Pam will come down and make sure the delivery gets to all of the areas/floors. **Once we know the exact delivery date for the night delivery, we need to call Pam, and she will give us the contact for that evening (it will be whichever assistant nurse manager is on duty).** Then the delivery person will once again go to Guest Services and have them call that person who will come down and coordinate the delivery from there. My recommendation is that whenever the delivery date is determined, you call Pam to not only find out the name of the night contact but also to confirm that she will be there the next day for the day shift delivery.

*Note: This is the part of the plan to thank the nurses who are a part of their hospital community.*

---

*Used with permission of Partners in Women's Healthcare.*

**EXHIBIT 8.7 ■ Steps for the Office Manager to Implement Nurse "Thank-You" Plan**

- Select a date for the deliveries (sometime BEFORE the week of Thanksgiving).
- Research and select a good restaurant near Orange Avenue that will deliver (including the 11 p.m. evening delivery). We believe there is an Italian restaurant near the ER that is open late and may be a good option (don't know the name). Recommend something easy like pizza or lasagna.
- Visit the restaurant manager to place the orders. Need to ensure the food will be boxed and labeled with the appropriate quantities for each area/floor.
- Work with the physicians to draft twelve personal thank-you notes on new PWHC note cards to go with each floor/area delivery for each shift. Clearly label the envelopes with the appropriate area/floor name and shift.
- Make sure these note cards are delivered to the restaurant manager and that they know to attach them to the order for each floor/area and shift.
- Follow up with Pam Moreland at APH to confirm the delivery (let her know date and name of restaurant/contact, find out APH night person contact, etc.).
- Follow up with the restaurant manager day before to confirm delivery, contacts, procedure, etc.
- Follow up with restaurant after each delivery to ensure the delivery is completed.

*Used with permission of Partners in Women's Healthcare.*

## EXHIBIT 8.8 ■ Talking Points on Why to Advertise

**PARTNERS IN WOMEN'S HEALTHCARE**

*Talking Points on Why to Advertise*

- PWH wants to be a unique OB/Gyn practice with its own image. It does not want to be just another OB/Gyn practice.
- The practice is the right size: big enough to meet all their patients needs and give them service of the highest level and small enough that "everybody knows your name" kind of feel.
- There are other aspects to their practice as well: expert care, accepting new OB-patients, convenient hours and locations, multilingual, additional services (laser hair removal and Iso therapy) and products (prenatal and multi-vitamins).
- We want to be able to tell all this because it is part of all PWH offerings and the total makes the PWH product so unique. We want several different ads and mediums for the following reasons:
  - There are different target groups for the different services that PWH provides.
  - It enhances the belief that the Partners in Women's Healthcare can meet all your needs, because the potential or existing patients see all kinds of ads or other printed matter talking about different aspects of the practice.
  - It is not very practical to put everything you offer in one ad, there is no space and nobody would even start reading it.
  - Not every aspect is suitable for an ad. For example, we may never make an ad for the laser hair removal or the vitamins. But if there is a nice poster, in the waiting room or other rooms, in the same visualization as the rest of the campaign, people will see it as part of the total package instead of just an afterthought, thereby enhancing the broad scope of products "their" doctor offers.

*(continued)*

# EXHIBIT 8.8 ■ Talking Points on Why to Advertise *(Continued)*

- We have to determine what medium is the best for what message, but it should always have the same look and feel. So wherever the patients look, in the media or inside the practice, they see the same expressions, one familiar theme.
- This will give us enough frequency to give them a chance to see and understand the messages. And act upon it.
- The whole intention of advertising is to put you in the forefront of patients' minds when they need a doctor. This requires, especially with small budgets, a constant look so that whatever the message in the ad or poster is, even if that specific message is not for them, they always will recognize and register the source. One little pinprick and delivery (no pun intended) at a time. But constantly seeing all these pinpricks will result in a positive thought when they do need a doctor, or at least the logo will look familiar when they look for a doctor in the Yellow Pages or on the Internet. Because that's what it does: it creates name recognition, and that counts when they are looking for a doctor. Also do not underestimate the effect those frequent messages have on your existing patients. They like to be reaffirmed in their choice of being with the good doctors, and it doesn't hurt to tell them about aspects of the practice they do not use at this time. That's why it makes good business sense to invest in the development of one look that can be used for all communications.
  - It really does the "1 + 1 = 3 trick." It can and should be used for years. One common look for all expressions of the practice is "what advertising for women's healthcare should be."

*Used with permission of Partners in Women's Healthcare.*

**EXHIBIT 8.9** ■ **Sample Ads**

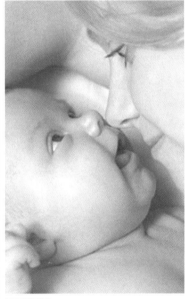

(continued)

## EXHIBIT 8.9 ■ Sample Ads *(Continued)*

Ads used with permission of Partners in Women's Healthcare.

## EXHIBIT 8.10 ■ Patient Survey

Dear Patient,

Please take a moment to review the list below and check off ALL of the areas where you have read, seen, or heard information about our practice.

___ *Orlando Weekly*

___ *Our Town*

___ *The Heritage Jewish News*

___ *Watermark*

___ *Tre* magazine

___ Partners in Women's Healthcare Magnet

___ Referred by a friend or family member

___ Referred by my primary care physician: _____

___ Referred by a specialist physician: _____

___ Referred by Arnold Palmer Hospital for Children & Women

___ Telephone book

___ My health insurance plan

___ Other(s): _____

We realize you may not have exposure to all of the publications or media outlets listed above, so please let us know if there are other local publications or directories you read or use on a regular basis:

_____

_____

_____

_____

Thank you!

*Used with permission of Partners in Women's Healthcare.*

CHAPTER 9

# Expecting the Unexpected— A Guide to Meeting Specific Challenges

This chapter is dedicated to two specific marketing challenges many practices face today that fall outside the other chapter subjects: marketing on the Internet and opening a new office.

## CHALLENGE #1: USING THE INTERNET TO MARKET YOUR PRACTICE

Just 10 years ago, who imagined the dynamic impact the Internet would exert today? That it would permeate every segment of our lives, from personal to professional—even to medicine and medical group practices?

It should come as no surprise that your customers, particularly patients, are navigating the Internet to research medical practices. They search for everything else, so why not health care information? These days, it's only natural to most people.

Patients surf the Web as they once did the Yellow Pages® looking for physicians, office locations, hours, and even doctors' credentials. And they often make a choice based on what they find on your Website. And if you don't have one, you're at a distinct disadvantage when it comes to Web-savvy patients. But you may ask, "How do I develop it, let alone maintain it, if I'm not a techie and, especially, with everything else I have to do?"

Here are a few important hints to help you set up and maintain an effective Website and keep you from making some simple mistakes.

The number one thing I'd recommend: hire a professional. Let me repeat—hire a professional. You're a practice administrator or manager, not a Website designer. You should not even attempt to do it yourself. Yes, a professionally designed Website can be expensive up-front, but I assure you, in the long run, it will be the right step to take.

However, I also want to emphasize that hiring a professional doesn't get you off the hook. He or she still will need your guidance to do a good job. That's why I've included some important guidelines for you to follow as you consult with the professional you choose.

First, be sure you select a company that can accommodate your Website and your budget. Check MGMA resources and ask for recommendations from your colleagues at other successful practices. Before you choose, be sure to interview several design companies and always ask to see samples of their work. Always ask for references and check them out, just as you would any other provider or new hire.

Finally, choose a designer or design company that you feel comfortable with. Ideally, you'll have a long-term partnership with them because your Website is not just a one-time purchase. To be effective, it must be maintained properly and regularly.

After you've chosen your Website designer, it's time to get to work. Remember, one of your primary goals is to have a home page that grabs your customers' attention and holds them there. Put yourself in their place and think about what they want. Make it exciting and easy to use.

Your patients, referring physicians, and others looking at your Website want it to meet their needs quickly. It's critical that you position important information appropriately on the top half of the page. You don't want your customers to have to scroll all the way down to the bottom to get the information that's very important to them, such as your telephone number and your locations.

You'll also want to have control over your Website. When you use images or graphics, you want them to be in proportion, and they should be sized to download quickly and easily. (By the way, remember to get permission for any outside images you use.) You want your home page menus to be easily navigated. You want links on your Website that help your patients visit other Websites.

Many people surf the Internet at work, so it's very important that you make your site as unobtrusive as possible. Skip the audio, as well as fun splash pages and pop-ups, which really are not necessary for your health care practice Website.

Another important thing to remember is to make sure your site is user-friendly. Sites display differently through different browsers, so ask family and friends to test your site using a variety of browsers, such as Netscape, Internet Explorer, or AOL.

Before you sign a contract with a Website designer, make sure you'll get a hard copy and a CD-ROM of your Website. You don't want to be held hostage for maintenance contracts, but you have to remember that building a Website is just the beginning. You do need to pay for Web hosting and for appropriate updates to keep your Website current. You don't want your site to become obsolete or boring—that's the death knell for a Website in today's fast-paced world.

A good designer will be able to make sure your Website appears high on search engine lists—and that's an important consideration in your hiring decision. People must have a way to find you, and you know from your own experience that the sites that are highest on the list of search results are more likely to be utilized.

For your information, I've included a typical contract for Web design (Exhibit 9.1). It does not include terms and costs because they will vary from area to area. However, I believe this example will give you some basic information to help you understand what to expect in your situation.

The final thing to remember is that your Website provides free advertising for your practice. Incorporate your Website address in all your practice marketing materials. Be sure it's included on everything you do, from business cards and brochures to print or broadcast advertising.

Never forget—the Internet is a valuable marketing tool for your practice.

I've asked Kristin Weissman, who also contributed to Chapter 8, for more of her practical advice, this time concerning Website development. I think you'll appreciate how empowered you'll feel after reviewing her information. Here's what she has to say.

## EXHIBIT 9.1 ■ A Typical Contract to Enhance an Existing Website

**WEBSITE DESIGN AND DEVELOPMENT FOR ABC ORTHOPAEDIC CLINIC: SAMPLE PROPOSAL**

*Overview*

With seven locations and as an innovator in orthopaedic practices, ABC Orthopaedic Clinic is one of the largest and most respected orthopaedic clinics in the southeastern United States. As such, the clinic needs a Website that represents the business properly and addresses the needs of current and future patients. This proposal covers the redesign and redevelopment of the Website for ABC Orthopaedic Clinic.

*Outline*

The following is a recommended outline based on the current site and recommendations by the ABC staff. The site may contain up to 30 pages (of 500 words and 5 unique photos per page), plus administrable areas as described below. This outline can be adjusted if needed during development of the site.

1. Home Page
2. Services
   - Sports Medicine
   - Joint Replacement
   - Foot & Ankle
   - Surgery and Rehabilitation of the Hand
   - Spinal Services
   - Orthopaedic Convenient Care Center
3. Physicians
   - Multiple Physician Biographies
4. Physician Assistants
   - Multiple Physician Assistant Biographies
5. About ABC Orthopaedic Group
   - News
   - Press Releases
   - Upcoming Talks
   - Advertisements and Media Spots

While there will not be a particular focus on designing the site to gain search engine prominence, it will be designed to meet current search engine standards and the amount of information included will assist in making the site easier to find by people who are searching online.

*Hosting*

We can provide monthly hosting services for your site, billed quarterly. Mail (MX) records will be pointed back to your in-house Exchange Server. We will also assist in the setup of Google Analytics in order to allow in-depth tracking of your site visits and users.

*Development Schedule*

We estimate that the site will take 4–6 weeks to develop, including timely review and approval of deliverables made to the customer. Project updates will be delivered to customer at key stages in the process, including design, programming, and outline. ABC will provide materials such as photos and text. We will provide guidance on placement and selection of this content for various pages, such as:

- Locations
  - Multiple Locations
- Employment Opportunities
- Contact Information
- Registration Packets
- Notice of Privacy Practices
- Site Map

*Design*

We will provide a design for the site based on your preferences. The design will incorporate the ABC logo, as well as logos for various areas of practice, and will complement other collateral and advertising materials. We understand that the design and layout should be easy to use and incorporate the ABC colors of black and yellow while maintaining a clean and professional feel. After the design is developed, you will be able to review it and make changes before it is approved and site development work begins.

A unique design will be provided for the home page. Interior pages will be designed to match each other. Common navigation will be included on all pages using a "collapsible" menu system to make navigation simple.

The home page may also feature a Flash animation that creates interest in the site and includes information such as "70 years in operation," etc. Within the site we will provide appropriate "cross-links" to different areas so that information is easy to

*(continued)*

## EXHIBIT 9.1 ■ A Typical Contract to Enhance an Existing Website
*(Continued)*

access and organized logically. Pages will be developed to meet current Web design standards and will be compatible with all common browsers.

### Features

The site will feature a password-protected administration area that allows the Website owner to perform maintenance securely through their browser by entering a username and password.

The following areas will be able to be updated:

- Physicians and Physician Associates pages. Physician and PAs will be able to be ordered (you can choose to order them by seniority)
- Announcement area on home page (new Physician or PA, new clinic, etc.)
- Press releases and talks
- Location information and physicians associated with these locations (in order you select)
- Include location photos and link to Google Maps* for each location
- Employment opportunities

### Search Engine Optimization

We have included Google's features as a convenience and cannot be responsible for changes in or service provided by this outside vendor.

### Ongoing Service and Support

After the development of your site, we will be able to provide ongoing development services on an hourly as-needed basis.

*Used with permission of Monty Hood, Website designer, E-mail: monty@monty.net.*

## KRISTIN WEISSMAN: THE INTERNET IS HERE TO STAY

You understand the power of the press. What about the power of the Internet—specifically, the power of an effective Website?

We've all visited an online site and may have found that it seems that everyone has a Web presence—and for good reason! Having a Website today is the fastest, most effective, dynamic way to transfer information and represent your business to your current and prospective patients.

Think about your daily life. As consumers, we're always on the hunt for information, whether in our personal or professional lives. We want information quickly and easily, which is why the Internet has turned into the most successful and progressive medium of our time. As you go through your day, you pop online to check everything from the stock market to the news, research, and fast data. Today consumers can do everything from ordering a pizza to transferring precious funds, all with the click of a mouse from the convenience of their home.

With this thinking in mind, it also must seem apparent that medical information should be found quickly and easily on the Internet. It also should be evident that putting your business online is one of the most powerful tools your medical practice can use.

With the continual strides in the Web, a Website can be published online in a matter of minutes. If you're computer savvy and believe you have the talent and resources to create your own Web page, there are a variety of programs you can use to put together a streamlined site, or you may hire a professional who can produce a site in a vast range of prices. It's all about knowing what to look for and truly assessing your needs to deliver a site that best suits your practice.

The first step in putting together any site is to know what your Web address or URL should be. It should be something clear and effortless to remember, and it should be as close to the name of your practice as possible. For example, if you were the Florida Cancer Center, you would want a Web address such as: www.flcancercenter.org. Your medical practice would most likely take on the ".org" address rather than the traditional commercialized ".com." However, you will need to research how other similar sites are listed and find the names available that most closely match your practice.

There is a wide range of possibilities for putting together a Website, and it can seem intimidating. Remember that you are trying to put information out to your patients about your services—who you are, how to contact you, and even valuable information about what to do in time of an emergency.

Your site should be an extension of you and your practice. It should reflect your commitment to exceptional patient care, and it should be maintained and updated frequently. It's not only a tool to bring you more business and make people aware of what you offer, it's also a tool to simplify and assist your business and enhance the experience of care for those you serve.

Who should you hire to create your Website and how much should you pay? Depending on your marketing budget, a quality site can be designed by either a graphic design student freelancing on the side, all the way to a full-service marketing firm that will provide the highest level of quality. There are many options to review. However, the more elements you add, the higher the price, and that may not be what you need.

You can drastically cut costs by knowing what to ask for. Many design firms will present a uniquely designed specialty site with a variety of features, which can run thousands of dollars. With a little research, you'll realize you can have a site very similar in style with fewer features, designed using a Web template from a site such as www.templatemonster.com. Using this option, either you or someone trained in this field essentially can drop in the content you supply, cutting your cost from thousands to a few hundred dollars.

And where do you find the right person to complete your site? Look online, call your local university, or ask your colleagues for a recommendation for the firm that created a site you admire. A Website is easily within your reach.

No matter how it's designed, the most important element is your content. Make sure your messaging is clear, easy to understand, well written, and useful. Picture yourself as a person on the other side of the computer trying to find information for medical care or a mother in the middle of the night wondering how to calm her newborn's cry. You can put as much information as you'd like on your Website to help and assist your patients. Again, it's an extension of you and your quality of care.

So what if you're feeling really proficient on the Web and want to take your site to the next level without the cost? The most successful way to do that on the Internet today is through a blog. Blogging is a way to comment on issues relevant to your practice and an outlet to express your thoughts to a wide audience on a daily or weekly basis. You're identifying your voice in the medical community.

Doctors can blog about new medical techniques and services, medical research, or information on prescription care. It's a way to reach out to your patients in a very personal way and help them understand a bit more about who you are and the information you strive to provide. The content of your blog is entirely up to you.

The media is also very connected to the blogging community, and today 32 percent of all mainstream media receive all of their factual information through blogs. However, only 2 percent verify that information to be true. The power of blogging is so incredible that those who create a valid, well-maintained blog receive a high level of attention.

Blogging also is an enormous effort in the pursuit of community relations. An example of this type of blog is written by the McDonald's Corporation (http://csr.blogs.mcdonalds.com). It is consistently recognized as a blog leader and model to emulate across every genre of business today.

There are a few final Internet tools you can use to fully benefit your practice. Although your message still can be crafted and shared traditionally through a press release to the media, many public relations professionals realize that they can share the same information with a very high level of success through the Internet.

The following are easy solutions: ensuring that your press release is fully optimized to guarantee that it is reaching important industry or community targets by using Really Simple Syndication (RSS) feeds that deliver only information the user selects to receive; setting keywords so that when your medical facility, services, or unique human interest story is researched on any network engine such as Google, it places your medical practice at the top of a search engine list; and linking to your industry through additional outside Websites, such as any of the community relations efforts you choose to support. Each of these methods is a piece of your intricate Internet puzzle.

I encourage you to log on and claim your Web identity. Provide easy-to-understand, user-friendly information, and, if you're feeling daring, post that blog and allow your patients to look a little deeper inside to be further educated, informed, and well cared for.

The power to heal is vastly changing every single day, but the one element that has remained the same through time is the simple power of good care. Keeping up with technology to share that care and enhance your level of service is what will keep you on the cutting edge and healing a growing number of patients for years to come.

## CHALLENGE # 2: OPENING A NEW OFFICE

With the addition of demographic research and the plan to hire a fifth physician, Eye Physicians of Central Florida made a decision to open a third office in a planned community in southwest Orlando. We developed a plan of action to integrate into the community with the goal of making the new office and the new physician busy immediately.

Exhibit 9.2 is a briefing that describes the basic marketing stepping stones we created for introducing the new office; Exhibit 9.3 is the actual action plan.

The rest of the exhibits are samples of specific plan implemenation material. Exhibit 9.4 is the ad that introduces the new office in a community newspaper. Exhibit 9.5 is a direct mail postcard that was sent to referring physicians' offices and the community at large. We added the tagline "Come see us!" to all projects relating to opening the new office.

St. Luke's is the largest church in the new neighborhood. We approached them about doing talks on pediatric eye care for their preschool teachers and for parents. As a result of Eye Physicians becoming involved in their new neighborhood, they were able to put posters (Exhibit 9.6) in the church to promote their practice to families. We used this opportunity to list the services provided by the practice and to add a map to the poster.

To continue our introduction to the new office and the branding effort, the poster reprinted as Exhibit 9.7 was created and hung in patient rooms in the two existing offices. We encouraged satisfied patients with family and friends who live in southwest Orlando to tell them of our newest office. The poster also served to communicate to existing pediatric eye patients who had traveled across the city to see the pediatric ophthalmologists that they now could schedule an appointment for their children and family members closer to home.

The goal of all of our efforts was to create both a matrix of layers and assert their brand each time we could communicate about the new office. This layering helped new and potential patients become familiar with the message due to the repetition.

## EXHIBIT 9.2 ■ New Office Briefing

**EYE PHYSICIANS OF CENTRAL FLORIDA: NEW OFFICE BRIEFING**

Eye Physicians of Central Florida will be opening a third office in the MetroWest area of Central Florida. This will complement and provide additional coverage beyond the Winter Park and Longwood area. Competition for pediatric ophthalmology in the MetroWest area is limited, and the referral sources will be attracted from Downtown Orlando into Kissimmee. The following are the basic stepping stones to create the marketing steps to introduce the new office.

*Our Targets*

- Existing patients—existing patients must feel they are informed by the practice prior to any media announcements.
- Referring physicians—referring physicians must have multiple communications to "get" the message about the new location.
- Individuals in the community and private, public, and pre-K schools
- Community—will be informed by direct mail, advertising, community relations, promotional items, billboard
- Managed care plans
- Employers/coalition
- Internal staff
- Media

*Our Goals*

*Internal*

1. Serve our patients to reflect the mission and vision of the practice of Eye Physicians of Central Florida.
2. Secure a stable staff infused with a culture of patient sensitivity, convenience, and service.
3. Create a culture of ease of appointment for referring physicians and self-referred patients.

*External*

1. Achieve number one brand equity in pediatric and adult eye services throughout the community.

$$\text{Brand equity} = \text{awareness} + \text{usage} + \text{perceived quality}$$

To have value in the practice:

$$\text{Value} = \frac{\text{Access} \times \text{Service} \times \text{Quality}}{\text{Cost}}$$

*(continued)*

**EXHIBIT 9.2 ■ New Office Briefing** *(Continued)*

Therefore,

- If you increase access, you increase value.
- If you increase service, you increase value.
- If you increase quality, you increase value, and
- If you decrease cost, you increase value.

2. Attract new patients to the practice.
3. Grow the practice by a set % over the first 12–24 months. (TBD)

***Things to Think About***

1. Creating an e-mail database for referring physicians and patients
2. Defining what will be "special" about the MetroWest office
3. Developing a slogan to assist with the introduction, such as "Come, see us" at … on … "
4. Being involved in the community as a new neighbor
5. Including non-traditional contacts for your mailing announcement, such as: veterinarians in the appropriate zip codes, hair salons, church schools, and other places where moms congregate
6. Selecting a promotional item for adult and pediatric patients for the first 6 months
7. Creating a referral campaign for existing patients—"Tell a friend to come see us and you can see a … "
   a. Free movie pass
   b. Ticket to Science Center Imax
   c. Pass to visit the Science Museum
8. Holding a CME conference in SW part of town for physicians and optometrists

***Other Marketing Issues***

1. Add address to existing ads.
2. Update letterhead, business cards, appointment cards, envelopes for the new office.
3. Update brochure.
4. Update Website.
5. Create new ad for *Southwest Orlando Bulletin* insertion—March thru December.
6. Revise Yellow Page® ads.
7. Consider drive time radio IF it will capture women.

*Used with permission of Eye Physicians of Central Florida.*

**EXHIBIT 9.3 ■ Action Plan for Office Opening**

**EYE PHYSICIANS OF CENTRAL FLORIDA METROWEST OFFICE OPENING: ACTION PLAN**

| Strategy | Steps |
| --- | --- |
| Update Corporate Identity Package w/ New Office Info. Letterhead and Envelopes, Business Cards, Appointment Cards, Note Card w/ Envelopes, Brochure | Revise layout/design<br>Print |
| Printing | Get quotes |
| Announcement Card Mailing—referring physicians (FP, IM, Peds, Endo, Neuro, Neuro Surg, Optometrists, Rheum), nursery schools, veterinarians, private and church schools, senior centers, and consumers in target zips: 32835, 32819, 32836, 34761, 34734, 34786, 34787 | Finalize target audiences<br>Rent Mail List<br>Develop/approve Copy<br>Layout/Design<br>Print<br>Mail (mail house fee + postage)<br>We are estimating 11,000 (6 × 9) oversized announcement postcards will be mailed in mid-May |
| Letter to Existing Patients | Develop/Approve Copy<br>Mail Merge<br>Mail |
| Update Website | Update Website to reflect new office |
| Announcement Ad in *Southwest Orlando Bulletin* to run April, May, and June | Develop Copy<br>Layout/Design<br>Placement<br>Update/revise ad to reflect all 3 offices for July–Dec. run |
| CME Conference in SW Orlando for physicians and optometrists | Set date and location (late May or early June)<br>Confirm speakers/program<br>Develop/approve invitation copy<br>Invitation design/layout<br>Printing<br>Identify invite list<br>Secure/rent mailing list<br>Mail (mail house fee + postage) |
| Promo Item for Adult and Pediatric Patients | Set budget<br>Review ideas<br>Select product<br>Develop necessary artwork<br>Produce/order |

*(continued)*

EXHIBIT 9.3 ■ **Action Plan for Office Opening** (Continued)

| Strategy | Steps |
| --- | --- |
| Press Release | Develop copy |
| | Approve release |
| | Distribute |
| | Follow-up as Needed |
| Create and Post Flyer at St. Luke's Methodist Church<br><br>Note: They have already given us permission to do this. | Develop/ approve copy.<br>Layout/design<br>Post |
| PTA/Teacher Presentation(s) at Target Schools (private, public; Pre-K and Elementary)<br><br>Note: St. Luke's Methodist has a huge Pre-K program. | 1. Identify target schools<br>2. Set up time to speak (i.e. back-to-school meetings/orientations?). Position EPCF as a neighbor and resource.<br>3. Create fact sheet on how to identify if a child has a vision problem/what to look for (signs/symptoms/ effects).<br>4. Print copies as needed. |
| A Gift For Teaching "Healthy Kids" Corner—Can provide information for distribution to area teachers. | Create fact sheet on how to identify if a child has a vision problem/what to look for (signs/symptoms/effects).<br>Print copies as needed. |
| Dr. Phillips YMCA—Research speaking/program/information opportunities | Research opportunities and position EPCF as a neighbor and resource.<br>Fact Sheet—Create fact sheet for adults if needed. |
| Speaking/Program Opportunities at Sand Lake Hospital—i.e., senior programs | Research opportunities and position EPCF as a neighbor and resource.<br>Fact Sheet |
| Ad/slide in West Oaks movie theater (before previews/movie)? | Develop/approve copy<br>Layout/design<br>Production |
| Revise Yellow Pages Ads | Revise ads to reflect new office |
| WDBO—Ad flight running May–July, 30-sec. spots | Develop ad copy/creative<br>Produce ad<br>Place ad<br>Update/revise as needed |

*Used with permission of Eye Physicians of Central Florida.*

EXHIBIT 9.4 ■ **Ad to Introduce the New Office in Community Newspaper**

*Used with permission of Eye Physicians of Central Florida.*

**EXHIBIT 9.5** ■ **Direct Mail Postcard**

*Used with permission of Eye Physicians of Central Florida.*

**EXHIBIT 9.6** ■ **Ad Integrating Community Service to Neighborhood Church**

Used with permission of Eye Physicians of Central Florida.

**EXHIBIT 9.7** ■ **"Our Newest Office" Poster**

**OUR NEWEST OFFICE**

1781 Park Center Drive
Suite 220, Orlando FL 32835

To schedule an appointment, call (407) 398-7730.
For more information, please visit us at www.eyephy.com

 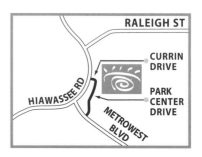

Winter Park ■ Longwood ■ MetroWest

## Come see us!

*Used with permission of Eye Physicians of Central Florida.*

CHAPTER 10

# Maximizing Your Practice's Profit Potential—A Guide to Retail Medicine

Early in this book, I said that marketing is remarkably unchanged over the past decade and, at least in terms of basics, not much is new. However, one area has changed dramatically. It's the increase in retail medicine, along with the marketing and price competition that accompany it.

As the American Medical Association defines it, retail medicine offers unique services for patients and families who can manage their health care with personalized, tailored services.[1]

According to David W. Hilgers, consumers have become much more aware of health care marketing and advertising of services and costs. In his article, "The Rise of Retail Medicine: Adding New Complexity to the Practice of Healthcare Law,"[2] he suggests this is a result of health plans requiring consumers to absorb more of the first dollar's coverage.

A couple of important things are happening in this arena. First, many consumers are becoming more sophisticated and, as such, realize and accept that many types of primary care ailments can be treated adequately by extenders under the supervision of a physician. Extender trade associations are marketing more and positioning to raise the awareness of their constituents, such as physician assistants, nurse practitioners, and nurse anesthetists. With their fast-paced lives, consumers frequently look for quick and easy access for ailments, even if it means seeing a physician extender and paying retail.

In addition, many physicians and entrepreneurs are choosing to meet consumer needs in very creative ways. Some are new ways and some we've seen for years. Areas that you'll find familiar are the sale of eyeglasses within ophthalmology practices, sleep clinics, fertility clinics, medi-spas, executive health screenings, direct sales of vitamins, and travel medicine.

Other new areas of retail medicine include boutique or concierge medicine, full-body scanning, 64-slice computed tomography cardiac scanning, cosmetic dentistry, cosmetic treatments such as Botox and Restalyn, general wellness programs, and retail health clinics in drug stores, including Sutter Health (in Rite-Aid in Sacramento), Solantic Clinics (in Super Wal-Mart), and other similar clinics in certain grocery stores.

In a November 30, 2006, *New York Times*[3] story on retail medicine, writer Natasha Singer interviewed two obstetricians/gynecologists who gravitated to the business of retail beauty. They're franchisees of Dermacare Laser and Skin Care Clinics, one of the nation's largest medical spas, with 38 franchises operated by 32 physicians. The obstetricians/gynecologists she interviewed said they turned to this area of medicine to enhance their ability to work with female patients, open their medical spa to men, and be able to spend more time with their young children and families.

In the article, Ms. Singer also wrote about MedSurge Advances, a Dallas company that offers physicians training in beauty procedures and then sells them devices, such as lasers, to perform the procedures. According to the article, MedSurge Advances helped more than 300 doctors go into the beauty business between 2002 and 2006.

Robert Huckels, MedSurge Advances' vice president for marketing, explained that noncosmetic surgery specialists are turning to this retail medicine to alleviate heavy patient caseloads, long work weeks, high medical malpractice premiums, and the paperwork and payment structure imposed by Medicaid and managed care. Others in the insurance industry believe physicians are turning to retail medicine to generate new revenue streams.

When we talk about retail medicine as a need for **Access** and **Availability,** it's easy to picture the primary clinics found inside shops we've grown to know and trust, such as CVS Pharmacy, Rite-Aid, Kroger, and Super Wal-Mart.

Suppose you're a consumer and you begin to feel ill at work. Your throat hurts, your glands are enlarged, and you're about to leave for vacation in 2 days. You call your regular doctor's office and are told you can't get an appointment until the next week. But you're ill now! You have a long awaited vacation in 2 days! You want someone to see you and get you past these symptoms so you'll feel better and enjoy your time off. And you expect this from your own personal family physician on your timeline—when you have a need.

But no go! No matter how much you negotiate with the staff person on the phone, they have no way to see you and suggest you can go to urgent care if you can't wait another day or two.

Along comes Minute Clinic, Solantic, the Little Clinic, or any of a number of similar health care clinics found inside retail locations. All of these clinics know the importance of the cornerstones of marketing, **The Four A's—Access, Availability, Accountability,** and **Accommodation.** They're all created to meet the needs of busy individuals and families who need health care delivery on their personal schedules when their doctors are not available.

Here's how it works. You show up at the retail center and sign in. At that time, you're told exactly what they can provide to you and what it will cost. Most of these clinics accept some insurance and all credit cards. If they cannot see you within 5 minutes, they'll make you welcome in their reception area or give you a beeper and send you roaming the aisles in the store. When your beeper goes off, you return to the clinic and are seen immediately.

Under the supervision of a physician, you may be given a script to be filled or other suggestions to help you feel better and improve your health. Then you can make a stop at the pharmacy, pick up water or Gatorade, throat lozenges, ginger ale, or the like. You check out, get in your car, and go home. And it all happened within an hour!

Is this service **Accessible?** Yes. **Available?** Yes. **Accountable?** Yes. **Accommodating?** Yes. It meets all **The Four A's,** plus it's convenient and affordable. And it's expanding throughout the country at a rapid pace.

Because of this rapid expansion in the vision and reach of retail medicine, I've asked two colleagues to provide their expertise on the subject. The first, Richard Sandlin, is the chief researcher at Sandco International, Inc., Manufacturing Services Division, located in

Northport, Alabama. He also operates a nationwide dietary and nutritional supplement and health and wellness consulting business.

As a research scientist, developer, and marketer of health care and nutritional products, Richard specializes in developing functionally unique proprietary products utilized by physicians, medi-spas, wellness centers, and ancillary services. His primary areas of research and development have been weight loss, longevity, cosmetics, joint movement, cardiovascular health, type 2 diabetes, and sports performance. Under current regulatory guidelines, all can be marketed without prior Food and Drug Administration (FDA) approval.

## RICHARD SANDLIN: REAL-WORLD ADVICE FOR PHYSICIANS SEEKING TO ESTABLISH AND MARKET THEIR RETAIL MEDICINE VENTURES

Health care providers traditionally have exchanged their time for money, providing one-on-one patient care. But in the past few years, as reimbursements have spiraled downward and overhead has skyrocketed, physicians have begun to look for other ways to legally make up for the shortfall.

They tried to leverage time for money by hiring nurse practitioners and physician assistants to assist in daily patient care, in effect increasing the volume of physician services. But as the number of uninsured and underinsured Americans grew, managed care plans pressed providers for lower rates and restrained the utilization of physician services, effectively holding down spending for medical care. At the same time, Medicare also lowered its fees. The result has been a decline in real income for physicians.

Additionally, higher deductibles and substantial copays have forced patients/consumers to be more concerned about the actual cost of health care services. They've become much more sophisticated regarding the many types of primary care ailments. The use of nonphysicians to diagnose non–life-threatening complaints and resolve them efficiently and expeditiously has led patients/consumers to question the true cost of services and become more discriminating about health care goods and services. The steady shifting of cost to patients/consumers to pay more of the first dollar spent on health care has pushed medicine further and further into a "retail" environment.

As patients/customers are forced to pay more and more out-of-pocket dollars for services, they've become less tolerant of lengthy appointment lead times, excessive waiting times, and unfriendly staff members who don't make them feel valued. They've begun to "vote with their feet," choosing urgent care centers or retail clinics for less serious problems and only visiting their personal physicians for more serious or life-threatening complaints. And as you know, this often creates a void in service—when patients don't see their personal physicians regularly for small problems, bigger problems may go undetected.

The greater financial problem for physicians is that their patients learn to shop elsewhere for services they typically would look to their personal physicians to provide. Obviously, this results in further income declines.

Savvy physicians are reclaiming lost dollars by offering so-called concierge care that caters to the upper-middle class or wealthy, as well as by finding new value-added services and products that are attractive to all their patients/consumers. These physicians recognize that getting the customer from the waiting room to the billing window without a complaint is only the first step in good service.

Americans want more value for every health care dollar spent, so innovative physicians identify services to complement and add value to their practices. They realize that satisfaction with service and better outcomes are key elements to attracting and retaining new customers. So they incorporate services or products that fit their practices and virtually sell themselves after their initial introduction.

Entrepreneurial physicians who realize their patients/customers have become more sophisticated regarding their health care and appearance don't hesitate to offer aesthetic and preventive medical services to meet this demand. Many prepackage these services to offer more value for the health care dollar. Because the managed health care system is not interested in the delivery of these services, but customers demand them, there is a growing retail medicine market.

Let's take a closer look at some of these new forms of retail medicine.

### *Medical Spas or Medi-Spas*

According to the International Medical Spa Association, these are facilities that operate under the full-time, onsite supervision of a licensed health care professional who offers traditional, complementary, and alternative health practices and treatments in a spalike setting.

These may include lasers and intense pulsed-light technology for wrinkles and skin treatments, such as microdermabrasion, fillers/injectables, chemical peels, tattoo removal, hair removal, and other beauty procedures. Some establishments even offer traditional spa services such as facials, massages, and body treatments. Regulations on these services vary from state to state.

Many offer a line of private skin care products to generate additional residual income after the initial treatment to restore and maintain skin health. Done correctly and compliantly, physicians who market retail skin care products can produce a tremendous passive income stream.

However, one of the nuances of skin care products is determining if the product is a cosmetic, a drug, or both. Or is it soap? The difference between a cosmetic and a drug is determined by a product's intended use. Different laws and regulations apply to each type of product. Physicians sometimes violate the law by marketing a cosmetic with a drug claim, or by marketing a drug as if it were a cosmetic, without adhering to requirements for drugs.

Skin care and prescription-strength skin health systems have proven to be profitable passive income streams, but it is advisable to seek a qualified consultant or company that develops, manufactures, markets, and sells skin care and proprietary prescription skin care systems to help integrate them into your practice.

### *Wellness Clinics*

Wellness clinics tailor lifestyle programs to meet patients' or customers' health needs or personal goals built around life-enhancing components. These include health and fitness assessments, personal nutrition counseling, diversified strength training, and exercise instruction.

They can range from weight-loss clinics to highly sophisticated testing that caters to corporate wellness, or to advanced centers for longevity and general wellness. They focus on lifestyle modification and have been spurred on by the Baby Boomer generation that wants to look younger or better and live longer. Most programs are designed to screen for potential health problems and risks.

The health and cost impacts of being overweight and obese are the major driving market forces behind these clinics, and the clinics are poised to become a residual income cash cow that may either replace or increase revenue for physicians. As the rates of obesity and overweight continue to climb at their alarming pace within the United States, the demand for services that focus on these health issues should continue to grow.

Even the US Centers for Disease Control and Prevention report that the key factor influencing an individual's state of health is everyday lifestyle choices (55 percent). The other key factors such as quality of medical care (10 percent), environment (19 percent), and heredity (18 percent) have not really changed in more than two decades.

The message for savvy physicians is that the choices patients or customers make about their lifestyle open a window of profitability. Plus, the passive income potential from residual monthly membership fees and other health-related products and services has transformed physician-associated wellness clinics from simply a good idea to a major income generator for practices—when done correctly and compliantly, of course.

## *Other Lines of Service*

Many physicians are unaware that they can legally provide other lines of service through their practice to make up for the shortfalls caused by declining reimbursements and skyrocketing overhead. Some try to increase practice revenue by seeing more patients per day, working more hours, and performing more procedures. Most see only a minimal increase in net revenue for the increased effort.

However, savvy physicians now provide nutritional products and services appropriate for their patient's/customer's health condition or disease propensity to increase practice revenue. The patients or customers see this as a value-added service, which is a nominal investment in physician time that results in residual practice profitability.

The retail medicine concept for this practice marketing model is new, but physicians providing medicines and other health care products dates back before the introduction of health insurance in 1950. Then pharmacies took over as the primary dispenser of most medications and other health care products, including nutritional products.

But before the 1960s, patients received medications and other health-related products from the physician's office or famous black bag. So, the retail medicine strategy of providing patients various products certainly is a legal and ethical practice.

By providing the medical services (covered and uncovered) and other health-related goods baby boomers seek, physicians will see an increase in practice income that long outlasts the initial office visit. This is called residual or passive income. Residual income is a recurring income a physician receives long after the initial effort to generate it has ceased. After the initial effort has been made, the residual income can be considered passive because the physician is not actively involved.

Traditionally, passive income is generated from a person's investments, such as interest, dividends, or real estate rentals or selling anything that is automatically renewable, or consumables where the reordering recurs. This contrasts with what most physicians do—swap their time for money. A major benefit for physicians of pursuing passive income streams in the practice setting with patients is once physicians set up one income stream, they're free to set up many more, generating multiple income streams.

## *The Baby Boomer Impact*

America's largest generation is growing up. In 2008, the oldest of the baby boomers, the generation born between 1946 and 1964, turns 62 years old. Among the Americans celebrating their 62nd birthdays are our two most recent presidents, George W. Bush and Bill Clinton. Other well-known celebrities reaching this milestone include Cher, Donald Trump, Sylvester Stallone, and Dolly Parton.

Because of its sheer size, the baby boomer generation has had enormous impact throughout its life cycle on trends in popular culture, consumer spending, demand for services, product development, and now retail medicine. And there's no sign that they're about to change now.

But, they don't want to get old! They're uneasy about aging, which they fear will lead to loss of attractiveness or contracting a debilitating disease. *This should send out buying signals to innovative physicians who are seeking new sources of income.*

Baby boomers have a can-do mindset that there must be something that can be done to improve or preserve their quality of life. This is a generation accustomed to using ingenuity and initiative to find solutions to breakthrough barriers. Baby boomers adopt a similar approach to remain healthy and youthful and do not react well to being told no. The impact this aging market will have on medical retailers everywhere, on everything, is enormous.

Baby boomers are an affluent generation, and they're more health conscious and health wary than previous generations. This population boasts more than 76 million people in the United States and is at its peak of earning and spending years. They're wealthy, sophisticated buyers of products and services making up 51 percent of the total US population, and they control 75 percent of the country's wealth!

Their demand for nontraditional health care and nondiscretionary health services, combined with their tendency to be self-conscious about their appearance and health, is a perfect market combination for savvy physicians to address with their practices' retail medicine strategies.

Not only do these consumers have disposable income, they're willing to pay for uncovered medical services, such as cosmetic medicine, including skin care and dermatologic services; weight management programs and dietary counseling; evidenced-based vitamins and nutritional supplements; massage therapy; sleep therapy; medical spas; and wellness programs. And because these types of treatments and programs many times are not covered by insurance, these consumers are much more aware of alternative health care, pricing of services, and treatment quality and outcomes.

Although baby boomers have the largest disposable incomes in history, they also impact the direction of health care decisions for their now multigenerational families. One baby boomer family member can influence the health care decision of many other members and directly impact practice income positively or negatively based of their perceived satisfaction of service.

Adding value to a patient's/customer's visit with nontraditional services that can be added on to their basic visit is a forward-thinking approach that may have an enormous impact on practice revenue. Physicians are limited by the number of hours in a day to the economic benefits their practices can achieve. Physicians seeking out new residual income streams that require a nominal amount of time after the initial visit that focus on loss of attractiveness and/or healthy aging with the baby boomers should find their services in high demand.

## LEGAL ASPECTS OF RETAIL MEDICINE

Michael R. Lowe, Esq., is the other colleague I've asked to contribute to this chapter. Michael is a board-certified health law attorney by the Florida Bar and a shareholder at Michael R. Lowe, P.A., located in Longwood, Florida. He specializes in health care law, with a heavy emphasis on the representation of physicians and physician group practices.

Licensed in both Florida and Georgia, he regularly represents physicians and physician group practices in all aspects of health care law, including regulatory and transactional health law matters, government investigations and professional licensure disciplinary cases, marketing matters, litigation, managed care contracting, Health Insurance Portability and Accountability Act (HIPAA) and privacy matters, Medicare and Medicaid reimbursement matters, federal and state fraud and abuse law matters including Stark Law analysis, and medical malpractice prevention, defense, and insurance matters.

I've asked him to participate in this chapter on retail medicine, because it is an area in which he excels, both in his writings and his speeches. I believe his input will raise your awareness of the legal issues that have been and will be faced as physicians begin to be involved in retail medicine and its marketing.

## MICHAEL R. LOWE: HEALTH LAW

Declining reimbursement. Skyrocketing overhead. Constant pressure to see more patients, generate more revenue, practice good medicine, and do it all in less time than ever before. In today's ultracompetitive and risk-laden health care market, physicians and physician group practices face nearly insurmountable challenges to keep their practices viable and to maintain, much less increase, their incomes.

To meet this challenge, many physicians are looking to create passive income streams through a variety of health care goods and services, and in doing so are engaging in retail medicine ventures. Popular retail medicine ventures include, among others, diagnostic imaging modalities, pharmacy, medical spa, skin care and dermatologic services, weight loss and dietary counseling programs, vitamins and nutritional supplements, and DME.

Although clear distinctions previously existed between the practice of medicine on one hand and ancillary services or retail medicine products and services on the other, the line between them is becoming increasingly blurred and more difficult to manage. With a huge baby boomer population possessing significant discretionary income to spend on health care, Americans more than ever are seeking healthier lifestyles, more youthful appearances, alternative medical treatments, and one-stop shopping for their medical care whenever possible. Savvy physicians are rapidly entering retail medicine to take advantage of this market.

However, physicians and physician group practices offering retail medical services to generate passive income streams need to identify and evaluate the numerous regulatory and liability risks associated with retail medicine ventures, and in particular, the regulatory and compliance requirements for advertising and marketing retail medicine products and services.

Failure to do so can result in physicians and their group practices being exposed to a variety of potential or actual liability, disciplinary action, regulatory scrutiny, patient dissatisfaction, government intrusion, and negative publicity. But done correctly and compliantly, physician marketing for retail medicine products and services can produce tremendous financial and public relations results for physicians and their group practices.

More important, by properly advertising and marketing retail medicine products and services, physicians and physician group practices can increase patient satisfaction by drawing new patients to their practices, increasing the range of services, and adding value for their existing patients. Furthermore, physicians who offer retail medicine services and advertise them properly will enjoy tremendous opportunities to either replace or increase revenue for their practices, thereby freeing up more time to spend with their patients in order to "reconnect" with them.

But unwary physicians may expose themselves to needless regulatory issues by failing to account for applicable federal and state laws and regulations governing marketing and advertising by physicians, as well as those advertising laws and regulations that are more general in scope and application. Thus, before placing advertisements or releasing marketing materials, physicians should have them reviewed by legal counsel who is both competent and experienced in the areas of physician advertising and marketing laws and regulations to ensure compliance with and to prevent unnecessary regulatory agency scrutiny.

## *False Advertising and Unfair and Deceptive Trade Practices Laws*

Almost every state has laws regulating and prohibiting unfair and deceptive trade practices and false advertising. Additionally, the federal government, and in particular the Federal Trade Commission, closely monitor and regulate advertising and marketing of dietary and nutritional supplements as well as cosmoceuticals, nutraceuticals, laser hair removal equipment, DME, and skin care products.

Failing to understand the intricacy of or to comply with the multiple state and federal laws and regulations governing unfair and deceptive trade practices and false advertising can be potentially disastrous for physicians.

For instance, the Florida Deceptive and Unfair Trade Practices Act (FDUTPA) is designed to protect consumers, including patients, from unfair, unconscionable, and deceptive methods of advertising. FDUTPA not only permits the Florida attorney general to bring regulatory and civil actions against alleged violators, but also permits consumers to sue alleged violators of the statute for damages caused by unfair and deceptive trade practices, including false advertising.

Additionally, FDUTPA permits plaintiffs to recover their actual damages and their attorneys' fees and litigation costs. This alone has spurred a tremendous interest by trial lawyers in Florida to pursue consumer class action cases against perceived violators of FDUTPA because of the potential for them to recover statutory fees and costs in addition to damages for their clients. Moreover, FDUTPA includes enhanced penalty provisions for violations involving senior citizens and handicapped persons and provisions, which allow Florida regulatory agencies to recover their attorneys' fees when they successfully prosecute alleged violators.

False or deceptive advertising is a very subjective concept. However, courts and regulatory agencies often adopt the views of the consumers or patients when analyzing whether particular marketing materials or advertisements are deceptive because laws such as FDUTPA are designed to protect patients and consumers. Also, laws such as FDUTPA often contain vague definitions of what constitutes unconscionable, deceptive, or unfair advertising or trade practices, and laws such as FDUTPA are closely tied to federal trade practices acts and Federal Trade Commission regulations.

Physicians who advertise health and wellness, nutritional and dietary supplements, free services, and other types of retail medicine must bear in mind that it is the patients' perspective, not that of the doctors, that matters when analyzing whether a particular advertisement is to be considered false or deceptive. Many physicians have geared their marketing and advertising materials toward traditional medicine and the types of medical and health care services that their practices provide to patients on a regular basis.

Retail medicine products and services cross over into a gray area in which issues of patient satisfaction arise and blur the lines between what may constitute simple statements regarding products and services versus representations concerning quality and results of certain products and services.

Therefore, physicians and their group practices should carefully analyze the types of representations they make to ensure that they do not cross into this gray area and make statements that could be perceived as false or deceptive by patients.

One of the best ways to test whether patients might perceive something as false or deceptive is to run draft advertisements and marketing materials by a small sampling of "average" patients to obtain their thoughts and perceptions of such advertisements. Failure to properly analyze advertisements and their potential impact on patient perception could lead to allegations of unfair and deceptive trade practices and false advertising.

These allegations, in turn, can expose physicians and their group practices to civil litigation and regulatory enforcement, which can lead to having to pay civil damages, regulatory fines and penalties, and attorneys' fees and costs for opposing parties in both civil and regulatory administrative litigation proceedings.

Also, physicians should never discount the fact that they will have to pay for their own attorneys' fees to defend themselves, and many times insurance policies do not cover the cost of defending actions brought under statutes such as FDUTPA or for false or deceptive advertising claims.

Taking proactive steps to analyze proposed advertisements and marketing materials should help protect physicians and their practices while also increasing patient awareness of retail medicine products and services, as well as their satisfaction with those products and services.

## Board of Medicine/Board of Osteopathic Medicine Advertising Rules and Regulations

All states have licensing boards that govern medical doctors and osteopathic physicians, as well as other health care professionals and providers, such as chiropractic physicians, licensed massage therapists, podiatric physicians, acupuncturists, physician assistants, advanced registered nurse practitioners, and even aestheticians in many states.

In many cases, these licensing boards promulgate rules and regulations governing various types of conduct by licensed health care professionals, including advertising and marketing practices.

Additionally, many state statutes and codes include laws that govern the practice of medicine and other health care professions that establish disciplinary provisions under which physicians and licensed health care professionals and providers may be disciplined for false or deceptive advertising.

For instance, the Florida Medical Practice Act (Chapter 458, Florida Statutes), the Florida Osteopathic Medical Practice Act (Chapter 459, Florida Statutes), and the Florida Chiropractic Medical Practice Act (Chapter 460, Florida Statutes) all contain provisions that allow their respective licensing boards to take disciplinary action against medical doctors, osteopathic physicians, and chiropractic physicians for false, deceptive, or misleading advertising.

The penalties for violating these provisions can include fines, payment of administrative costs and expenses incurred by regulatory agencies in investigating and prosecuting false advertising cases, suspension or revocation of a physician's license, licensure probation, reprimands, and requirements to obtain additional continuing medical education credit hours. Moreover, disciplinary action taken against a physician's or health care professional's license is required to be reported to the federal Healthcare Integrity and Protection Data Bank (the sister databank to the National Practitioner Data Bank) and, in many instances, state practitioner profiles and licensing databases.

Although the federal databases are not accessible by the general public, many state databases and practitioner profiles containing disciplinary actions are accessible by patients and the public. Furthermore, credentialing entities, such as hospitals, ambulatory surgical centers, health insurers, and managed care organizations, can access the federal Healthcare Integrity and Protection Data Bank and do consider disciplinary actions and professional licensure investigations as part of their credentialing process.

For physicians and group practices wondering what types of advertising and marketing actions might violate professional licensing board rules and regulations, the rules promulgated by the Florida Board of Medicine and the Florida Board of Chiropractic Medicine provide some enlightening illustrations. The Florida Board of Medicine rules on advertising state that no physician shall disseminate or cause the dissemination of any advertisement or advertising that is in *any way* false, deceptive, or misleading.

These rules go on to state that any advertisement or advertising shall be deemed by the Florida Board of Medicine to be false, deceptive, or misleading if they:

- contain misrepresentations of facts;
- make only partial disclosures of relevant facts;
- create false or unjustified expectations of beneficial assistance;
- contain representations or claims referred to in the advertising that a physician does not expect to perform or meet;
- state or imply that a physician has received formal recognition as a specialist in the practice of medicine unless the physician has in fact received such recognition and such recognizing agency is approved by the Florida Board of Medicine;
- represent that professional services can or will be completely performed for a stated fee when that is not the case or make representations with respect to fees for professional services that do not disclose *all* variables affecting such fees that will be charged to a patient;
- convey the impression that a physician possesses qualifications, skills, or other attributes that are superior to other physicians other than providing a simple listing of earned professional postdoctoral or other professional achievements recognized by the Florida Board of Medicine;
- imply that a physician has earned a specialty or subspecialty when such specialty or subspecialty is not recognized by the Florida Board of Medicine; and
- fail to conspicuously identify the physician by name in the advertisement.

The Florida Board of Chiropractic Medicine's rules and regulations contain many of the same provisions. Recent professional licensure disciplinary cases involving the Florida Board of Chiropractic Medicine's dissatisfaction with the "DRX9000," a traction machine used to treat lower back pain and herniated discs, illustrate the specific types of advertising and marketing that will draw the ire of professional licensing boards.

In the DRX9000 cases, the Florida Board of Chiropractic Medicine and the Florida Department of Health have alleged that chiropractic physicians have made representations about the clinical efficacy and success rate of the DRX9000, advertised the machine as being "FDA approved" when it is only "FDA cleared," failed to identify themselves as chiropractic physicians in the advertisements, and failed to include proper disclaimers required under applicable Florida law for free services.

Many other state licensing boards are taking similar actions against chiropractic physicians and medical doctors for similar advertising violations.

It is important to note that many state laws include statutory provisions that require doctors and other licensed health care professionals to include disclaimers in their advertisements when offering free services. These disclaimers are often contained verbatim in state statutes and require physicians and licensed health care professionals to identify which specific services will be offered free of charge and which specific services may be charged to patients.

To prevent and avoid disciplinary action being taken against a physician's license for alleged false, deceptive, or misleading advertising, physicians and group practices should engage legal counsel and marketing consultants and advisors who regularly work with physicians and physician group practices on marketing and advertising matters and who are familiar with applicable state laws and professional licensing board rules and regulations on advertising and marketing.

Additionally, it is important to note that many state licensing boards will permit physicians to submit draft advertisements and marketing materials for review before disseminating them to the general public.

Physicians would be well advised to take advantage of such review processes if they exist in the state in which they practice.

## Use and Advertising of Physician Extenders and Ancillary Providers

To address lack of time, skyrocketing overhead, and declining reimbursement issues, many physicians and physician group practices are turning to physician extenders and ancillary health care professionals and providers such as advanced registered nurse practitioners, physician assistants, licensed massage therapists, aestheticians, and radiology technicians. Additionally, many doctors and their group practices are entering into integrated group practice models with chiropractic and podiatric physicians.

When advertising the use of such physician extenders, physicians must be careful to ensure that they comply with the rules and regulations of the respective licensing boards that govern and regulate physician extenders and other licensed health care professionals in their respective states. Many states, including Florida, have disciplinary statutes, which permit professional licensing boards to discipline medical doctors and osteopathic physicians for aiding and abetting the unlicensed practice of medicine, osteopathic medicine, and other health care professions.

Innocent and simple advertisements that focus on the use of physician extenders and other licensed health care professionals can lead not only to false, misleading, and deceptive advertisement allegations, but also allegations that physicians may not be properly supervising physician extenders and other licensed health care professionals. These allegations in turn can spawn allegations that physicians are aiding and abetting the unlicensed practice of medicine and osteopathic medicine by their physician extenders.

In this regard, advertisements and marketing materials that include the names and qualifications of physician extenders in the same advertisements and marketing materials that reference medical doctors and osteopathic physicians must clearly indicate the types of qualifications the physician extenders possess and the types of services they will be providing.

If these physician extenders require particular types or levels of supervision while rendering their services, the physicians also must ensure that they provide this supervision or risk allegations that they are allowing their physician extenders to practice without appropriate supervision or to engage in the unlicensed practice of medicine or osteopathic medicine.

These types of allegations can arise from dissatisfied or unhappy patients who seek various forms of retail medicine, medical spa, cosmetic, or other types of health care goods and services and expect to be treated by a medical doctor, osteopathic physicians, chiropractic physician, or podiatric physician only to find that they are "downstreamed" to an ancillary provider or physician extender. Many patients still want to be seen and treated by their doctor only and cannot understand why a physician assistant, advanced registered nurse practitioner, licensed massage therapist, or other type of physician extender is providing their care and treatment or their cosmetic or medical spa procedure.

Therefore, marketing and advertising materials should clearly delineate not only the types of ancillary professionals and providers used by physicians and their group practices, but also the types of services that such physician extenders and ancillary professionals and providers will provide directly to patients.

Although the task of complying with these recommendations is often daunting and limited by the amount of space available on a cost-effective basis when designing advertising and marketing materials, physicians and physician group practices can use informed consent forms, disclaimers, and notices within their practice to further disseminate this information and clarify their relationships with and the types of services provided by physician extenders.

Well-drafted forms and effective methods of communication with patients concerning these matters can help prevent patient dissatisfaction and complaints to state licensing boards and regulatory agencies.

Finally, physicians and physician group practices need to be aware of potential fee splitting and kickback issues that can arise from compensation and productivity of bonus arrangements with physician extenders and ancillary health care professionals and providers.

Specifically, many physicians and physician group practices enter into employment and independent contractor relationships. This creates an incentive for physician extenders and ancillary health care professionals and providers by offering commissions and percentage-based productivity bonuses for selling medical spa and cosmetic packages and dietary and nutritional supplements to patients.

As with Florida, many states have laws prohibiting fee-splitting by physicians. Such state laws often include prohibitions on and professional licensure disciplinary actions for engaging in split-fee, bonus, kickback, and commission arrangements that pay individuals or entities for referrals of patients.

Although these statutes and laws do not always establish "blanket" prohibitions against such types of arrangements, most include very narrow exceptions to fee-splitting prohibitions. These must be carefully analyzed by physicians and physician group practices when structuring bonus and other compensation arrangements for their employees and independent contractors who engage in selling or promoting retail medicine products and services to their patients.

## HIPAA Privacy Regulations and State Medical Record Confidentiality Law Considerations

Many times physicians and physician group practices include patient names and faces or likenesses in their marketing and advertising materials. Additionally, many physicians and group practices like to advertise or market results obtained for patients. In doing so, physicians and physician group practices need to be keenly aware of the restrictions placed on the use of patient names, photographs, and information by the federal HIPAA privacy regulations and applicable state medical record confidentiality laws.

Specifically, many state laws applicable to physicians and physician group practices prohibit them from releasing patient medical record information to anyone other than a patient or another treating physician or provider without *written* authorization from their patients.

In some instances, physicians are under the mistaken impression that verbal authorization for the release of patient medical record information is permissible. However, many states like Florida have medical record confidentiality laws that require *written* authorization for the release of such information and, in particular, for the use of such information in marketing and advertising materials. Additionally, as many physicians and physician group practices are aware, the HIPAA privacy regulations require written authorization from patients to release or use their information for marketing purposes.

Therefore, physicians and physician group practices would be well served to develop and use well-drafted authorization forms for their patients to sign for the release of their information for marketing and advertising purposes. Because of the technical and legal nature of these documents, it is strongly recommended that physicians always have such authorization forms reviewed by competent and experienced legal counsel.

## *Marketing and Advertising Contract Considerations*

When negotiating and entering into marketing and advertising contracts with marketing consultants, Internet and Website development companies, and other marketing and advertising vendors, physicians and group practices should be aware of certain types of provisions that need to be carefully considered as part of such contracts.

Provisions concerning cost, type, and size of advertisements and marketing materials, and deadlines for the delivery of products and services must be carefully negotiated and clearly understood by physicians or group practices, and then accurately memorialized in the contracts. Nothing can ruin or negatively impact a physician's or physician group practice's marketing and advertising efforts faster than the failure of a marketing or advertising company or vendor to deliver the expected materials and products on time, at the negotiated price, and in accordance with the specific instructions and expectations for appearance, quality, and functionality by the physician or group practice.

Thus advertising and marketing contracts should include appropriate provisions to ensure compliance with these types of provisions by marketing and advertising vendors, as well as liquidated damages provisions, which require either a reduction in price or payment of damages to a physician or physician group practice for a vendor's failure to deliver appropriate marketing and advertising materials on time.

Additionally, physicians and physician group practices should carefully negotiate breach and termination provisions in such marketing and advertising vendor agreements. If a physician or group practice is dissatisfied with a particular marketing or advertising vendor, termination of that vendor's agreement may not be an option if the physician or group practice wants to obtain their marketing and advertising materials from the vendor without forfeiting fees or costs paid in advance to the vendor.

Many times a physician or physician group practice cannot practically terminate an advertisement or marketing contract without risking a complete loss of the materials being produced or developed, as well as costs and fees already paid to the vendor. Moreover, in situations involving Website development contracts, physicians and physician group practices should include provisions in Website development agreements that ensure that they take possession of the Website and all source codes and links in the event of a termination of the development or support agreement. These types of provisions will prevent leaving a physician or group practice without access to their Website or partially developed Website material in the event of a contract dispute with a Website development vendor.

Physicians and physician group practices should also be wary of automatic or evergreen renewal provisions in marketing and advertising agreements. These types of provisions usually state something to the effect that unless one of the parties specifically terminates an agreement before its anniversary date, the agreement will automatically renew for an additional term or terms.

Physicians must have clearly delineated termination provisions that allow them to exit from and terminate marketing vendor agreements for a number of reasons, including failure by the vendor to perform appropriately under the agreement and regulatory or other violations caused by a marketing or advertising vendor to avoid being trapped in an agreement for an indefinite or prolonged period.

Physicians and physician group practices also must be aware that many state laws—in particular, professional licensing board rules and regulations—place the responsibility for inappropriate or volatile advertisements on the physician's shoulders.

Specifically, many state licensing boards have promulgated rules and regulations that state that physicians are always ultimately responsible for advertisements or marketing materials, which violate applicable state laws or licensing board rules and regulations.

In particular, the Florida Board of Medicine has promulgated rules that state that:

- a physician who solicits patients personally or through an agent shall be responsible for any advertising promulgated or used by such agents to solicit or advertise to patients;
- any physician who advertises by or through a referral service will be held ultimately responsible for the content of any advertising or advertisements promulgated by such advertising or referral service; and
- physicians shall be ultimately responsible for all electronic media used for the purpose of advertising and to ensure that an exact

copy of all such electronic media, including audiotape and videotape, is maintained and preserved for at least 6 months from the date that the advertisement or electronic media is aired or shown to the public.

The failure of an advertising or referral agency to ensure that physician advertisements and marketing materials meet the requirements of regulatory agencies such as the Florida Board of Medicine can cause physicians to incur professional licensure disciplinary action even though they may not be at fault for mistakes or errors contained in advertising or marketing materials.

State regulatory entities such as the Florida Board of Medicine usually take the position that a physician is the "captain of the ship" and ultimately responsible for any advertising violations caused by marketing and advertising vendors retained by the physician. Therefore, physicians and their group practices always should carefully review drafts of advertisements and marketing materials before releasing them for dissemination to patients and the public.

## *Other Considerations*

There are a number of other considerations that physicians and physician group practices should be aware of when conducting marketing and advertising for their retail medicine goods and services.

On the federal level, the US Department of Health and Human Services Office of the Inspector General has issued a number of advisory warnings about health care professionals and providers purchasing contacts and leads from advertising and marketing agencies when such lists of contacts and leads include patient contact information.

In particular, the Office of the Inspector General has focused on the DME industry and the diabetic testing supply market where unscrupulous marketers have compiled and sold lists of potential patients who may be interested in receiving information from DME and diabetic testing supply companies. The Office of the Inspector General has previously taken the position that the purchase and use of such lists would most likely violate the federal Anti-Kickback Statute (AKS).

Additionally, many states have statutes or laws similar to the AKS, which prohibit the payment or solicitation of any type of remuneration in exchange for referrals of health care goods and services.

Although the AKS only applies to referrals of health care goods and services reimbursable under federal health care beneficiary programs, such as the Medicare and Medicaid programs, many states' statutes such as the Florida Patient Brokering Act prohibit this type of conduct regardless of the payment source a patient may be using. State statutes and laws similar to the AKS may apply to self-pay patients and patients who are insured by managed care organizations and health insurers.

Therefore, physicians and physician group practices should be very careful in purchasing patient lists and information from marketing and advertising vendors for use in contacting, soliciting, or marketing to potential patients. It's important to note that many of these state laws, and the AKS and federal regulations, contain exceptions that allow health care providers and professionals to market to existing or former patients without the fear of violating these laws.

Physicians and physician group practices also should be wary of including superlatives or representations about superior quality and service in their advertisements. As noted previously, many state laws and licensing board rules and regulations prohibit this type of advertising and marketing or provide venues to punish and discipline physicians for making unfounded or unsupportable representations about the quality of their services.

Additionally, physicians and physician group practices must be careful of making such representations and using superlatives in their advertising because patients who may be dissatisfied with their results or outcomes may attempt to sue a physician or physician group practice for professional negligence or medical malpractice.

In these situations, patients and their attorneys may use representations about the quality of the physician's services or superlatives contained in advertising and marketing materials against a physician defendant in a medical malpractice or professional negligence case. For instance, patients or their attorneys may ask a physician in a deposition or at trial whether they met the highest quality or standard of care when treating their patient, and if the physician answers that they believe they did, then the question becomes why has the patient been injured or achieved a bad outcome?

These are very difficult questions to work around in medical malpractice and professional negligence cases, and physicians and physician group practices are well-served to carefully evaluate their advertisements and marketing materials in this regard.

### *Concluding Remarks*

Although the information provided in this chapter seems daunting, physicians should not let it intimidate or deter them from marketing their practices. Well-crafted advertisements and marketing materials can significantly enhance physician practices, their reputations, and their retail medicine and passive income streams.

For the careful practitioner, violations of state and federal advertising laws and regulations should be a minor concern and never affect their practices. Marketing is now an essential function for most, if not all, physicians and their group practices. Focused and carefully designed marketing programs for retail medicine products and services will not raise the types of concerns noted herein. Rather, they should lead to successful passive income stream opportunities and, most important, happy and satisfied patients who will seek out you and your practice.

## SUMMARY

As you've read, this chapter focuses on various areas of the law and the practical considerations physicians should be aware of when designing and implementing retail medicine programs. It focuses on these practical and legal aspects to provide a comprehensive primer on the issues facing physicians and their marketing advisors when designing their retail marketing and advertising programs.

Because Michael is licensed to practice law in Florida and primarily focuses his practice there, his examples were based on Florida law. However, physicians and physician group practices located and practicing in other states are subject to many of the same laws and regulations as physicians practicing in Florida or have similar legal considerations and prohibitions under the laws of the states in which they are practicing.

This chapter is intended to provide guidance to you and your physicians as you build your retail marketing programs and to make you aware of the various potential legal pitfalls that can be involved in advertising and marketing programs. That said, although you should be aware of the laws and regulations applicable to your practice, you should not be intimidated by them.

Now more than ever before, you must market your practice to stay on the cutting edge and attract new patients to your retail medicine ventures. Laws and regulations, although at times daunting, are not impossible to work with and should not stop you from engaging in compliant and effective marketing campaigns.

As we have just read, lots of physicians and entrepreneurs are engaging in meeting consumer needs in very creative ways—some new and some we've seen for years. Areas that you will find familiar are the sale of eyeglasses within an ophthalmology practice, sleep clinics, fertility clinics, medi-spas, executive health screenings, direct sales of vitamins, and travel medicine, to name a few.

Let's look at a specialty group that found a way to be more creative and convenient for their orthopedic patients. Jewett Orthopaedic Clinic, team physicians for the Orlando Magic, UCF Knights, Rollins Tars, and the Orlando Ballet, is well branded in the community. The clinic is totally subspecialized with centers in the following areas: total joint replacement, sports medicine, spine, hand and upper extremity, foot and ankle, and general orthopedics. Physicians and physician assistants are frequently booked four weeks in advance.

Yet, when an existing patient or a new patient had an acute accident or orthopedic issue, it was difficult to get worked into the daily schedule. The practice realized they were not mastering **The Four A's** under these circumstances. That's when the group decided to meet that need in a big way, by opening the Orthopaedic Convenient Care Center. See Exhibits 10.1 through 10.10 for Jewett's marketing plan, press releases, advertisements, and Website information:

- Exhibit 10.1 Marketing Plan
- Exhibit 10.2 Newly Created Logo
- Exhibit 10.3 Map
- Exhibit 10.4 Ad in High School Booklet
- Exhibit 10.5 Press Release
- Exhibit 10.6 Letter Sent to Coaches and Trainees on Orthopaedic Convenient Care Center Letterhead

- Exhibit 10.7 Flyer Used as Community Handouts
- Exhibit 10.8 Ad Placed in Middle School Planner
- Exhibit 10.9 Managed Care "Blast Fax"
- Exhibit 10.10 Orthopaedic Convenient Care Center Ad on Website

OCCC has been accepted by the community and exceeded the Jewett Orthopaedic Clinic's expectations.

## REFERENCES

1. Wormon III, Isaac L., *Ramifications*. Richmond Academy of Medicine, Richmond, Va. 2003; XIV:1–2.
2. Hilgers, David W., "The rise of retail medicine: adding to the new complexity to the practice of health care law." Presented at the Law Institute's National CLE Conference, Aspen, Colo., January 2005.
3. Singer, Natasha, "More doctors turning to the business of beauty." *New York Times*. November 30, 2006. Available online at www.nytimes.com/2006/11/30/us/30plastic.html?_r=1&oref=slogin online. Accessed September 10, 2007.

## EXHIBIT 10.1 ■ Marketing Plan

**ORTHOPAEDIC CONVENIENT CARE CENTER:**
**A JEWETT ORTHOPAEDIC SERVICE MARKETING PLAN**

*Goals*
- Create awareness of this new center/service.
- Secure brand name identity for the Orthopaedic Convenient Care Center.
- Position in consumers' minds as the "first stop" when you experience an unexpected injury.
- Attract new patients with acute orthopaedic injuries to Jewett through the OCCC.

*Target Audiences*
- Parents (moms)
- Weekend warriors
- Referral sources: employers, physicians (PCP, pediatricians), athletic trainers/coaches

*Challenge*

Consumer and referral sources will not necessarily use this service immediately upon learning about it. We must continually create awareness so it becomes second nature, "top of mind," for when they do need it.

| Strategy | Person(s) Responsible | Notes |
| --- | --- | --- |
| Develop logo | Andrea/Berto | |
| Determine phone # | Jay | Try to get one that is easily remembered. |
| Seminole County Schools Planner book ad | Andrea | Half page, inside back cover ad in books for three schools<br>Ad due in March; will come out in August |
| Develop Corporate Identity Package: Letterhead, envelopes, business cards, and prescription pads? | Andrea/Jay | Need separate materials from Jewett with new OCCC logo, address, phone #, etc. |

*(continued)*

## EXHIBIT 10.1 ■ Marketing Plan *(Continued)*

| Strategy | Person(s) Responsible | Notes |
|---|---|---|
| Develop materials to educate managed care companies? | Andrea/Jay | Do we need to create any targeted pieces (letter/fact sheet) to help educate managed care companies/ensure coverage and panel inclusion? Key messages for managed care: reduces overall cost of care and treatment; provides cost-effective, efficient alternative to ER and urgent care centers; improves quality of care for patient; improves patient satisfaction; improves access to timely treatment; reduces unnecessary medical tests and procedures/duplication of services that often occur in the ER and urgent care centers. |
| Update Jewett Website | Jay/David | Update Jewett Website to include OCCC: hours, location, services, directions, etc. Consider separate "splash page" for OCCC (ties to Jewett site but appears separate). |
| Develop creative announcement card | Andrea | Develop creative piece to announce opening/attract attention. Send to key referral sources/Jewett "friends": physicians (FP, GP, IM, Peds), key employers, sports contacts (Magic, UCF, Rollins, area high schools, youth leagues, golf club managers, etc.). Could also serve as invitation to open house if holding one. Make piece creative and eye-catching (i.e., Ace bandage: "We are unwrapping a new service"). Include leave-behind that can be posted somewhere to remind them of the OCCC (with phone #, location): decal, magnet, flyer. |
| Hold open house? | Andrea/Jay | Do we want to hold an open house for key referral sources and Jewett "friends"? |

| Strategy | Person(s) Responsible | Notes |
|---|---|---|
| General flyer | Andrea | Distribute to local referral sources: physician offices, gyms, RDV Sportsplex, Winter Park YMCA, golf courses, restaurants, etc. Goal: to have them post it or provide copies for their waiting areas. |
| Mailing/e-mail to current Jewett patient database? | Andrea/Jay | Educate current Jewett patients about this new service. Need to make sure they know this is for new, urgent acute injuries and not an alternative to receive care for existing problems/follow-up. |
| Employer letter and flyer | Andrea/Jay | Develop a targeted piece to educate key employers (both major employers and those smaller employers within a 3-mile radius) about the benefits of the OCCC. Personally visit those nearby the OCCC and drop off flyer/decal (leave-behind) that can be posted in area visible to employees/managers to serve as ongoing reminder. Key messages for employers: Save time, save money, improve access, improve quality of care, and reduce unnecessary tests and expenses. |
| Create billboard | Andrea | Secure key billboards in 1-mile radius of facility to generate ongoing, "top of mind" awareness. Consider one directional billboard near the center (if available)? |
| Develop drive-time radio campaign | Andrea | Determine stations to reach desired target market (i.e., 104.1: men; 105.1, 103.1, 98.9: moms; etc.). Key is ongoing frequency to generate "top of mind" awareness. Keep ads brief for greater frequency and run only in drive time. |
| Create magnet | Andrea | For distribution to key referral sources and consumers. Idea is to provide a leave-behind that people can reference and quickly access when needed (i.e., when an injury occurs). |

*(continued)*

## EXHIBIT 10.1 ■ Marketing Plan *(Continued)*

| Strategy | Person(s) Responsible | Notes |
|---|---|---|
| Consumer direct mail piece | Andrea | Consider direct mail to families/residents in target zips and income levels (include magnet). Could use creative from announcement card. |
| Research signage/sponsorship opportunities for local athletic facilities and events (football fields/tracks, soccer fields, baseball fields, gyms) | Andrea | Examples: Showalter Field, Winter Park High School, Ward Park (soccer), Winter Park YMCA, Cady Way Trail, Track Shack races, etc. Can also investigate ads in programs for key community/youth sports events. Idea is to promote awareness among target audiences at sights where injuries may occur. |
| Area schools/sports teams: public and private | Andrea/Jay | Need to educate coaches, athletic trainers at key schools. Take advantage of any opportunities from current Jewett relationships. Need to determine best approach: letter with flyer (need some sort of leave-behind to serve as ongoing reminder/reference)? Is there an association or meeting that they all attend? If so, could consider sponsorship. |
| Youth sports leagues/sports camps | Andrea/Jay | Once again, may want to educate coaches, organizers of key youth leagues (i.e., soccer, volleyball). |
| Employer health fairs | Jay/David | Promote at any employer health fairs Jewett participates in and at Worker's Comp fair in the fall. |
| Orlando Magic games | Andrea/Jay | Take advantage of opportunities from current Jewett relationship. Consider creating new rolling billboard for games to promote OCCC. Opportunities on WDBO? Good way to reach "weekend warriors" market (i.e., those who play pick-up BB games). |

| Strategy | Person(s) Responsible | Notes |
| --- | --- | --- |
| Develop new Yellow Pages ad | Andrea/Jay | Consider a new ad and listing for the OCCC separate from Jewett. Need to position under "Clinics" heading to compete with Centra Care and other urgent care centers. |
| Develop news release | Andrea | Announce new facility as first of its kind in the area. Consider creative angle/mailing (i.e., "Weekend Warrior," beginning of fall sports season). |
| UCF athletics | Jay/Andrea | Take advantage of any opportunities from current Jewett relationship. |
| Rollins athletics | Jay/Andrea | Take advantage of any opportunities from current Jewett relationship. |

*Used with permission of Jewett Orthopaedic Clinic.*

### EXHIBIT 10.2 ■ Newly Created Logo

*Used with permission of Jewett Orthopaedic Clinic.*

**EXHIBIT 10.3** ■ **Map**

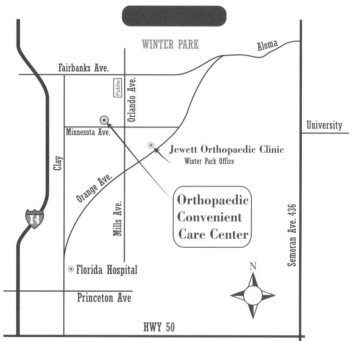

**MOST INSURANCE ACCEPTED**
**NO APPOINTMENT NECESSARY**

801 S. Orlando Ave., Suites A-K, Winter Park, Florida 32789
(407) 599-3710 • fax (407) 599-3711
ENTRANCE ON MINNESOTA AVENUE, 1 BLOCK WEST OF SOUTH ORLANDO AVENUE

www.jewettortho.com

*Used with permission of Jewett Orthopaedic Clinic.*

**EXHIBIT 10.4** ■ **Ad in High School Booklet**

## NO APPOINTMENT NECESSARY

*A Service of the Jewett Orthopaedic Clinic*

The Center is staffed to provide diagnosis and care for a wide variety of school, sports, work and every day injuries.

### 407-599-3710

801 S. Orlando Ave., Suites A-K, Winter Park, Florida 32789
(407) 599-3710 • fax (407) 599-3711
ENTRANCE ON MINNESOTA AVENUE, 1 BLOCK WEST OF SOUTH ORLANDO AVENUE
www.jewettortho.com

*Used with permission of Jewett Orthopaedic Clinic.*

## EXHIBIT 10.5 ■ Press Release

**MEDIA CONTACT:**
Andrea Eliscu
407-629-0062/mmiandrea@sprintmail.com

### JEWETT ORTHOPAEDIC CLINIC OPENS ONE OF THE COUNTRY'S FIRST WALK-IN CONVENIENT CARE CENTERS DEDICATED TO TREATING ORTHOPAEDIC INJURIES

WINTER PARK, Fla.—Jewett Orthopaedic Clinic recently opened the Orthopaedic Convenient Care Center in Winter Park, Central Florida's first walk-in center dedicated solely to treating broken bones, sprains, strains, and lacerations.

Until now, when someone broke a bone, their only option was usually a visit to an emergency room where they might wait six hours or more for treatment. This is because most orthopaedic physicians' offices are booked up two to three weeks in advance. In addition, traditional urgent care centers typically don't treat broken bones because they lack the necessary orthopaedic specialists on staff. Meanwhile, Central Florida's emergency rooms are overwhelmed with patients, and because they are not life-threatening, orthopaedic problems typically fall to the bottom of the triage list. With weekend hours, the new Orthopaedic Convenient Care Center located at 801 S. Orlando Avenue, Suites A-K (entrance on Minnesota Avenue), offers a convenient, cost-effective alternative.

"This innovative center really fills a critical and growing gap in our community—making high-quality orthopaedic care easier and more affordable to access," said John McCutchen, M.D., Jewett's CEO.

The Center is staffed to provide diagnosis and care for a wide variety of school, sports, work, and everyday injuries. The new center houses an MRI as well as digital imaging, including a state-of-the-art PACS (picture archiving and communications system), a technology that some local hospitals have secured in recent years but is rarely found in physicians' offices. Additional services include physical and occupational therapy, an in-house pharmacy, and a full range of orthotic devices.

Before she retired at the end of May, Windermere resident Margie LeBarge worked as an administrator with Orange County Public Schools (OCPS) and suffered a bad fall after tripping over a chair as she was getting up from a meeting. LeBarge injured her left knee, foot, and shoulder, and had a difficult time walking. She called the OCPS employee health department, and they suggested she go directly to the Orthopaedic Convenient Care Center.

"I was so impressed by the Center's efficiency, professionalism, friendliness, and compassion," said LeBarge. "I was seen right away and felt immediately that everyone on the staff, from the front desk to the physician assistant, was there to take care of me. I have been in this community for a long time and injured before. This was better than any medical facility I have been to in the last 40 years."

The Orthopaedic Convenient Care Center accepts most major insurance plans and charges the same co-payment as a doctor's office visit, which is less expensive than an emergency room or urgent care center co-pay. Current hours are Monday–Friday, 8 a.m.–4 p.m., and Saturday, 9 a.m.–3 p.m., and no appointment is necessary.

Founded in 1936 by Eugene L. Jewett, M.D., the Jewett Orthopaedic Clinic has been recognized internationally as a pioneer and leader in orthopaedic care for more than 70 years, performing some of the first total knee replacements in the state of Florida and some of the first arthroscopic knee surgeries in the Southeast, as well as designing and developing several innovative joint replacement systems used worldwide. The Clinic's 23 board-certified/board-eligible, fellowship-trained physicians, 10 physician assistants, and team of healthcare professionals provide a full range of orthopaedic care, specializing in sports medicine, joint replacement, foot and ankle care, surgery and rehabilitation of the hand, and care for spinal injuries and conditions. Jewett serves as the team physicians for the Orlando Magic, the University of Central Florida, Rollins College, the Orlando Predators, the Orlando Ballet, and Cirque du Soleil. The practice has seven offices throughout Central Florida.

For more information or to reach the Orthopaedic Convenient Care Center, call 407-599-3710 or visit www.jewettortho.com.

*Used with permission of Jewett Orthopaedic Clinic.*

## EXHIBIT 10.6 ■ Letter Sent to Coaches and Trainees on Letterhead

Dear Coaches & Athletic Trainers,

As you are gearing up for another school year and the fall sports season, Jewett Orthopaedic Clinic is pleased to announce a new service designed to better serve the needs of your injured student athletes.

The Orthopaedic Convenient Care Center is located at 801 S. Orlando Avenue, Suites A-K, in Winter Park. Its entrance is on Minnesota Avenue, 1 block west of Orlando Avenue.

The OCCC is Central Florida's first walk-in, urgent care center dedicated solely to treating orthopaedic injuries, including broken bones, sprains, strains, and lacerations. It offers a convenient, high-quality, and less costly alternative to the emergency room. Current hours are Monday–Friday, 8 a.m.–4 p.m., and Saturday, 9 a.m.–3 p.m., and we plan to add evening hours in a few months. No appointment is necessary. Most major health plans are accepted, and the center charges the same co-payment as a doctor's visit, which is typically much less expensive than an emergency room or traditional urgent care center co-pay.

The Center is staffed to provide diagnosis and care. The new center houses an MRI as well as a new PACS (picture archiving and communications system) digital imaging system. Additional services include physical and occupational therapy, an in-house pharmacy, and a full range of orthotic devices.

We've enclosed a magnet for you to put up in your office or training room. Feel free to contact me with any questions or to reach the Orthopaedic Convenient Care Center directly, call 407-599-3710.

Cordially,

David Cassidy, M.Ed., ATC/L, CSCS
Director of Marketing

*Used with permission of Jewett Orthopaedic Clinic.*

MAXIMIZING YOUR PRACTICE'S PROFIT POTENTIAL

**EXHIBIT 10.7** ■ **Flyer Used as Community Handouts**

## NO APPOINTMENT NECESSARY!

It's all well and good... until your shins get kicked.

Broken bones, sprains, strains, or lacerations are bad enough!

Now you can have them treated by an orthopaedic specialist at Jewett Orthopaedic Clinic's new Orthopaedic Convenient Care Center.

The care you need... when you need it! From the area's most experienced orthopaedic team.

**407-599-3710**
No appointment necessary.
Most major health insurance plans accepted.
*Open Monday through Friday*

Orthopaedic **Convenient Care Center**
*A Service of the Jewett Orthopaedic Clinic*

801 South Orlando Avenue, Winter Park, Florida 32789 • www.jewettortho.com
**ENTRANCE ON MINNESOTA AVENUE, 1 BLOCK WEST OF SOUTH ORLANDO AVENUE**

*Used with permission of Jewett Orthopaedic Clinic.*

EXHIBIT 10.8 ■ Ad Placed in Middle School Planner

Used with permission of Jewett Orthopaedic Clinic.

## EXHIBIT 10.9 ■ Managed Care "Blast Fax"

United Healthcare is pleased to announce the addition of the Jewett Orthopaedic Convenient Care Center, providing walk-in orthopaedic care for broken bones, sprains, strains, and lacerations. The location is as follows:

**Orthopaedic Convenient Care Center, A Service of the Jewett Orthopaedic Clinic**
801 S. Orlando Avenue, Suites A-K
Winter Park, FL 32789
407-599-3710
www.jewettortho.com

Entrance on Minnesota Avenue, 1 block west of Orlando Avenue

Business Hours: Mon.–Fri., 8 a.m.–4 p.m., Sat., 9 a.m.–3 p.m.
(Evening hours will be offered within a few months.)

Jewett Orthopaedic Convenient Care Center can be used in many cases as an alternative to the hospital emergency room. The out-of-pocket expense is lower for members as the physician visit co-payment applies versus a more costly emergency room or urgent care co-payment. The Jewett Orthopaedic Convenient Care Center medical staff will stay in close communication with the patient's primary care physician.

- Wide range of services
- Rapid diagnosis and care for broken bones, strains, sprains, and lacerations
- Treatment of school and sports injuries
- Walk-in, no appointment necessary
- Physical therapy
- Occupational therapy
- Orthotic devices such as splints
- MRI
- Digital x-rays/imaging—PACS (picture archiving and communications system)
- In-house pharmacy
- Follow-up care
- Treatment for workers' compensation injuries

*Used with permission of Jewett Orthopaedic Clinic.*

**EXHIBIT 10.10** ■ **Ad on Website**

## NO APPOINTMENT NECESSARY!

It's all well and good… until you plant your face in the dirt.

Broken bones, sprains, strains, or lacerations are bad enough!

Now you can have them treated by an orthopaedic specialist at Jewett Orthopaedic Clinic's new Orthopaedic Convenient Care Center.

The care you need… when you need it! From the area's most experienced orthopaedic team.

**407-599-3710**
No appointment necessary.
*Most major health insurance plans accepted.*

Orthopaedic **Convenient Care Center**
*A Service of the Jewett Orthopaedic Clinic*

801 South Orlando Avenue, Winter Park, Florida 32789 • www.jewettortho.com
ENTRANCE ON MINNESOTA AVENUE, 1 BLOCK WEST OF SOUTH ORLANDO AVENUE

*Used with permission of Jewett Orthopaedic Clinic.*

CHAPTER 11

# Final Words of Advice

As I asserted in the introduction to this book, successful medical group marketing today is all about understanding and effectively meeting the needs of your customers—whether they happen to be patients, referrers, staff, vendors, or others who interact with your practice. In other words, it means providing excellent *customer service* in each of the four cornerstones—what I call **The Four A's—Accessibility, Availability, Accountability,** and **Accommondation.**

My aim is to provide a practical "how-to" guide that will allow you to implement *effective* marketing programs in your practice on your own or with the help of other professionals. Most measures I recommend can be implemented by almost any practice in the United States, no matter how large or how small.

In this book, I've gone a step beyond the basics, which are covered in my two previous books published by MGMA.[1-2] Although the basics are still important, particularly as they apply to building and maintaining your brand identity, that topic has been well covered by hundreds of books. This time, I've concentrated on customer service.

To review, you begin by understanding your customers, and after you know them well, you try your best to meet their wants and needs, even as you evolve your practice. A practice assessment is another vital step of any effective marketing plan. In a very practical sense, you must assess where you are before you can move forward.

One way to assess your practice is by conducting a retreat—getting away from your practice with others—to spend time considering how to develop and sustain a competitive advantage in spite of the never-ending challenges of practicing medicine in today's environment.

Also, in today's new reality, it's more important than ever that you focus on building and maintaining relationships—whether it's with patients, referring physicians, internal staff, outside vendors, or the community as a whole.

I've presented a number of recommendations on how to position your practice and physicians as leaders through community integration. These include how you can serve as a valuable resource to the media—to work effectively with radio and television stations—as well as how to craft your message exactly as you want it through the use of print advertising.

And throughout the book, I've offered specific examples of actual campaigns to illustrate how to accomplish my recommendations, including using the Internet to market your practice and opening a new office. I've also included the professional expertise of several of my esteemed colleagues, including the increase in retail medicine, along with the marketing and price competition that accompany it.

I hope I've helped empower you to take charge in your practice and, ultimately, your own destiny. I believe the secret to successful medical group marketing today is to understand what your patients/customers want and then find creative ways to provide it. Practices that can do this, plus deliver cost-effective health care, have a much better opportunity to control their own destinies.

Remember, satisfied customers are your best marketing tools of all.

## REFERENCES

1. Eliscu, Andrea T., *Ready-Set-Market!* Medical Group Management Association, Englewood, Colo. 1999.
2. Eliscu, Andrea T., *Position for Success.* Medical Group Management Association, Englewood, Colo. 1995.

# About the Author

Andrea Eliscu, BS, RN, is president of Medical Marketing Inc., a marketing and public relations firm that she founded in 1984 to respond to the changing marketplace. She serves as a facilitator and consultant to physician groups, managed care companies, hospital systems, pharmaceutical companies, health care attorneys, and health care management companies, as well as a respected resource to local and national electronic and print media.

Eliscu has authored two books—the popular *Ready-Set-Market!* and *Position for Success! Strategic Marketing for Group Practices,* both published by Medical Group Management Association. Throughout her career, she has received numerous professional awards and recognition, including being named a finalist for the 2007 Women Who Mean Business—Business Owner of the Year award by the *Orlando Business Journal* and Orlando Regional Healthcare System. Other awards include the Outstanding Woman in Orlando Business; the Most Innovative Small Business in Florida; the Presidential Citation for Exemplary Service to the Health Care Marketing Discipline; and the Friend of Medicine Award.

As a registered nurse with 42 years experience in the health care field, Eliscu is frequently invited to share her vision and problem-solving skills with clients throughout the country and through professional presentations and trade publication articles. She also is actively involved as a volunteer in the business community, providing a unique insight into the needs of the health care purchaser/customer. She is on the Council of Governors of the MD Anderson Cancer Center, Orlando, and currently serves as an advisor to the College of Health and Public Affairs, University of Central Florida. In addition, Eliscu serves on the Board of Directors for Women Playing for T.I.M.E. and Hospice of Polk and Sumter Counties. She has been a director on the Board of A Gift for Teaching and the Healthy Florida Foundation as well as the Florida Chamber of Commerce. Eliscu was an appointed member of the WorkForce on Certificates of Need for the State of Florida.

# Index

## A

access
  customer service as, 23, 36
  as marketing cornerstone, 1
  in retail health care facilities, 32–33
  retail medicine as, 206–207
accommodation, 1, 36
accountability, 1, 36
added value
  nontraditional health care as, 212–213
  physician income and, 211–212
  in retail medicine, 209
  in television advertising, 140
advertising. *See also* television advertising
  authorization for release of patient information, 223–224
  community relations and, 181–182
  contract considerations for, 224–226
  false or deceptive, 216–218
  legal considerations for, 226–228
  patient review of ads, 217
  physician extenders and, 221–222
  physician responsibility for content, 225–226
  purchasing of contacts and leads, precautions, 226–227
  rules and regulations of licensing boards, 218–220, 225–226
  state laws affecting, 220
  use of superlatives or quality of care representations in, precautions, 227
advocacy, 67
aestheticians, 221
altruism, 63
Anti-Kickback Statute (AKS), 226–227
availability
  customer service as, 36
  as marketing cornerstone, 1
  retail medicine as, 206–207
awareness, 66

## B

baby boomers, 212–213
behavioral styles, 59
blogs and blogging, 194–195
brand-name identity. *See* practice identity
Bruns, John, 37–38, 39–40
buzz sessions, 40–41

## C

Calato, Tom, 127–128
change, in referral relationships, 64
chiropractors, 221
communication
  examples of methods for, 77–83
  with patient, 5–6
  referral relationships and, 63, 70, 73–76
community assessment, 48
community offices, terminology for, 2
community relations, 149–186
  ads targeted for specific groups, examples, 183–185
  basics of, 150–153
  case studies, 153–157
  crafting message, 150–151
  logo and letter head reinforcing corporate identity, examples, 176–177
  as marketing, 150
  marketing and public relations plan, example, 158–161
  marketing tips, 8
  opening new office, 195–204
  opportunities for, 178
  patient survey about ads, example, 186

community relations, *(continued)*
  planning guide, example, 162–175
  reasons for advertising, 181–182
  sponsored events as, 152–153
  thanking community nurses, examples, 179–180
concierge care, 209
contracts
  marketing and advertising, considerations for, 224–226
  for Website design, example, 190–192
customer service, 35–43. *See also* patient satisfaction
  customer satisfaction assurance surveys, 38, 42
  four A's of marketing and, 245
  Harrah's Entertainment (gaming industry) example, 37–42
  Hyatt Hotels (hospitality industry) example, 36–37
  internal, quality components, 40
  issues in, 35
  marketing tips, 6
  as most important element of marketing, 36
  Red Lobster (restaurant industry) example, 36
  service culture, 40–41
  service process, 41–42
  strategies for improving, 23–25
customers
  broad definition of, 35
  lifetime value of, 64–65
  patients as, 23
  perceptions of brand identity, 2–3

## D

diabetic testing supplies, 226
direct response, television advertising and, 140–141
DISC (dominance, influence, steadiness, compliance) assessment, 58, 59
durable medical equipment (DME) industry, 226

## E

employers, marketing strategies to, 49–51
environmental changes, 46

## F

familiarity, in referral relationships, 66–67
Federal Trade Commission, 216
fee-splitting prohibitions, 222–223
Florida Deceptive and Unfair Trade Practices Act, 216–217
four A's of marketing, 1–2, 206–207, 245
franchise, creating, 139

## H

Harrah's Entertainment
  customer satisfaction assurance surveys, 38, 42
  customer service model, 37–42
  service culture, 40–41
  service process, 41–42
  service profit chain (SPC) model, 39
health care costs, retail medicine as response to, 208–209
health insurance, instability of coverage, 46
Health Insurance Portability and Accountability Act of 1996 (HIPAA), 223–224
Hilgers, David W., 205
Huckels, Robert, 206

## I

image, 67
internal relations, 7–8
internal service quality, 40
Internet. *See also* Websites
  blogs and blogging, 194–195
  as marketing challenge, 187–195
  in multi-media promotion, 145, 148, 244
  patient use of, 187
  RSS feeds, 195
  Web address as advertising, 189, 193

## K

Kodzis, Bob, 61–65
Konsens, Richard, 120, 121–122, 126

## L

lifestyle choices, 211
logos, 55–56, 57, 235

# INDEX

Loveman, Gary, 37–38, 39
Lowe, Michael R., 214

## M

managed care, 47, 49
marketing
  basic tips for, 3–8
  contract considerations for, 224–226
  four A's of, 1–2
  in-office, tips for, 4–5
  market research tips, 4
  practice assessment and, 47
marketing plans
  example of, 9–21
  opening new office, 195–204
  orthopedic convenient care center, 229–235
massage therapists, 221
Maynard, George, III, 64
media management, 115–148. *See also* television advertising
  making contacts with media, 117–118
  media relations planning, 116–120
  medical expertise and, 115, 117–118, 120, 132–134
  multilevel promotion, example of, 142–148
  press releases, use of, 115, 120–127
  public relations and, 150–151
  sample print ads, 143–144
  sound bytes, 118
medical records confidentiality, 223–224
medical spas, 209–21–
Medicare, 46, 120, 208
Mertz, Gregory, 45
Mitchell, Ken, 120–127
mutual benefit, in referral relationships, 62–63

## N

newsletters, 77–78, 81
nurse practitioners, 208, 221

## O

one-on-one relationships, 62
*The One to One Future* (Peppers and Rogers), 62

opening new office
  ads introducing, examples, 200–204
  marketing plan, 195–204
  marketing stepping stones, example of, 197–198

## P

passive income streams, 210, 212, 214, 215, 228
patient satisfaction
  factors in, 25–26
  marketing and physician extender use, 222
  retail medicine and, 209
  surveys, example of, 28–31
patients
  confidentiality and retail medicine, 223–224
  cost-consciousness and growth of retail medicine, 208–209
  as customers, 23
  desires of and marketing strategies to, 48
  marketing tips and communication, 5–6
  meeting needs of, 26–27, 32–33
  scheduling and practice assessment, 45
Peppers, Don, 62
personal contact, 63
physician assistants, 208, 221
physician extenders
  advertising and use of, 221–223
  compensation and fee-splitting prohibitions, 222–223
  primary care by, 205
  supervision of, 221–222
physician income. *See also* retail medicine
  ancillary services and, 211–212
  concierge care and, 209
  decline in, 47, 208
  passive, 210, 212, 214, 215, 228
  skin care products generating, 210
podiatrists, 221
practice assessment, 45–60
  audit list, 51
  changing environment in, 46
  community assessment, 48

practice assessment, *(continued)*
   employer priorities and marketing strategies, 49–51
   example of, 52–53
   factors in, 45–46
   guidelines for, 50
   identification of customers, 48
   managed care needs and marketing strategies, 49
   marketing plan and, 47
   mission statement, reexamination of, 51
   needs of referral physicians, 49
   patient desires and marketing strategies, 48
   patient scheduling, 45
   population assessment, 46
   practice identity, 51, 53–55
   revenue cycle activities, 45
   staff assessment, 45, 56–59
   SWOT analysis, 47
practice identity
   assessment of, 51, 53–55
   building, 2–3
   communication tools, 54–55
   community relations and, 150
   customer perceptions of, 2–3
   differentiation of, 54
   logo, 55–56, 57
   terminology and, 2
practice retreats, 85–113
   benefits of, 3, 86–87, 245
   facilitator's role, 88
   identifying location for, 87
   indicators for, 85
   length of time for, 88
   preparation for, 87–88
   staff-only retreat, example, 89, 101–113
   strategic planning facilitation retreat, examples, 89, 90–100
   types of, 88–89
   who should attend, 87
preferences, in referral relationships, 67
press releases
   examples, 121–122, 238–239
   limitations of, 115
   newspaper article using, 123–127
primary health care centers, retail, 32–33
proactivity, 69
promotional events, 139

public relations. *See* community relations; media management

# R

radiology technicians, 221
*Ready-Set-Market!* (Eliscu), 23, 37, 61
referral relationships, 61–84
   added value of, 69–70
   advocacy in, 67
   awareness in, 66
   behaviors fostering, 70–76
   common traits of, 62–64
   communication in, 63, 70, 73–76
   communication methods, examples of, 77–83
   familiarity in, 66–67
   image in, 67
   lifetime value of customers, 64–65
   marketing tips, 7
   needs of referring physicians and marketing strategies, 49
   power of, 61–65
   preference in, 67
   proactivity in, 69
   referral enhancement program, example, 72
   relationship continuum model, 65–68
   survival of, 63
   as two-way street, 68–69
   utilization in, 67
The Relationship Continuum model, 65–68
retail medicine, 205–244
   advertising considerations, 226–228
   ancillary services, 211–212
   anti-kickback statutes, 226–227
   baby boomers and, 212–213
   blurring of lines between medical practice and ancillary services, 215
   definition of, 205
   expansion of services, 206
   false advertising and deceptive trade practices laws, 216–218
   fee-splitting prohibitions and, 222–223
   four A's of marketing and, 206–207
   HIPAA regulations and confidentiality laws, 223–224
   legal aspects, 214–228

# INDEX

liability for deceptive ads, 217
marketing and advertising contracts, 224–226
marketing materials, examples, 236–244
marketing plan, example, 229–235
medical spas, 209–210
physician extenders and, 205, 221–223
products and services, gray areas in, 217
regulatory and liability risks of, 215
as response to patient concerns, 32–33, 208–209
skin care products, 210
wellness clinics, 210–211
retreats. *See* practice retreats
revenue cycle, assessment of, 45
Rogers, Martha, 62
RSS (Really Simple Syndication) feeds, 195

## S

Sandlin, Richard, 207–208
satellite offices. *See* community offices
Satre, Phil, 37
senior citizens, 46
service profit chain (SPC) model, 39
service statement, example, 3
Singer, Natasha, 206
staff
   assessment of, 56–59
   behavioral styles, 59
   clinical and nonclinical roles, 45
strategic planning
   sample action plan, 9–13
   sample objectives, strategies, and participants/notes, 14–21
   tips for, 4
surveys
   customer satisfaction assurance measurement, 38, 42
   patient satisfaction, example, 28–31
   patient survey about ad exposure, 186
survival of referral relationships, 63
SWOT analysis, 47

## T

talent recognition, 140
television advertising, 127–141
   added value in, 140
   advertising buys, 134–135, 137
   ancillary opportunities in, 141
   buying promotional event, 139
   costs of, 132, 138, 145
   creating franchise, 139
   credit process, 138
   direct response to, 140–141
   Internet tie-in, 145, 148
   localism in, 131–132
   making commercials, 137–138
   medical expertise and news air time, 132–134
   multilevel promotion, example of, 142–148
   negative views of, 127
   owning show, 139–140
   pre-emptible time, buying, 141
   programming and, 129–131
   radio exposure and, 145
   schedules, 138
   stations as local businesses, 128
   talent recognition, 140
   talking points for, 145, 146–147
   working with account executive, 136–137, 138–139
   working with ad agencies and public relations firms, 135–136
trust, in referral relationships, 63

## U

uninsured population, 46
utilization, in referral relationships, 67

## W

Websites
   basics of design, 188–189
   contracts for design, 190–192, 224–225
   effective, power of, 192–193
   importance of content, 194
   templates for design of, 194
   working with Website designer, 188–189, 194
weight-loss clinics, 210–211
Weissman, Kristin, 149–150, 189, 192
wellness clinics, 210–211
Wilson, Annetta, 56–57, 59, 115–120